ROOTS AND BRANCHES

THE RELIGIOUS HERITAGE
OF WASHINGTON STATE

By
David M. Buerge and Junius Rochester

Church Council of Greater Seattle
SEATTLE

Church Council of Greater Seattle, Seattle 98105

©1988 by Church Council of Greater Seattle.
All rights reserved, including the right of reproduction in whole or in part in any form. Published 1988.

Designed by Adrian Kalar

54321

Library of Congress Cataloging in Publication Data

Buerge, David M.
  Roots and Branches.

  Bibliography: p.

  Includes index.
  1. Washington (State)—Religion. 2. Indians of North America—Washington (State)—Religion and Mythology. 3. Indians of North America—Washington (State)—Missions. I. Rochester, Junius, 1934- . II. Title. BL2527.W2B84 1988
291'.09797 88-71090 ISBN 0-9619863-0-1

Printed in the United States of America

Dedication

This history of religion in the state of Washington is dedicated to the panelists on the pioneering television program, *Challenge,* a weekly interfaith television program on KOMO-TV from 1960-1974. The program featured a Jewish rabbi, a Catholic priest and a Protestant minister. Rabbi Raphael Levine and the Reverend William Treacy were regular panelists for the entire fourteen years of the program's life. The program drew weekly 300,000 faithful viewers.

We honor these religious leaders who have done so much to nurture the interfaith climate in the state of Washington.

Rabbi Raphael H. Levine, Jewish
Father William Treacy, Roman Catholic
The Reverend Dr. Martin L. Goslin, United Church of Christ
The Reverend Dr. Oscar R. Rolander, Evangelical Lutheran
  Church of America
The Reverend Robert M. Fine, Free Methodist
The Reverend Dr. Lynn H. Corson, United Methodist

Table of Contents

Foreword

Our celebration of the Centennial of the statehood of Washington State in 1989 provides the appropriate occasion for the writing of a comprehensive summary history of religion in our state. Centennial celebrations provide a time for remembering. We do not have a lengthy religious history in the Pacific Northwest. We have known people who have personally experienced much of this historical period.

Religion is an integral part of the complex forces that shape a society. Any historical account of our past that does not include the religious people and spiritual forces that helped to shape the society is woefully inadequate. Happily, *Roots and Branches: The Religious Heritage of Washington State,* portrays the religious events of Washington State history in the context of the social, economic and political history of each successive period. The authors note the manner in which the frontier ethos has affected the religious communities. Similarly, they depict the way in which the religious groups helped shape other aspects of our society.

The frontier was settled primarily by sect-type churches which were individualist in nature and tended to separate themselves from the "world". This past has resulted in a largely secular society in our state in which two thirds of the people are not related to any religious group. The sectarian image of the church lingers into the present. On the other hand, the major institutions of the Pacific Northwest, such as schools, hospitals and mutual aid agencies, were created by religious groups in order to make our society more humane. The early religious pioneers considered themselves to be the bringers of salvation and civilization to Washington State.

This book is unique in that it reminds us that our entire society rests on a highly developed foundation of Native American traditional spiritual religion. This perspective has shaped the manner in which we view and experience the Pacific Northwest environment in the present.

As one who has struggled for several decades to understand religion in the Pacific Northwest, I eagerly await this book. Only in knowing our religious history can we begin to shape our religious and social future. We can thank David M. Buerge and Junius Rochester for this important gift to us all.

William B. Cate
President-Director
Church Council of Greater Seattle

November, 1988

Preface:

W ith family roots in the Pacific Northwest, and life-long interests in researching, writing, teaching and eavesdropping on the historical minutiae of our verdant strand, we undertook the Church Council's offer to write a Washington State Religious History with one reservation: will it interest the reader?

Working in tandem, integrating personal profiles with the sagas of religious development since pre-history, we discovered that Pacific Northwest religious tracks lead in every direction. This project turned out to be an adventure in historicity. We were frequently delighted—and entertained—to find the trails that our state's religious characters followed. Sometimes secular and religious events were blurred. Great piety and fervency could occur next door to hocus pocus and chicanery. In other words, the religious path breakers and leaders of our state were dedicated, often frail, human beings. Their adventures were essentially our own. And it all, thankfully, looked like great fun for the reader.

Reared in Roman Catholic (Buerge) and Episcopalian (Rochester) religious traditions, and having had educational and employment experiences in the Pacific Northwest and abroad, we found the diversity of local religious activity fascinating. Maybe Washington State's gleaming mountains, colorful prairies and relentless waters offered extraordinary challenge to our forebears. Something certainly inspired and tested them. Similar forces seem to create independent Washington State residents today. We, the authors, feel those same tremors, and therefore can empathize, but not always agree, with the religious upheaval and change marking our far corner.

Though most religions seek to direct our gaze to another reality, and claim to be not of this world, they exist within it. That worldly connection is the subject of this book. One volume (or two or ten) cannot adequately describe the historical riches to be found in this lode. Our intention is to entertain, educate, and stimulate readers to dig deeper into our religious heritage. Though our story is based on fact, the sources are human beings—and often human beings dedicated to tenets of a particular faith. Now and then a source may inadvertently embellish or sound a shrill note when straight narrative would have been enough. We have tried to respect all religious sources, while nevertheless recognizing their worldly connections and bias.

Washington State has been described as the most unchurched part of the nation. Though the population may have the lowest per-capita membership in religious bodies of any region in the country, that fact doesn't tell us much about the impact of these bodies on the state's history. American immigration into the Pacific Northwest began in part as a religious crusade; much of Washington's health, educational, and welfare establishment owes its existence and character to religious groups, and some of its politics turned on issues generated from within religious organizations. With few exceptions, the sense of community within ethnic groups coalesced around a church, temple or synagogue.

In 1689, English jurist and scholar John Selden, wrote "Religion is like the fashion: One man wears his doublet slashed, another laced, another plain; but every man has a doublet; so every man has a religion. We differ about the trimming." Washington State's past is in large measure a tailor's shop full of religious trimming, with national and economic issues strewn about. The most colorful and memorable figures behind the shop's counter are religious characters. Our state has recognized that unique link with religious origins by choosing two unusual representatives for perpetual honor in Statuary Hall, U.S. Congress: Marcus Whitman, M.D., pioneer Protestant missionary; and Esther Pariseau—Mother Joseph, Catholic founder of numerous health institutions, including the Providence Hospitals.

Roots and Branches may be the first of its kind: a summary, a detailed sketch, of religious institutions and characters that were important to our state's history. The reader may choose an era, a decade, a favorite religious figure, or follow the whole story from aboriginal Winter Dance to New Age. Whichever, we hope the pleasure of reading this story equals our interest and excitement in setting it forth.

David M. Buerge,
Seattle, Washington

Junius Rochester,
Walla Walla, Washington

November, 1988

Introduction

Church histories are nothing new in Washington. Most denominations have written material documenting their growth and experiences in the Northwest, in which their authors often seek to show the hand of Providence at work in their group's successes. In this book, however, we tried something a little different. Instead of writing a history of a church or even a group of them, we attempted instead to examine in general the history of religions in Washington.

There are good reasons for doing this. Every history of Washington or the Northwest includes a part dealing with the early missionaries who created an American colony in the Oregon Country and were in large part responsible for the development of its first institutions. But after the Whitman massacre in which missionaries Marcus and Narcissa Whitman and several others died at their mission station, Waiilatpu, on the Walla Walla River in 1847, the missionaries virtually drop out of the picture, and picturesque lumbermen, settlers, railroad men, financiers and politicians step up to take their places in the narrative.

Look out on any town or city in Washington today, however, and you will see an assortment of steeples, towers or otherwise imposing structures calling attention to a bewildering variety of religious congregations. Obviously the missionary churches did not disappear: instead, they grew and multiplied. Churches are often in the news today for one reason or another, not all of them positive, but no one can deny their influence. Washington is said to be the most unchurched state in the Union, but the part that is churched, the thirty or forty percent of the population that belongs to any of several hundred denominations, has a loud voice. They may not speak as one, and their members often squabble among themselves, but they are heard. Churches, by which we mean organized religious bodies representing varieties of Protestant, Catholic, Orthodox, Jewish, Buddhist, Hindu and Muslim faiths, as well as a host of others including native American and some uniquely local sects, are significant, and on occasion powerful instutions. An appreciation of Washington's history during this centennial year, therefore, cannot be complete unless we examine their history.

We decided against writing a history of each denomination. That would be too cumbersome, and one finds that, in general, church histories read similarly. Because they are institutions, they tend to follow the same patterns of growth, decline, division and renewal that characterize other institutions here and elsewhere. A person who seeks the history of his particular denomination in this book will be disappointed: it is simply too small to accomodate them all or even only a few of the major ones which, for the most part, are amply documented elsewhere.

What this book attempts instead is to trace the complex and fascinating history of religion in Washington State, organized and in some cases disorganized. Religion is a profound phenomenon, one that has public and private aspects that cannot be separated. To write a religious history of the state without examining the lives of some of those who gave it form would do violence to both aspects. To address this problem, biographical vignettes have been placed at strategic points within the historical narrative. The book is a cooperative effort and it does not pretend to be complete. The subject is too large for that, but we hope it will serve as a provocative and interesting introduction to a topic not generally covered, but one worthy of interest and further study.

Just as Washington has its share of famous timber barons, railroad magnates, civic leaders and politicians, it also has had the benefit of a wide variety of extraordinary religious figures. Some of these have had influence beyond the boundaries of the state. Marcus and Narcissa Whitman are as significant to Oregon and Idaho history as they are to Washington's, and native American religious leaders like Smohalla and John and Mary Slocum inspired movements that still command followings throughout the Northwest and much of the larger West. Presbyterian Reverend Mark Allison Matthews gained national recognition as a pastor in the early decades of this century just as Catholic Archbishop Raymond Hunthausen has in our own time.

To avoid the kind of rivalry that comes from congregations which dote on their present pastor, priest or rabbi, the leaders profiled in the vignettes are deceased, but even within this limitation, there was a problem selecting a relative few from a host of deserving candidates. Some, like Mother Joseph, the Reverend John Wilbur and Rabbi Raphael E. Levine, are fairly well known and their work well documented, but others like the Reverend Gertrude Apel, Abraham

Huppin, the Reverend Fred Shorter and the Buddhist Reverend Tatsuya Ichikawa are more obscure and undeservedly so. Many of those profiled are distinguished by their vision and hard work; others for their skill and personal flair, and others still for a rare and dramatic enthusiasm. All helped build and mold the religious institutions that enrich the state and help give it its heterodox character.

The roles they played are part of an extremely long story. One of the advantages of writing on a universal topic like religion in a local setting is that it allows one to bridge the boundary dividing the periods before and after white settlement.

The first chapter seeks an understanding of native American religious traditions, and the intimate connection native beliefs had with the land the people lived in for at least ten millenia. If these traditions are still imperfectly understood, none can deny their significance, vitality and enormous durability. The chapter can offer only a brief outline of what beliefs and customs were prevalent or could be recalled at the time when the first records of them were written, but it is important to understand that the nineteenth-century missionaries did not step into a spiritual vacuum when they entered the Northwest.

The second chapter examines the role of the missionaries and their churches in the area now called Washington state, beginning with the first efforts by the Spanish in 1790. The missionary chapter in Washington's history began with high hopes but ended in the blood of martyrs and victims. The source of the tragedy was the fact that missionary work was intimately involved with the furtherance of national ambition. The rivalry between the English and French in Canada, and between the United States and Great Britain in the Oregon Country, had strong religious overtones which powerfully affected the history of the Northwest. Key roles in the unfolding drama were played by religious figures such as Jason Lee, Pierre De Smet and the Whitmans. Sadly, the struggle for the native soul turned too quickly into a struggle for his land, and for their part in the contest, the Whitmans paid dearly.

The real victims, however, were the native people who died by the score, who lost their lands and much of their culture. One of the few consolations left to them was religion—that introduced to them by the missionaries, but also their own which survived in many forms into the new dispensation. It helped keep alive the people's most cherished cultural possession, the hopeful spirit that had sustained them for thousands of years.

The blood of conflict marked the birth of Washington Territory, and the third chapter follows the history of the churches when most histories abandon them. Pioneering church men and women worked alongside other immigrant builders to raise the foundations of their institutions in the new land. Necessity inspired cooperation, and the work of the churches was furthered enthusiastically by pioneer women anxious for a stable environment in which to raise their families. To provide education for the children, church men and women took the lead in developing many of Washington's first schools and institutions of higher learning, many of which survived into the period of statehood. In the vital flux of frontier life, church leaders took an active role in civic affairs, supporting a successful but shortlived effort to extend the vote to women in order to gain votes for temperance legislation.

Although these efforts failed, the churches persevered, and chapter four examines their response to the multitudes of problems and opportunities that confronted them as the frontier gave way to the complexities of urban, industrial life. The phenomenal growth at the turn of the century was matched by an exuberant idealism that found expression in the efforts of several denominaitons to build hospitals, orphanages and homes for the region's sick and abandoned. As new groups of immigrants entered Washington, many denominations sponsored missions to them, and the ethnic church often served as a nucleus around which a sense of community, be it German, Scandinavian, black American, Italian or Japanese, developed. Many of the new peoples brought new faiths with them, and the period saw growth in Jewish, Orthodox and Buddhist congregations. There was continuing ferment among native Americans as well as new prophets who rose to call their people to honor the old traditions. The spiritual idealism of the time also expressed itself in renewed efforts by the churches to seek passage of legislation extending the vote to women and enacting laws prohibiting the manufacture and sale of liquor, both of which were crowned with success before World War I.

If these successes were a measure of the churches' influence in the state, an influence all the more surprising for the relatively small number of their adherents, the end of prohibition in 1933 was seen by their critics as a sympton of their decline. The final chapter examines the profound, often wrenching changes that have affected religious bodies in Washington as they have affected the rest of society in the twentieth century. In spite of wars, economic disasters and severe social tumult, the religious impulse continued to impel individuals to action, and churches continue to play an important role in society. In an effort to pool their slender resources and become more effective, churches learned to work together, and some merged into larger bodies. One of the more notable expressions of the cooperative spirit was the television program "Challenge" which went on the air in 1960. Protestant, Catholic and Jewish clergy who participated in that program gained national recognition for their efforts to further ecumenical understanding between denominations. At a time when many regarded religion as an anachronism, their efforts and the efforts of others gave the churches a renewed credibility that made them potent forces for social action and reform.

The events and individuals chronicled in this book are part of the larger history of Washington whose character they helped shape. The modern period has witnessed the appearance of Hindu and Muslim congregations so that now every major faith on the planet and a host of minor ones are represented in the state. Those faiths present a rich spectrum of belief, and their influence is likely to grow, to the delight of some and the dismay of others. The carryings-on of some in the so-called electronic church confirm in many the suspicion that the churches are bastions of hypocrisy and forces for reaction. On the other hand, the recent statement of apology by many of the pioneering denominations to native Americans whose spiritual heritage they demeaned, now points toward a healing of the ancient wound that has scarred Washington state since its birth. Washington's religions today present a picture as varied as their history is long. Their roots reach deep into the soil of the past and their branches are spread wide. And bitter or sweet, the fruit they bear provides nourishment to many.

David M. Buerge
Seattle, Washington

Junius Rochester
Walla Walla, Washington

Acknowledgements

Special thanks to Church Council of Greater Seattle and its Washington State Centennial Celebration Committee headed by the Reverend Ron Marshall of the First Lutheran Church of West Seattle. We are also grateful to the Reverend Dr. William B. Cate, President-Director of the Church Council, who undertook many tasks on behalf of *Roots and Branches* with humor and a keen sense of priority, aided by the Church Council staff.

Thanks to our skilled professionals: Adrian Kalar, regarding the artistic and printed work; Judy Pickens directed marketing and coordination efforts, plus firmly holding us to a time-line; Dan Peterson, editor, provided historical review and graciously assumed most of the detail work involved in book editing.

Unstinting cooperation from individuals representing many religious organizations extended the scope of our project while helping reduce errors. The authors assume responsibility for any remaining errors or omissions.

Ron Marshall's Committee not only regularly attended meetings, but also provided helpful information and read draft copy. The active committee included:

Rev. Dr. A. J. Fjellman	Lutheran (E.C.L.A.)
Jessie Kinnear-Kenton	Presbyterian (Church Council Historian)
Chester Kingsbury	Methodist Layperson
Rev. Timothy Nakayama	St. Peter's Episcopal
Rev. Paul Pruitt	United Christian Church
Lavern Ricke	Lutheran (E.C.L.A.)
Rev. Richard A. Seiber	Epworth Le Sourd United Methodist Church

Contacting a wide variety of religious groups was one of the challenges and rewards of this book. In alphabetical order the following religious institutions or individuals with access to specific religious data were contacted:

Baha'i: Robert Stauffer, Wes Dyring and Janet Tanaka all offered draft reading and bibliographic suggestions.

Baptist: Rev. Peter Koshi read several biographical sketches, and Rev. Lemuel Peterson offered help on recent Seattle church religious activism and about Rev. Gertrude Apel.

Buddhist: Sat Ichikawa and Etsuko Osaki edited the sketch about their father, Tatsuya Ichikawa, while Adrieene Chan (Sakya Monastery) offered information on Buddhism in the Pacific Northwest.

Catholic: Sister Rita Bergamini and her archival assistant Loretta Green helped with photos from the Sisters of Providence archives, as did Christine Taylor, archivist for the Archdiocese of Seattle. Wilfred P. Schoenberg, S.J., Gonzaga University, provided critical reviews and suggested sources.

Christian Church: Frances A. Hare and Dr. and Mrs. Douglas Corpron of Yakima provided photos and expertise on the Corpron family.

Christian Science: Linda DiBiase and William R. Thompson shared their research and suggestions.

Episcopalian: Duncan A. Bayne, Seattle, and Peggy Ann Hansen, Ven. Paul Langpaap, Joyce McConnell, all of the Diocese of Olympia, gave critical reviews and suggestions regarding Bishop Stephen F. Bayne Sr. On behalf of the Cathedral of St. John the Evangelist in Spokane, B.T. and V. Whithouse provided Cathedral photos and information on Spokan Garry.

Jewish Community: Gene Huppin and his daughter Beth helped with the Abraham Huppin sketch, Xeno York added insight on Rabbi Raphael H. Levine, the office of Rabbi Earl S. Starr was very cooperative, and Julie Eulenberg read and proofed several chapters plus offering her research on Rabbi Koch.

Latter-day Saints: Carol O. Hinckley provided research and advice as did Dwaine Hatch, while Leora Clawson and her son Jack reviewed the material on James H. Clawson.

Lutheran: Retired Bishop Dr. A. G. Fjellman offered research materials and information on Lutheran mergers and Dr. Philip Nordquist, Pacific Lutheran University historian, reviewed the biographical sketch on Dr. Hans A. Stub.

Methodist: Chester Kingsbury read the entire rough draft and offered help from his experience as a printer as well as an active layman. Rev. Richard Sieber proofed Chapter Two as well as provided us the Methodist archives photo collection at the University of Puget Sound. LouAnn Bivins also helped with Methodist archival material.

Presbyterian: Jessie Kinnear-Kenton reviewed and proofed the Gertrude Apel sketch.

Quaker: Rich Beyer provided original ideas about the Friends.

Seventh-day Adventist: Elwood L. Mabley and Lee Johnston of the Walla Walla College library provided photo and archival data.

Unitarian: Clarice Wills and Rev. Peter Raible gave help on historical and current Unitarian activities.

Vedanta: Devra Freedman of the Seattle Vedanta Society provided information and later reviewed Vedanta materials.

A large measure of help came from the academic community. In addition to Gonzaga University and Walla Walla College, already credited, Whitman College's Prof. G. Thomas Edwards offered critical reading on the Whitman and Eells missionary families, while archivist Lawrence L. Dodd, librarian Henry M. Yaple and the staff of Penrose Memorial Library opened their materials to the authors. Paul Buell, Western Washington University, helped with Asian religions. From Seattle Central Community College, Ben Yorita read several biographical sketches, James B. Baenen and Dr. Astrida Onat read Chapter One from anthropological perspectives. John Doty read all of the first draft material and Nada Oakley read the second draft copy and helped clean up copy for the typesetter.

Native American traditional educator Mrs. Cecelia Eli helped our understanding of native Washani religion. Jon Magnuson also read topics dealing with Native Americans with a critical eye.

Several members of the University of Washington library faculty offered suggestions, while Northwest Collection archivists Carla Rickerson and Gary Menges helped with the photo collection materials.

The Museum of History and Industry (Seattle) and the Washington State Museum of History (Tacoma) staffs were generous with time and materials.

Other institutions that were helpful included the Seattle Art Museum; Peterson Memorial Library, Walla Walla College; the public libraries in Walla Walla and Seattle; the Penrose Memorial Library at Whitman College; Northwest Collection, University of Washington; and the Public Relations Office of the University of Puget Sound.

Archives of the diocese of Olympia, Episcopal Church in Western Washington, Seattle Catholic Archdiocese, Sisters of Providence and Methodist archives at University of Puget Sound all provided generous help.

The Yakima Valley Museum and Historical Association sent us photos and research material. Members of the Pacific Northwest Historians Guild were helpful, including Murray Morgan, dean of regional historians, Charles P. LeWarne, Doris Pieroth, Esther Mumford who shared her research on the early black community in Seattle, and finally Doug Honig's insights and materials.

From the National Park Service's Whitman Monument near Walla Walla Roger L. Trick and June Cummins provided valuable missionary materials. Stephanie Toothman of the National Park Service's Seattle office offered assistance.

Individuals such as Frances Owen, Al McVay, David Brewster, and R. Mort and Bob Frayn offered suggestions, support and counsel. Guela Gayton Johnson was helpful with materials on Sister Emma J. Ray and other black religious leaders. Florence Peterson shared some of her minister husband's materials on Grand Coulee Dam. Gary Darragh, KOMO-TV Tape Librarian, provided photos of members of the Challenge panel.

North Seattle Community College provided work space to assemble and review copy. The University Bar and Grill was the convivial site of a number of author-editor-professional meetings.

Wilma Schmerer did much of the word processing; Whitman College student Matthew Sabin organized the index; Doug Wainwright worked on printing problems; Susan Batchelor helped on the photo captions and proofread many pages. Shari Peterson proofread the majority of these pages and typed a good many more in re-writing. Janet Jensen did all of the typesetting, and Larry Cort of Rainier Mapping developed the maps.

In case we have forgotten a specific person or act of kindness, all those involved in the work of this book thank the unknown person or persons in the style of St. Paul who observed the Athenians and their altar to the unknown god.

Finally, the authors personally thank their families and special friends for love and support. For David Buerge that includes Mary Anne, David John, Katie Em, and Catherine Callaghan. For Junius Rochester: Janice, Tommie, Julie, and Steven, as well as Marguerite and Alfred R. Rochester. Tom Kuebler and Denis Ostermeyer get a special salute.

1

The First People

Ten thousand years ago, a body was burned in the harsh landscape of eastern Washington. When the wind cooled the last embers, the charred bones were lifted from the feathery ash, carried into a rockshelter and buried. Buried with them was a talisman, an owl claw with a hole bored through its leg bone and flanked by two pieces of flaked stone. Once these rituals for the dead were completed, the people carried on with the work of living in the huge, windswept land.

Ten thousand years later, archaeologists discovered the burial in the lower levels of what had become known as the Marmes Rockshelter. To their trained eyes, the claw flanked by its stones looked very much like a medicine bundle, a ritual object worn by modern Native Americans, the probable descendants of those first people who buried their dead in the rockshelter. The archaeologists found other artifacts revealing of how the people lived in those distant times. We know they possessed weapons to hunt large animals, and delicate, eyed needles to sew clothing. We know they also shared a set of beliefs that bound them to act in certain ways: a belief that events could be affected supernaturally through the use of talismans, and that the dead should be cremated and buried. As it was elsewhere in the prehistoric world, the development of culture at the time was intimately bound up with the phenomenon of religion.

Only a few clues give us any idea about the nature of that religion during the long millenia of human residence here. The people built no temples, pyramids or churches as a testament to their faith. The presence of grave goods, however, indicates a belief in an afterlife, and the documentation of different styles of burial suggests the belief had variations. A remarkable collection of carved bone figures found in graves throughout the state suggests the widespread popularity of at least one supernatural figure about 1,000 years ago, but its identity is unknown.

Rock art—petroglyphs carved onto rock surfaces or pictographs painted on them—survives at several sites throughout the state, and some of it may be thousands of years old. Much rock art may commemorate spiritual events like vision quests and initiations or honor supernatural beings associated with certain places. In eastern Washington, vision quests involved the creation of rock cairns that survive in isolated spots.

Indeed, our ability to identify many ancient objects and practices by comparing them with more recent examples suggests that there are more similarities than differences between the prehistoric religion and what was observed in historic times. Having said this, we must immediately qualify the statement by noting that the historic period wrought profound and often catastrophic changes in the lives of Washington's native people that were reflected in their religious beliefs.

The historic period began in the late 1700s when the first European and American explorers arrived. In 1788, the American trader Robert Gray saw evidence of smallpox among native groups along the Pacific coast, and when British explorer George Vancouver saw skeletal remains scattered along Puget Sound beaches in 1792, he concluded, correctly, that the area had been recently visited by an epidemic. Lewis and Clark made similar observations entering the Pacific Northwest in 1805 where they also found native groups in possession of the horse. These two things, the introduction of the horse and western diseases, had a profound impact on native life, producing social revolution in the first case and causing severe depopulation in the second.

These changes complicated an already complex situation. As information about Northwestern native life accumulated in the eighteenth and nineteenth centuries, its enormous variety became apparent. Linguistically the people were divided into several major groupings and a host of minor ones. Much of the Pacific shore of what is now Washington, the Olympic Peninsula, the Puget Basin, and the northern two-thirds of the state's interior were occupied by groups speaking tongues belonging to the Salish language family. On the western margins of this language territory were pockets of other linguistic groups: the Wakashan Makah, Chemakuan Quilleute and Chemakum of the Olympic Peninsula, and the Penutian Chinook and Athapascan Willapa of the lower Columbia River. The southern Cascade mountain region and interior were occupied by Shahaptin groups like the Klikitat, Yakima and Nez Perce.

Such complexity suggests a complicated past, but language was only one factor dividing the people. Just as geography and environment west of the Cascade Mountains differed from that east of them, so did the life-ways of the people. West of the Cascades people traveled long distances in large dugout canoes, lived in cedar plank longhouses and wore clothing made from cedar bark. As one moved eastward, however, the horse became the dominant mode of transportation; people lived in semi-subterranean pit houses or, more recently, mat lodges, and they wore clothing made from animal hides. Socially, too, there were major differences. In the west there was heavy emphasis on class, status and the importance of property, while in the east, a greater sense of equality prevailed.

Throughout the region, people showed little inclination to organize themselves into groups larger than those occupying winter villages, the cluster of houses where groups of families spent the winter months. Only the Umatilla and to a lesser extent, the Nez Perce, east of the Cascades organized themselves into tribes, but this was a fairly recent development evidently brought about by the introduction of the horse. The picture of native life in Washington that emerges for the early historic period is a complicated one, with literally hundreds of autonomous groups living in their own unique ways, each with their own traditions that were developed over a long period of time.

A few elements, however, did bring a measure of unity to certain areas. Some groups shared a linguistic or an ethnic identity. More significant was the unifying effect of water. East and west of the Cascades, sustenance was derived most importantly from bodies of water, from the great Pacific Ocean to the smallest creeks. The region's most important food source, the salmon, congregated in rivers to spawn and were caught there in the greatest numbers. Even with the introduction of the horse, rivers continued to be major arteries of travel and communication, and kinship patterns followed their flow. The rivers' role in providing many indpendent and often contentious village groups with a sense of common identity is apparent in the remarks of informants like John Sams, a Swinomish elder, who observed that, "every river has its people," or another man who attributed the sense of affinity shared by the Puget Sound peoples to the fact that its rivers, "flowed in the same direction," that is, toward the Sound.

If we cannot speak of a single people, a single society or even a single culture when we describe Washington's native peoples, neither can we speak of a single religion. But an examination of several widespread practices and beliefs may give us a sense of the rich religious heritage of Washington's first people.

If every river had its people, each people appears to have had its own myth of creation. Generally, each family had its own version of the myth which it passed down through its generations like a sacred heirloom and which its members regarded as their own property to be recited by them alone. These myths were localized; that is, the events and characters in them were associated with specific landmarks like certain hills, rocks, lakes and other features located within the area the people regarded as their traditional homeland. In this way the landscape was given a potent supernatural dimension, and the prerogative of reciting the myths associated with its features strengthened the group's claim to it and its resources.

This is in keeping with religious tradition throughout the world. Jews and Christians, for example, share a sacred landscape described for them in the Old Testament. Just as these groups associate important events in their common heritage with landmarks like Mt. Ararat, Jacob's Well, Mt. Sinai and Jerusalem, the native people here celebrated landmarks that were equally important to them. The major difference, of course, is that while Jews and Christians living here must make a long and expensive journey to visit their holy land, Native Americans live in theirs. Their homeland is also their holy land.

A sacred landscape did more than evoke a sentimental response or strengthen claims to an area's resources. It and the myths that sacralized it served also as a working model of the universe. As such it enabled the people to participate in the drama of nature, and by providing them with a shared vision of the world, strengthened the bonds that gave them their sense of identity. Two examples out of the many show how this was done and how different their approach could be.

The first features a cluster of low hills and rock formations that straddle the Duwamish River in the present communities of South Park, Allentown and Riverton, south of Seattle. These landmarks figure prominently in a group of myths collected by ethnographer Arthur Ballard from native informants early in this century that seek to describe the origin of the weather cycle in the Puget Basin.

A small knoll west of the river in South Park is identified in one myth as Sba'bateel, the "little mountain," the center of the world. This is where the Ancients, probably the four winds, are said to have lived and made the four divisions of the world. The number four, a sacred number, refers to the four cardinal directions, and the act of dividing the earth into quarters is a sacred action common to many Native American creation myths. As the story unfolds, one of the winds, cold Northwind, attempts to dominate the others. According to one version of the myth, he sought to marry Mountain Beaver Woman, but she refused him and married Chinook Wind instead. Enraged, he killed Chinook Wind and all his people except an old woman who took refuge on a hill in Riverton. Northwind tormented the old woman by sending ravens to defecate on her face, hence her name, "Dirty Face," or "Marked Face." Then, Northwind covered the land with ice and snow and built an ice fishweir across the Duwamish River from his village at Sba'bateel to keep the salmon from going upstream.

In time, Mountain Beaver Woman, gave birth in hiding to a son by Chinook Wind. Although warned to keep away from the hill at Riverton, he inevitably visited it and discovered the old woman, miserable and filthy, weaving baskets. From her he learned the fate of his father's people. Washing her face, a purifying act enabling her to manifest the power to bring the rain, he took the name "Stormwind," and set out to do battle with Northwind.

Sensing a threat, Northwind tried to ally himself with Stormwind by offering his sister in marriage, but Stormwind refused. The sister, described as an evil temptress, is identified with a small hill on the east bank of the river. Eventually, Stormwind fought Northwind and drove him from the country, and the old woman shook the rain from her baskets, melting the ice and snow and washing away most of Northwind's fishweir. The remnant, transformed into rocks, still lies on the river's east bank.

The myth describes a crucial time of the year when the Chinook winds of fall are superceded—'killed'—by a northerly surge of Arctic air that often plunges the Puget Sound region into sub-freezing temperatures. Winter's grip is loosened by a southerly surge of warm maritime air, generally stormy and rainy—the successor to the rain storms of the fall—that ushers in the spring.

Cold winters were hard on a people who lived in drafty houses and were drawing on the last supplies of food collected during the previous summer and fall. Food would not be abundant until spring, and since salmon did not begin their up-river migrations until the spring floods had ceased, the people eagerly awaited the end of winter and the onset of the spring rains. To hurry them along, the people recited the myths and performed rituals by which, through the agency of sympathetic magic, they sought to call on Stormwind and the old woman to manifest their power. Duwamish women went to the hill at Riverton and washed a part of it that was streaked with mineral stains just as the old woman's face was marked by filth. Thus purified, she could bring on the rain. Boys swung bull-roarers, blades of wood attached to strings, mimicking the sound of Stormwind. Dramatizing another version of the myth, men captured sparrows and rubbed their faces with charcoal. In this version, Sparrow took the role of the old woman, and when the birds flew to the riverside to wash the charcoal from their faces, they recapitulated the action that enabled Sparrow to manifest his power.

Ultimately these myths were concerned with the timing and success of the salmon runs. This concern is also part of another very different creation myth centered on the Sacred Island at Priest Rapids on the Columbia River, a great slab of basalt now submerged behind Priest Rapids Dam. It was passed down through the prophets of the Washani or Dreamer religion of the area, and was recorded by the newspaperman and writer, Click Relander, in the 1950s. It tells the story of the creation of successive worlds by Nami Piap, the creator god, and their destruction by fire, flood and terrible windstorms. The Sacred Island survived them all, the mythic pivot around which the storms of creation rolled. It was called Chalwash Chilni, the name of One-legged Abalone Man, who in an early age lived there with his friend, Anhyi, the Sun. Their friendship lasted until they fought over the use of the dip net to catch salmon. The dip net was used by people lower down on the river but was tabu at Priest Rapids where people use seines. Chalwash Chilni killed the Sun, decapitated him and threw his parts into the river where they became a group of rocky islands next to the Sacred Island.

When this happened, Nami Piap became angry. He plunged the world into darkness and filled the land with fire and ashes. Chalwash Chilni escaped downriver to join his people in the ocean, and Nami Piap created a new race for the Sacred Island. The world he created for them was a paradise, and to give it light, he transformed Anhyi into a heavenly lamp. But over time the people forgot to pray the prayers of thanksgiving, and to punish them, Nami Piap had the sun hide behind a hill and blasted the world with cold. Only a remnant survived to live in the next world which was not as perfect as the previous one had been. The Sun was released but gave light for only part of the day. To help at night, however, the creater put the moon and the north star into the sky. The people were taught anew the proper way to live and to honor the salmon and were warned that if they did not do as they were commanded, a flood would come, the salmon would die and their world would be destroyed.

The Sacred Island was important to people over a wide area. There were at least 150 petroglyphs and pictographs on it and many were associated with events and figures in the myth. It was used as a burial place, and youths carried out vision quests on its boulder-strewn surface. More importantly, as we shall see, it served as the mythic setting for a religious movement that had a profound impact on the lives of native people in much of the Northwest.

The battle between Northwind and Stormwind and the events that took place on the Sacred Island happened in a myth time believed to exist before human beings flourished in the world. In most myths, this time is brought into being by the creator god who unlike Nami Piap is generally described as a distant figure, an old or one-eyed man. Among the Spokane he is identified as Amotqen, the Sun, who lives at the top of a great tree. The various beings he creates are sometimes termed the Elipoo or Elip Tillikum, the "first people," titans who have the characteristics of humans and animals. Their nature and activity give the world its form; their battles produce its canyons, its rivers and its cyclic seasons, and later many become part of the earth, the sky and the heavens.

Figures associated with meteorological and celestial phenomena are generally male, but the earth is female, and like the triple-goddess of the Old World, it is perceived as having three aspects. These are personified as the anarchic maid of springtime, the nurturing mother of summer and fall and the hag of winter. Boulders that straddle the tideline, like Capstan Rock on Hood Canal, are sometimes identified as spring maids who leave their menstrual huts and copulate with a multitude of wind and water beings. Punished for their sins or otherwise abused, they weep down the rains. Hills or snow-capped mountains like Mt. Rainier are often identified as nurturing mothers or grandmothers. They plant gardens in the meadows around them and many carry children in the form of subsidiary peaks like Little Tahoma in the case of Mt. Rainier. In the summer, the white water streaming from their slopes is likened to milk pouring from their glacial breasts. They make fruit ripe, animals pregnant, and they call the salmon to spawn. The hag of winter carries a pitch-lined basket on her back in which she sticks children to take home and roast over her fire. West of the mountains she is identified as the bug-eyed Snailwoman; east of them, she is a terrible witch. The snailshell and the basket are symbolic of the womb, but the hag's is a carnivorous womb, devouring life instead of producing it. She is the earth in winter when leaves fall to the ground and disintegrate and salmon die in their streams.

Sometimes several aspects are combined in a single feature. A hill at Riverton combines aspects of the abused spring maid, weaving baskets in her menstrual hut, and the nurturing grandmother. Mount Rainier was maiden, mother and hag; creator and destroyer, as was a black boulder at Browns Point near Tacoma that was regarded with great awe.

In a world inhabited by such titans, human beings could hardly be expected to survive much less flourish, and to make creation habitable required the labors of another more powerful being. This was the figure known as the Changer, the Transformer or Coyote. He is called many names by many groups, but for all he is the culture hero, the demiurge who makes the world habitable for humanity.

Stories about him make up a large part of the regions' mythology. In the adventures of Coyote, he is desribed as vain and foolish, possessed of an unrestrained sexual apetite, but clever and ultimately wise. Stories about the Changer begin with an elaborate account of his birth as the Star Child, a being born of a union of heaven and earth. His most important work is carried out in an epic walk during which he battles the titans, defeats them and transforms them into natural phenomena. Some myths tell how he created human beings from a monster he killed and dismembered. The parts he throws to the four directions become the various peoples whose distinguishing character comes from the part out of which they sprang. It is he who marries into the race of Salmon People and establishes the covenant by which they agree to sacrifice their bodies yearly for the benefit of humanity. Every group celebrated his walk up their river in their myth of creation and in their sacred landscape. The transformation he wrought was a mythic cataclysm, a turning over or capsizing of the world, and with it, the myth time ends and the human era begins. By way of making the world habitable, the Changer transformed many of the Elip Tillikum into spirit beings that became benefactors to mankind. Many took the form of animals: Bluejay became a bird, Deer a quadruped and Skate a bottom-dwelling fish. As creatures, they could be used by humans for practical purposes, but their greater value lay in the supernatural gifts they offered. By communicating with a spirit being in a vision, a person could make it his guardian or ally and obtain the power that made it unique. Each spirit being had a particular song or dance that it taught the suppli-cant which when sung or danced enabled the person to manifest its power.

Ethnographers have collected long lists of these spirit beings from many groups, and the concept seems to have been open-ended. Distinguishing physical or character traits, from prowess in war to ownership of property, from generosity of spirit to craft skills, were attributed to the agency of spirit beings. Deer made one fleet; Blue-jay made one a talker; Grizzly Bear gave strength, Eagle courage. Fog enabled one to conceal himself while Hazelnut gave one the ability to get out of tight situations — just as the nut often shot away from a striking hammer. East of the mountains, where society was relatively egalitarian, the powers of spirit beings were judged roughly equal, but west of them, where rank and property were so important, some spirit beings, particularly the more abstract ones that made one wealthy, were believed to be more important and powerful than others.

Generally spirit beings were divided into two major categories: those that empowered lay men and women and those that empowered shamans. Shamans are more popularly if less accurately described as medicine men or witch doctors. They were important members of native society, and they often occupied positions of high rank. Shamanic powers were associated with the ability to diagnose and cure illness and sometimes to kill with witchcraft. Some also had the ability to influence nature, to see into the future and make journeys to the land of the dead. Although most shamans were men, women were not barred, and among the lower Chinook on the Columbia River, they outnumbered their male counterparts.

All native groups regarded the relationship an individual had with the spirit beings as the most important of his life. One could survive without such a realtionship, but one would never amount to anything. Spirit beings could be inherited; some liked to 'stay in the family,' and west of the mountains the more important wealth-giving spirit beings generally associated only with members of the highest class.

To make contact with the spirit beings, a person had to undergo a vision quest. Generally, this was done at puberty, although some groups believed that quests could only be carried out successfully before puberty when a person was free of sexual taint. Some allowed for only one quest for one spirit ally, while others, particularly west of the mountains, believed a person could make many quests and obtain several spirit allies.

To prepare for the initial quest, a child's parents or a trainer drawn from the extended family taught the novice how the quest should be carried out and how to deal with the different spirit beings that might be encountered. The quest might take one day or several and was usually made at some distant spot in which spirit beings were believed to reside. The child might be given an object to leave there or ordered to pile stones or bring back an object that had been placed there as proof that he had followed directions.

There was considerable concern about ritual purity during quests, since it was believed that spirit beings found uncleanliness offensive. Children were expected to fast and bathe after rubbing their skin vigorously with fir needles. Adults were expected to refrain from sexual activity, and many sought to purify themselves by taking steam baths in sweat lodges. The latter were generally small, conical huts in which steam was generated by pouring water over hot rocks.

The encounter with the spirit being often occured in a dream or a vision where the being spoke to the supplicant and, if judged worthy, taught him its song or dance. Sometimes contact required the supplicant to dive into deep bodies of water, enter the house of the spirit being and wrestle it for its power. One might go questing for a specific spirit being, but one might encounter another and receive its unexpected gift.

Both boys and girls made quests, but while in theory women could obtain powers equal to those of men, their inferior status, particularly west of the mountains, was believed to reflect the fact that theirs were generally weaker. Women, however, had the unique ability to produce life, and the onset of menarche which signalled the arrival of their power was regarded as an event of profound supernatural significance. On both sides of the mountains, menarche and subsequent menstrual periods were the occasion for ritual and the imposition of tabus. At menarche a girl was sequestered in a menstrual lodge, often for a lengthy period of time. This might be a screened-off section of a longhouse or a detached semi-subterranean hut. Certain types of clothing were worn; a ritual diet was prescribed, and her contact with the outside world was severely restricted. In some cases she could scratch her head only with a special scratcher or drink only through a drinking tube. Unless her power were thus restrained, it could prove dangerous. A hunter who somehow became contaminated with menstrual blood lost his power to hunt, and among the Spokanes and other interior groups, menstruating women were forbidden from approaching the fishweirs lest the salmon refuse to allow themselves to be caught.

During her confinement, a girl would be taught the responsibilities of womanhood and given materials with which to weave baskets. East of the mountains they were instructed to pray to the Day dawn. Her coming out was an occasion for celebration—a potlatch west of the mountains where that institution prevailed—and a sign that she had become a woman and could now receive proposals of marriage.

Powers obtained at pre-pubertal and pubertal quests often did not manifest themselves for many years, even decades, until the person matured. East of the mountains spirit beings were believed to remain close to a person, but to the west they were believed to lead a semi-migratory way of life, similar to their human hosts. In the spring, summer and fall when the people were out moving from camp to camp, the spirit beings traveled on the periphery of the world, in an anti-clockwise motion. In the winter, however, after the people returned to their longhouses, the spirit beings visited their hosts.

The arrival of one's spirit ally was counted as a momentous occasion. A symptom of its return was an illness described by some as a feeling of intense loneliness. A shaman was usually called upon to diagnose the condition, and once its cause was identified as spirit-possession, the 'patient' called upon his relatives and friends to join him in singing and dancing to control its power. These were the preliminaries to the winter dance, the most important religious celebration of the year. If a person did not heed his ally's return, the spirit being might abandon him, and he might die.

The weakening of one's faculties toward the end of life was perceived as the gradual dissolution of the bond between one's self and the spirit ally. In the end, death severed the relationship. When a person died, the soul left the body and traveled to the land of the dead where it became a ghost. Some groups believed that just as a person's soul went to live in the land of the dead, his spirit ally also died and its soul went to live in a ghost land of its own.

To some, the soul was a miniature version of the person that lived near the heart. The lower Chinook and the Twana of Hood Canal believed in two souls which the Twana described as a life soul that resided in the head and a heart soul. Some groups also believed in reincarnation, but this was thought to occur when children died. The Chinook believed that if parents did not care for their children properly, their soul would return to the spirit land to inhabit another body. Many groups believed that the souls of the dead returned in mid-winter to visit the houses of living relatives.

Throughout the region, the phenomenon of death provoked intense ritual behavior. Among some groups relatives' hair was cut and women were hired to wail. A tabu against speaking the deceased's name would be imposed so as not to call up his ghost. If a person died at home, the corpse might be taken out of the house through a specially made exit that was closed immediately afterwards so the ghost could not find its way back in. The house might be fumigated to drive the ghost away, disassembled and rebuilt at another spot or destroyed altogether.

West of the mountains the dead were buried in several ways. They could be interred in cedar boxes and wrappings over which large stones were heaped in a cairn, or in stone enclosures over which earth was heaped in a tumulus. Others placed their dead in elevated canoes or boxes. The differing modes may have been determined by family tradition, rank or an individual's special achievement. The bodies of children were often placed in boxes or baskets and secured in the branches of trees. After the flesh decayed, the bones of the dead would sometimes be cleaned and reinterred in a second burial, or they might simply be allowed to fall to the ground and be disturbed or preserved by local environmental conditions.

East of the mountains the dead were commonly buried on isolated islands, toes of cliffs or in open sandpits. Along the Columbia River, islands like Coffin, Memaloose and Blalock Islands, the Sacred Island and Rock Island served as communal cemeteries. For the rest of the interior, burial was in shallow graves, often in talus slides. Along the lower river graves were marked by elaborately carved and painted wooden figures, but further inland, a single painted pole sufficed. By the beginning of historic times, the Spokanes had begun the practice of hanging a horse's skin over the grave.

Just as the progress of a single life was marked by ritual observances, the passage of the year was measured by ceremonials. Many of these were inspired by the dramatic or long-awaited appearance of food sources. The beginning of the year, when the earth began to warm and new life appeared, was a critical time when supplies laid in from the previous year were nearly exhausted. When roots were ready to dig and berries were ripe, many groups performed simple first fruits ceremonies in which the first part of the crop was gathered and shared in a special meal. East of the mountains prayers might be addressed to the sun and a tray of food raised in its honor, or to a mountain peak or the four directions. Among some, the village head would lead his people in a thanksgiving dance when the crop was brought in.

The hunt, too, was inaugurated with ceremony. Among the Twana, elk hunters purified themselves by bathing, fasting and abstaining from sexual activity in order to enhance their hunting powers. A hunter's wife was expected to remain quiet and as still as possible while her husband was gone so as not to offend the elk spirit. These rituals were more developed along the coast where whales were hunted. Among the Makah, for example, harpooners spent long periods before the hunt purifying themselves and calling upon the whale's spirit. At home during the hunt, a harpooner's principal wife took the role of the whale, remaining docile and still so the kill would be successful.

The first whale killed was welcomed to the harpooner's village with great reverence and sprinkled with eagle down. The first elk or the first deer was boiled in its own skin and consumed in a kind of sacramental meal. Among the upper Skagit, the first bear of the season was similarly honored: its skull placed atop a pole and its flesh braided. The purposes of the rituals were to emphasize the importance of the food source and to insure the continued good will of the spirit governing its supply.

The most widely performed first fruits ceremony was held upon the arrival of the year's first salmon. For virtually every group that caught it, the appearance of the first salmon, the "crooked-jawed chief," was a joyous and important event, a witness once again to the covenant in which the Salmon People agreed to sacrifice their robes of flesh for the benefit of humanity. First salmon ceremonies made rituals of the catching, cleaning, preparation and consumption of the sacred fish. It was often ceremoniously welcomed and brought into the village by the headman in procession. It was cut lengthwise so the bones would not be disturbed, and after it was cooked and those assembled ate it, its skeleton was disposed of in such a way that its soul would be inclined to call the rest of the Salmon People upstream.

High up on the Columbia and its tributaries where the salmon ran later, and their appearance was even more critical, the ceremony was more elaborate. Fishing was supervised by a salmon chief: a shaman or a man who had Salmon as a spirit ally. Among the Nespelem and Sanpoil of northeastern Washington, the salmon chief set the time for the construction of fish weirs and supervised the first salmon ceremony and the subsequent distribution of fish. He also made sure that the tabus associated with the fish were rigidly observed.

Among these groups the first salmon was laid ceremoniously on a bed of sunflower stems and leaves. The head was broken off, and the back of the head and the backbone were preserved whole, wrapped and hidden. For the first four days of the ceremony, only the flanks of the fish caught were eaten—boiled during the first two days and roasted the second two. The heads, roe and other parts were put aside to dry, and on the fifth day they were mixed together with flanks and boiled in a soup. During this time only men ate the fish, but after the fifth day of the ceremony, women and children joined in the feasting.

Once ceremonies were done, fishing began in earnest and continued as long as the runs persisted, often well into November. Once the people returned to their winter houses well-supplied with food, they began preparations for the winter dances, held around the time of the solstice.

All native groups in Washington held winter dances, although as might be expected, they exhibited a great deal of variation. West of the mountains they were often closely associated with potlatches, during which the host would give gifts to acknowledge people and to thank them for their presence. Although the potlatch among the Salish was not as important an institution as it was further north, wealth-

giving spirit beings were still earnestly sought after, and the distribution of wealth at a potlatch was its own manifestation of power. Among
the Quinault of the Pacific Coast, the spirit-being came to its host and
told him, "You had better throw away our money now. I would like
to see the people enjoy themselves and hear all the shamans sing their
songs."

Singing, dancing and gift-giving made up the heart of the winter
dance ceremony, and the winter dance season took on a festive air
as people made the rounds from house to house and village to village
where relatives had announced the arrival of their spirit allies.

There were a number of spirit-allies who called upon their hosts
to perform extraordinary feats, and the demonstrations of these powers
was often the scene of great public drama. These might include feats
of strength or agility or demonstrations of an ability to inflict grievous
injury upon one's self without apparent pain or harm. One of the most
spectacular of these powers was the ability to animate objects and
have them move about a room, often dragging their holders after them.
Special objects: poles or hoops of vinemaple dressed in buckskin or
carved and painted cedarboards, were the centerpieces of these
demonstrations and were also used in healing ceremonies. They were
sacred, treated with the utmost respect as potent embodiments of
power, and they often had illustrious individual histories.

Winter dances west of the mountains also provided occasions for
performances by members of secret societies. Membership in secret
socities involved a complex initiation rite that might last several days
and included a public demonstration of power. Initiates were said to
be possessed by spirit beings that drove them out of their senses. To
keep from hurting themselves or others while in this state, they were
sometimes restrained by ropes or wrestled to the ground by society
members. By dancing and performing other rituals, society members
were able to calm the initiates and restore them to normalcy. These
ceremonies often involved the use of elaborate costumes and masks,
and among the Makah, members of several secret societies joined in
a dramatic masked procession.

Secret societies may have been introduced from further north on
the coast where in historic times they were notably secular and hierar-
chical. In Washington the initiation rites would appear to have been
regarded as social events as much as religious ones. One might

"become sick," that is, become possessed by the spirit being of a particular society, or simply request initiation. Ultimately, all who joined became "possessed" by the spirit being, and all had to pay a fee for the ritual entry period. Many secret societies appeared to cater to those who shared a particular skill like fishing, seal hunting or whaling.

Winter dances also provided an opportunity for shamans to demonstrate their powers to cure. Like most phenomena, illness was believed to have a supernatural origin. It might be caused by a spirit being having entered a person's body or having shot an object into the body. A shaman could cure the illness by extracting the spirit being or removing the pathogenic object. An especially powerful shaman could cure simply by extending his hands toward a patient, but generally they cured by either blowing on the affected part, rubbing the body to force the illness into one part from which it could be ritually extracted, or by finding where it was centered and sucking it out. The object removed might be a fragment of bone or wood that the shaman displayed triumphantly at the end of the session. Shamans were also schooled herbalists and cured by prescribing a wide variety of teas, purges and poultices, but this knowledge was not restricted to them.

The most dramatic example of shamanic curing involved the search and recovery of lost souls. Many groups located the land of the dead in the west, undergound or over the ocean. The Spokane believed souls traveled north to Amotqen's territory at whose boundary Coyote lived in a house of ice guarding the gate through which they had to pass. The land of the dead was often described as being opposite in character from the land of the living. Ghosts looked like skeletons, walked backwards and fished in canoes made of sticks. When it was day there it was night here; summer there—winter here, and the trail to the land of the dead was most easily traveled during our mid-winter. This is when the ghosts visited the land of the living, and to honor them, Puget Sound groups like the upper Skagit and the Nooksack prepared feasts for them in their longhouses. Sometimes, ghosts got lonely for human company and kidnapped souls to take home with them.

If a ghost kidnapped someone's soul, he became ill and began to lose property. Once this was diagnosed as soul-theft, a group of shamans was called in to make a journey to the land of the dead to retrieve the soul and return it to its owner. The best known examples of this ceremony, known as the "spirit canoe," were carried out by

Duwamish and Snoqualmie shamans. If the patient and his family could afford it, two teams of shamans were hired to make the journey in two spirit canoes. A large dance house was sometimes built to shelter the canoes represented each by a line of large spirit boards hewn from cedar slabs and painted with images of the spirit beings that enabled the shamans to make their journey, and smaller carved images of spirit helpers. An audience of relatives and associates would be invited to join the ceremony and help the shamans sing their songs.

The ceremony might last as long as six successive nights during which the shamans would follow the trail to the land of the dead. The topography of the spirit land was complicated, and they mimed the unique encounters they had with supernatural entities along the way. Once they arrived at the village, which stood on the bank opposite a river, they searched for the lost soul and finding it, fled, often fighting off an attack by the ghosts whose parts were played by young boys. All during these adventures the shamans and their audience sang their powerful songs to the thunderous accompaniment of poles pounded rhythmically against the roof planks of the house. The climax of the ceremony came when the shamans presented the soul to its owner. This was a moment of intense excitement: the singing had built to a crescendo; people were swaying to and fro; some were crying, and the patient was shaking uncontrollably. One who witnessed the ceremony as a child said it nearly scared him to death. If the song the shaman holding the soul sang was the same as the patient's spirit ally's, the cure was deemed successful.

East of the Cascades a person who sponsored a winter dance would distribute gifts to those who attended as a reward for their presence and help, but the institutions of the potlatch and the secret society were not a part of the ceremonies. Neither was it believed that the spirit beings returned from their peregrinations to possess their hosts. Rather, spirit allies were thought to be always present, but winter was the time their hosts were expected to demonstrate their power in ceremony.

Like their western counterparts, friends and relatives gathered at the house of a person who announced his desire to hold a dance over several nights to help in the singing and dancing. Shamans directed the ceremony, and a distinctive feature of many interior winter dances was the setting up in the middle of the house of a pole that represented the spirit being. Prayers were addressed to it, and small gifts: feathers, pieces of cloth, tobacco and other objects were attached to it, and at the end of the dance the pole and its gifts were covered, taken out into the woods and hidden.

Shamans were often called upon to cure, and in rituals reminiscent of those carried out along the Duwamish River, some also sought to hurry the departure of winter and the onset of spring. But the most remarkable participants in the winter dances of several interior groups were the individuals who assumed the character of the mythic figure, Bluejay. In myth Bluejay appears as a brash, noisy smart-aleck, but one who is also sharp-eyed and observant. Individuals who had Bluejay as a spirit ally would remove most of their clothing and blacken themselves as the winter dances began. They became like Bluejay, shunning normal human company, eating scraps or pine pitch and moving about in broad leaps, often roosting in trees. During the dances they acted as sentries perched in the rafters of the dance houses, watching for visitors and enforcing ritual etiquette, sometimes by swooping down and snatching food from the mouths of those who were breaking the tabu against eating. Some were believed to have the power to find lost objects and cure certain illnesses. They usually kept their identity until the end of winter when they were captured and forced to breath the smoke of burning roots, whereupon their Bluejay character 'died' and they resumed their normal human guise.

These annual rites celebrated the great rhythms of nature and the supernature world that empowered it just as those marking an individual's changing role in the community celebrated the tides of human life. The ceremonies dramatized the changes, celebrated renewal, but ultimately they sought to insure continuity. Their success could be measured against the continuing generosity of the environment and the vitality of the people in their long span of residence.

But there were also times when the great rhythms skipped a beat, when the environment failed and the salmon did not reappear or the deer and elk perished in a harsh winter. These catastrophes inspired desperate attempts to purify the community and appease the angry spirit beings. There were times, too, when the earth shook, the sky burned and darkened and the land was covered in ashes—times when the world seemed about to topple into cataclysm. Out of the depths of this terror came apocalyptic visions, and these inspired ceremonies of their own.

In the century leading up to the first appearance of the white man, native life was already beginning to experience revolutionary change. By the early 1700s, the horse was traded into the Columbia Basin and westward, and it began to transform life here as it had elsewhere on the continent. With increased mobility, the people were able to broaden their economic base and improve their life. Trips were made across the Rocky Mountains to buffalo country, and the customs and accoutrements of plains culture were brought back with the jerked meat. The great sun dance of the plains was celebrated by those who made the annual trek east as well as the hunting dances that were performed to ensure success. And because the hunt was often attended by violence as equestrian groups ran roughshod over old boundaries, war dances became more common.

Perhaps no more than two generations after the introduction of the horse, the people endured the first epidemic of western disease. The first scourge came out of the east in the 1780s, from the same direction as the horse had come. After that, epidemics of smallpox, measles and typhus came ever more frequently, and the results were terrifying. There was vast depopulation; in some cases entire peoples disappeared. In the vacuum groups wandered, carving out new homelands, desperately trying to regain their balance in a reeling world.

The first white visitors to the Northwestern interior observed many groups performing a dance ethnographers now refer to as the prophet dance. In it the people formed a circle and moved in a shuffling gait around a pole or the person who led them, a prophet who had received a vision and was impelled to proclaim its message. The prophet, and there were many of them, was one who was believed to have died and gone to the land of the dead. There, he received a message from the dead or from spirit beings who directed him to return to the land of the living and preach it. The prophets' messages were basically the same: the world was old and worn out and would soon be utterly transformed. When this happened, all those who had died would return to life. To hurry this, the people must dance.

It is possible to see even in this simplistic description elements that surely came from other seasonal rites, but the prophet dance had a distinctly apocalyptic tone, and it could be held at any time. As disaster was piled on disaster, it assumed greater importance. The return of the dead meant life without end, without want, and desperate groups sometimes danced through the time they would ordinarily have spent fishing or hunting, so that when winter came they faced starvation.

As the historic period approached and the whites drew ever closer, the visions and their messages became more specific. In the early 1700s, at a place called Sinielman, "the surrounded place," a valley near Flathead Lake in western Montana, a visionary named Shining Shirt prophesied that men with fair skins and black shirts would come to teach the people religion and give then new homes and new laws. His name may have come from a talisman he wore, a piece of metal inscribed with a cross. This may have been a religious medal traded in from the east or from the south, from the Spanish missions and settlements of New Mexico which was also the point of origin of the horse.

The Spokane recalled a similar prophecy made by one of their shamans, Yureerachen, "Circling Raven," in 1790. He had received a vision atop Mount Spokane where he had gone in despair in 1782 after a smallpox epidemic had decimated his people and killed his young son. He did not reveal its message until a fall of "dry snow"—volcanic ash—produced a panic among the remnant Spokane who were convinced the world was disintegrating. Yureerachen assured them that the end was not yet at hand. "Soon," he told them, "there will come from the rising sun a different kind of man from any you have yet seen, who will bring with them a book, and will teach you everything, and after that the world will fall to pieces."

Spokan Garry's Journey
Through Two Worlds

Chief Garry's father was called Illim-Spokanee—hence the origins of our word Spokane (Garry always dropped the "e"). His followers were called Salmon Trout people, and their influence matched the Northwest river systems of present-day Washington State and north Idaho. Garry was born into this rich tradition about 1811.

Spokan Garry in his later years.

Courtesy Penrose Memorial Library, Eells N.W. Collection, Whitman
College, Walla Walla, Washington.

In later years Garry would describe how his father prophesied that a people of different color would come and teach them many things. Illim-Spokanee's people, having seen a few "King George" men (British) and the occasional "Boston" (American) believed that the world would soon end. The old chief assured them that there was still plenty of time left.

When Garry was fourteen a decision was made in the white man's world that would literally change his life. Governor George Simpson of the Hudson's Bay Company asked his trader at Spokane House to find "two Indian boys...for the purpose of being educated at the school." The school to which he referred was a missionary institution under the aegis of the Church Missionary Society of the Church of England at Red River (Winnipeg).

Besides the Ten Commandments, Garry and his companion learned geography, English, writing skills and the difference between a Catholic and a Protestant. Not unlike a then prevalent view of "Roman" and "Boston" missionary thrusts into western lands, there was negative "feeling" between the two Christian faiths. The Anglican Catechism, Book of Common Prayer and church hymns were part of his daily academic diet. Garry and most of his Indian classmates seemed to feast on this austere, strange banquet. Their educational experience was, however, tantamount to a kind of benevolent imprisonment. For example, it was four years (1829) before Garry returned to visit his home. The old chief, Illim-Spokanee, had died while he was away.

Evidence suggests that Garry and his Spokane fellow student, Pelly, (those names were bestowed on Indian boys by Hudson Bay employees) immediately began to impart the Christian message to their Indian community. Their listeners were impressed. Thanks to these youthful Indian converts, this new and strange religion spread throughout the West. Garry was apparently the more articulate of the two. In fact, the historically famous Nez Perce and Flathead delegation of four Indians who appeared in St. Louis in 1831 looking for the white man's "Book", had heard the words of Garry and Pelly.

Spokane House had been abandoned in 1827. During the winter of 1831 Garry established a crude school and residence cross-river from the former Hudson's Bay post. Using an old bell, Garry summoned tribal members to Sunday services. Teaching his people to say grace at meals, observe the Ten Commandments and say the Lord's Prayer, Garry attracted followers from the Colville, Nez Perce, Coeur d' Alene, Pend d' Oreille, Flathead and Okanogan tribes. Catholic priests noted with some envy that Garry's error-prone, simple lessons were effective, in no small part because listeners were hearing these wondrous things from one of their own. One Indian observer of Garry's work said: "He told us of a God above...He said to us, if we were good, that then when we died, we would go up above and see God."

Spokan Garry's version of Christian tenets, usually mixed with native chants, shaking, monotonic hymns, bells and the up and down movement of arms, tended to attract Indian participants, while annoying white believers. This was evident in 1835 when Reverend Samuel Parker was dispatched as an observer to Oregon by the American Board of Commissioners for Foreign Missions. On September 5 he held a service for a band of Nez Perce. His congregation dutifully showed up in their best attire, kneeled or sat in a semi-circle, and then proceeded to murmur and hum throughout the service. Parker had the presence not to make an issue of this circumstance, and was otherwise favorably impressed. That amalgam of Indian and white, and the attentiveness, courtesy, and rough familiarity with the new religion, certainly stemmed from Garry's teachings.

In time Garry learned that there was a diversity of Christian faiths. His early exposure had been to three worlds: 1. his Indian traditions; 2. Anglicans—his new faith; and 3. Catholicism, which he viewed as "wrong". With arrival of the Marcus Whitman party the western religious landscape seemed to blur. Methodists, Presbyterians, itinerant preachers: these cross-currents, and then the Indian Wars following the Whitman murders in 1847, caused Garry's influence to decline. In fact, some of his followers, having found that not all white men lived by so-called Christian ethics, withdrew from the new religion. Indian prophets, many anti-white in character, gained favor in the early 19th Century. Later, the rise of Smohalla, legend-telling prophet of the Snake and Columbia River People, coincided with a decline of Pacific Northwest missionary influence.

Spokan Garry was also a human being. He married—at least twice—sired children, accumulated and lost wealth, and was known to enjoy gambling. Nevertheless, his stature among the Spokane Indian people, and in the eyes of white leaders, remained high. At a meeting near his village with territorial Governor Isaac I. Stevens, Garry eloquently asked the governor why he was "in such a hurry to have writings for your lands...?" Stevens was annoyed, especially when he heard the grunts of approval from other chiefs. During later Indian wars, Garry tried to act as mediator, based on his Christian beliefs. Such efforts were not always well-received by either friend or foe.

Famine, disease, liquor, the worst of the white man's world, now became his people's enemy. During the 1870s-80s western Indian reservations were firmly established. The long decline accelerated. Garry continued to oppose the "peagans" (Catholics) while attempting religious revival among his people. Referred to as "Chief" Garry by the whites, he was nevertheless growing old and frustrated by efforts to preserve his people's rights, especially their land base. Experiencing personal problems in establishing title to a small piece of property he owned, Garry lived in a teepee, virtually destitute. His wife Nina had gone blind. By the late 1880s his prairie had vanished. Instead, before him lay city streets, saloons, flour mills and plate glass windows. In 1890 Spokan Garry was still waiting for the $100 annuity promised by the white man's Congress.

On January 14, 1892, Spokan Garry died in his simple teepee. Despite his former influence, and his reverence for the Anglican faith, the Episcopal church in Spokane had never heard of him. Instead, friends from the First Presbyterian Church of Spokane arranged a funeral.

White injustices did not abate after Garry's death. His lands were seized, a few Cayuse horses he owned were stolen, and his old, blind widow Nina was removed to the Coeur d' Alene Reservation. Her Protestant remains were later interred in potter's field at Fairfield, Washington, because burial was refused at the Catholic DeSmet cemetery. It would be years before Spokan Garry would be honored as a Christian and defender of his people. Garry's old father, Illim-Spokanee, had told the truth: a people of a different color, he prophesied, would "come and teach them many things."

Smohalla, Indian High Priest and Dreamer

My young men shall never work. Men who work cannot dream, and wisdom comes to us in dreams...

Smohalla

A long the Columbia River banks, in today's Yakima County, a band of about 200 Indians followed the "Dreamer" teachings of a stocky leader called Smohalla. It all began in the 1850s near Wallula Gap, when Smohalla was thirty years old.

On the sacred mountain of LaLac, between modern day Prosser and the Columbia River, Smohalla received the visions that led him to become a twuteewit, or Indian doctor. Dissension among powerful chiefs forced him to move, and in time he led followers to the fishing station at Priest Rapids where the Wanapams lived. There he attracted more followers with his call to return to the ways of the ancestors and shun those of the whites.

According to newspaperman-historian Click Relander, Smohalla's life entered a critical period with the death of his dearly loved daughter. Devastated, he fell into a death-like swoon. Believing him dead, his followers prepared him for burial, but they were astonished when he stirred and even more astonished when he claimed that he had in fact died, that he had spoken with the spirits and had received from them a message for his people.

Earth as the center of all things was the core of Smohalla's dream-faith. Disturb the soil and great calamities will occur, he warned. Seasonal foraging by Indian tribes did not violate God's great creation, he said, but the daily, dawn-to-dusk digging, construction, cutting and planting by the whites was an insult to the earth.

Smohalla prophesied that an accounting was inevitable. Therefore, not unlike the millenium or Armageddon anticipated by other faiths, Smohalla's vision was also an admonition to his followers. Pervading his view was a deep suspicion of all white ways. Citing the "bottle of poison" that Dr. Marcus Whitman brought to the Cayuse, the white witch doctors were trying to destroy his people, he believed. Restoration of ancient, ancestral ways, was Smohallas's ultimate goal. It was clear, he believed, that the white man's ways had failed his people.

Army Major J.W. MacMurray was sent to Priest Rapids to meet Smohalla. His orders were to find out more about this aboriginal priest's religion and learn something of Indian restlessness in that region. What MacMurray found was a busy village with red-robed women chanting to the beat of drums. Trances were apparently induced during dances that occurred on special occasions and usually on Sunday—a possible influence from Hudson Bay Catholic priests.

Dressed in a white shirt, Smohalla oversaw these ceremonies while his son and heir to the priesthood knelt nearby. An interesting feature of these rites was the employment of an interpreter who loudly described the entranced utterances of each "speaker." MacMurray also learned that many of Smohalla's rituals were secret.

The Dreamer's religion spread to other Inland Empire tribes. The great leader Smohalla, who many believe never cut his thinning hair and fiercely retained anti-white sentiments, was said to live for many years as a recluse prophet along the cliffs of the Columbia River. His death in 1895 as a blind, impoverished leader of the Wanapums (River People), brought the old worshippers together again for a brief period.

Variations on Smohalla's doctrine have emerged in several Washington State Indian groups up to our time. Smohalla's spiritual world may seem less extraordinary when contrasted with the rich Indian myths of our mighty Columbia: e.g. the Watetach Monster with irresistible breath and the lyrical Bridge of the Gods legend. It was clear, however, that the Dreamer faith was more than legend. Its origins were founded in distrust and disappointment. The white man had not kept his promises. The land was gone. Smohalla's people had been decimated by disease and treachery.

Smohalla loved symbols and flags. The sacred colors of white, yellow and red were woven on buckskin with porcupine quill needles. Over his lodge fluttered a banner with a seven-point star, each point representing a day. On the seventh day, the Washat, a sacred dance was held. Two of these flags were buried with the dreamer high above the Columbia River.

John Slocum:
Hard Benches and Hand Bells

Sectarian disagreements proliferated among Puget Sound Indians of the mid 1800s. South Sound natives had their land bases threatened and divided. Liquor, disease, and the strange ways of white settlers further confounded Washington's original residents.

Catholic and Protestant missionaries plied their trade among the Indians on the heels of white settlers. John Slocum, father of thirteen children, and his wife Mary were members of the Squaxin Island band. John Slocum supported his large family (several children had died at birth) by logging. A simple man, his tribal instincts had been confused and diluted by the Christian ideas he encountered from roving white missionaries.

Slocum had also encountered, and as a youth failed to overcome, temptations of whiskey and gambling. Not distinguishing himself as a hard worker, and lacking education, his life might have passed unnoticed by history except for an exceptional physical experience which later assumed mystical proportions.

Described by the 1890s white chronicler James Mooney as "5 feet 8 inches high...stoop shouldered...with a shock of long black hair, a flat head (presumably caused by pressure as a baby—a common practice of some Northwest tribes), bright eyes..." Slocum lived with his family on the Skookumchuck, a stream near south Puget Sound.

In the fall of 1881 John Slocum became sick and died— or appeared to die. Later variations of this incident would attribute his "death" to a broken neck caused by shamans, Indian medicine men. Slocum miraculously revived after several hours. Friends and relatives en route to Olympia in quest of a coffin, had to be recalled by a runner. Upon reawakening, Slocum described a dream. He wanted a church, he said, and the good "power" for the church would come from "above your head." He fulminated against gambling, booze and smoking, and claimed that restorative powers lay in wait for those who followed the signs of his dream.

At this point, variations on the resurrection, or born again, theme of John Slocum become unclear. Second and third hand versions claim that Slocum's experience was accompanied by shaking or tremors.

Others said that as a shaman tended to her husband's lifeless body, Mary Slocum left the house. While washing her face in a creek she fainted. As friends carried her back to the house she trembled uncontrollably. It is clear, however, that the entire death and resurrection experience of the Slocum family was witnessed by a number of persons. Indian Shakerism was to grow from those events. Unrelated to the United Society of Believers in Christ's Second Appearing, or American Shakers, transplanted from England to the U.S. in 1774, Indian Shakers are an indigenous western messianic cult.

Mary and John Slocum may not have enjoyed a perfect marriage. Their various families were sometimes at odds. For example, rumors persisted that a shaman had caused the death of one of Mary's male relatives, with remarriage to the deceased widow as a motive. Despite John Slocum's visions and good intentions he may have lacked the talent or willpower to establish a new church. He was described as timid and taciturn. Mary stepped in, sometimes disagreeing with her husband's opinions about their new faith, and asserted herself as a co-founder of Indian Shakerism. Other "bishops" and Shaker leaders followed, such as John Smith and Louis Yowaluch (called "Mud Bay Louis") who helped spread Shakerism to tribes throughout Washington and into Northern California.

Shakerism capitalized on the ceremony of physically shaking, and also introduced bell ringing, foot stamping, hard backless benches and wailing. Catholic influences can also be seen in the use of candles, beads, white robes and kneeling. Prayer tables—not quite altars—are utilized for flower arrangements and to rest the bells and candle holders. A cross usually dominates the scene in typically simple clapboard churches.

John Slocum died around 1898. No one is sure of the exact date of his death or where he is buried. Mary died soon after. Indian Shakerism, however, survives. The hard benches and hand bells are still in use for healing and worship. Shakerism is, finally, a peculiarly Indian cult. White visitors attend Shaker services but are not encouraged to participate. As an anti-shaman faith Shakerism is sometimes accused of rejecting the aboriginal old ways. John and Mary Slocum didn't worry about such things. The old life had died, shaman medicine men, they believed, had been a nuisance in their time, and John's "death" was proof enough that a new path lay before them.

Relentless Paths:
The Eells Family and Dokibatl

Descended from pious English forbears and Massachusetts clergy, Eells family members rarely ventured far from a church door. In May 1776 Reverend Nathaniel Eells of Stonington, Connecticut, had his sermon interrupted by a horseman. After reading the rider's missive, Eells looked out at his congregation and said: "...General Washington and the sons and daughters of civil and religious liberty were...calling for help." He urged his listeners to "repair to the Public Green" and organize a militia. He then added: "I consider the cause of the Patriots as one that God will bless."

Cushing Eells, who was born at Blandford, Massachusetts, in 1810, also chose the profession of his ancestors. After graduation from Williams College, and following further studies at the Hartford

Cushing Eells, Northwest missionary A.B.C.F.M. Tshimakain Mission (1838-47) and founder of Whitman College 1859.

Courtesy Penrose Memorial Library, Eells N.W. Collection, Whitman College, Walla Walla, Washington

Theological Seminary, he married Myra Fairbank and dedicated his life to the church. Drafted for work among the Zulus, an African tribal war quickly changed the young couple's plans. Beginning in March 1838 they instead embarked on a year-long American "bridal tour", more or less following the tracks of Marcus and Narcissa Whitman to Oregon.

Eells' missionary work included the 1859 founding of Whitman Seminary at Walla Walla to commemorate the Christian martyrs of Waiilatpu (the Whitman party). Cushing's wife, Myra, teacher, opponent of slavery, and instigator of college scholarships, was also recognized as a consummate homemaker and church fundraiser—her churn was publicly credited with producing four hundred pounds of butter for sale in one season.

The Eells' two sons, Myron and Edwin, would choose teaching, writing, and missionary endeavors as their life's work. Edwin studied law and then received appointment as Indian agent to Skokomish, Hood Canal. Myron followed more closely in his father's footsteps by attending Hartford Theological Seminary, later undertaking missionary duties. Curiously, Cushing and his two sons would work together for a time with the Twana and Clallam Indians in south Puget Sound.

Confined to reservations by the 1855 Treaty of Point No Point, Olympic Peninsula Indians were undergoing a wrenching transition. Their land base was now specific, tribal sinews had been torn—or at least stretched, and the white man's culture was encroaching on every aspect of Indian life.

Myron Eells attempted to convert members of the Skokomish tribe at lower Hood Canal to Christianity. He was, in that endeavor, unsuccessful. He did, however, make an important contribution to the record of Indian life in western Washington State. His voluminous notebooks attest to a triumph of dedication and curiosity. Those writings constitute a fascinating and detailed record of Puget Sound tribes, especially, as he put it, "the Squakson and Clallam Indians, and...the few Chemakums who are left."

Myron Eells described the Indians' ideas of a Supreme Being as follows:

"The Clallams say the Being was a woman, but most other tribes say a man. The ideas about Him are confused. One of the Clallams,

a tribe which worshiped the sun, says that this Being was the sun incarnate, while many of the Twanas (an offshoot of Pacific Northwest Salish Indians who live around Hood Canal) say that He was the original creator of the sun, moon, man, woman, beasts, birds, and all things...A long time after the creation, say the Indians, the world became bad and the people became bad and foolish, whereupon Dokibatl (the Supreme Being) determined to come here and rectify affairs...One Skokomish Indian says of Dokibatl that He came first to create, second to change or make the world new, and that, when it shall become old, He will come a third time to make it over again."

Myron Eells, born 1843 at Tshimakain Mission. Later (1870s) missionary to South Puget Sound Indians.

Courtesy Penrose Memorial Library, Eells N.W. Collection, Whitman College, Walla Walla, Washington

Missions in the Wilderness

As Yureerachen proclaimed in his vision, a different sort of man was raising a cross on the shore of the western sea. On August 1, 1790, Alferez Manuel Quimper, commander of the Spanish vessel *Princess Royal,* entered what is now Neah Bay and claimed the northwest corner of the Olympic Peninsula for the King of Spain, Don Carlos IV. In his report to his superiors, Quimper described the ceremony of taking possession, taking pains to assure them that religion was properly honored in this affair of state.

"...immediately taking the large cross on their shoulders, the men of the vessel, being arranged in martial order, with their muskets and other arms, they carried this in procession, chanting a litany with all responding. The proession being concluded, the commander placed the cross and erected a pile of stones at the foot of it as a memorial and sign of possession of all these seas and lands and their districts, continuous and contiguous and named the bay Nunez Goana in honor of a respected real admiral of the Spanish navy. As soon as the cross was planted, they adored it a second time and all begged and supplicated our Lord, Jesus Christ, to be pleased, as this would be for his holy service for the exalting and augmentation of the Faith, and for the sowing of the Holy Evangel among these barbarous nations who up to the present have turned away from the true knowledge and doctrine."

The reaction of the Makahs to these extraordinary goings-on is not recorded, but they left the cross in place where it was seen two years later by crewmen on Robert Gray's ship, *Columbia Rediviva.* By then the Spanish garrison had built a fort and were tending gardens near its base. The fort at Nunez Goana was an outlyer of Fort San Miguel de Nutka which had been built at Nootka Sound on Vancouver Island in 1788. The Spanish had also built a chapel there, and Franciscan chaplains had begun the work of evangelizing the native people. Many including several Makah were baptized before the fort at Nunez Goana was abandoned in 1793. In 1795, Fort San Miguel de Nutka would itself be abandoned in accordance with the agreement between Spain and Great Britain known as the Nootka Convention. Although brief, the Spanish activity at Nootka Sound and Neah Bay represents the first Christian missionary work undertaken in the Northwest and Washington. Ironically, as the Spokanes looked expectantly toward the east, the white man and his holy book had arrived on the West Coast.

All nations whose imperial ambitions in the New World led them to the Northwest sponsored missions to the native peoples as part of the effort of colonization. These were inspired by genuine piety but also for the very practical purpose of securing allies in a wild and untamed land. Converts were expected to support those who preached the new faith against their unconverted kinsmen, or, as opposing faiths were introduced, against the purveyors of heresy.

By 1790 the stage was set for the final imperial contest over the new land. Despite its initial energy, Spain's aims in the Northwest exceeded its grasp, and after the abandonment of Nootka Sound, it eventually accepted the 42nd parallel as the northern limit of its claims. The Russians, whose activities in Alaskan waters had inspired the Spaniards to come to Nootka Sound in the first place, pressed southward along the coast. As early as 1790, an Orthodox parish had been organized at Unalaska in the Aleutians, and in 1794 Archimandrite Ioasaph and several other monks established the first mission to Alaska's native people on Kodiak Island. Thereafter, other missions and parishes were established as far south as California, but these were too remote to have any effect upon life in the Northwest until a later date.

From the east France and Great Britain aspired to dominate the continent. A Catholic power, France relied on religious orders, primarily the Jesuits, to conduct its native missions. These were undertaken with considerable success, but Catholicism was also transmitted to native groups by the Metis, a people born of French and native blood, whose attachment to their religion was as strong as their attachment to the French language. While the Jesuits converted the Hurons and founded the Caughnawaga Mission near Montreal to further their efforts among the Iroquois, French and Metis explorers and trappers carried Catholic practices westward to the Rocky Mountains with the La Verendrye expedition of 1742-43.

The dominant power, however, proved to be Great Britain, the major Protestant nation in Europe. In the early seventeenth century, England freed herself of the Puritans—troublesome religious reformers—by allowing them to emigrate to the American colonies where they created the holy commonwealth of New England. There, vigorous and intolerant, they became a potent religious yeast. In the early eighteenth century they inaugurated a period of religious ferment throughout the colonies known as the "Great Awakening," a surge of intense popular interest in religion that inspired some to believe the Kingdom of God would be realized in America. Subsequent victories of British and colonial arms over French forces in the French and Indian War, and the cessions of New France and Spanish Florida to the crown seemed evidence of God's agreement with their supposition.

In the years leading up to the American Revolution, British officials in French lower Canada resisted the calls from many Protestant colonials who wanted "Popery" expunged from the St. Lawrence valley. Quebec would remain Catholic and French, but the English conquest produced a cultural turning-inward, expressed among other ways by an increase in devotional religion. French Canadians would remember what had been and would dream of what might be yet again, if not in Quebec then, perhaps, somewhere further west.

After the Revolution, the fur trade attracted British and American traders and explorers to the Northwest Coast where the claims of each helped give form to the western ambitions of their respective nations. In 1792 Robert Gray discovered and named the Columbia River and claimed it for the United States. In that same year Captain George Vancouver claimed a vast stretch of the coast for the Crown. In 1793 North West Company explorer Alexander Mackenzie became the first white man to cross the continent north of Spanish territory, and he was followed eleven years later by Lewis and Clark who descended the lower Columbia to the sea. In 1811 New York fur trader John Jacob Astor had an American trading post, Fort Astoria, built at the river's mouth, but even as it was rising, the rival North West Company was building posts on the middle Columbia.

As the North West Company extended itself into the Pacific Northwest, its chief rival, the Hudson's Bay Company (HBC), put a strangle hold on the trade route from Montreal by sending colonists to the strategic Red River valley in what is now southern Manitoba where they could effectively control the flow of supplies. This move sparked a brief but bloody feud known as the "Pemmican War" between the colonists and the Metis and other employees of the North West Company, many of whom had settled in the valley with their Chippeweyan kin. In a bid to win the loyalty of the Metis and to support those of its colonists who were Catholic, the HBC erected facilities for a priest in the valley in 1815. In 1818 Bishop Plessis of Quebec sent two missionary priests to the area, appointing one, the Abbe' Joseph Norbert Provencher, vicar general. Four years later Provencher was consecrated bishop and served at Red River as Plessis' auxiliary and Vicar Apostolic for the District of the Northwest, a region encompassing almost everything north and west of the Red River including the Oregon Country which Great Britain and the United States had agreed to occupy jointly.

Both the North West Company and the HBC sought to keep employees from settling west of the Red River in hopes of keeping the hunting economy that supported their trade intact. Inevitably, however, many intermarried with native groups in the vast hinterland and stayed. Among these were a group of Iroquois who had left their homeland around 1812 and traveled westward to the Rocky Mountains where they settled among the Flathead people. They were led by Old Ignace, an imposing figure who had received religious instruction at the Caughnawaga Mission and who appears to have made a particular impression upon the Flatheads. To a considerable following he taught the Sign of the Cross and the Lord's Prayer. He seems to have given them some understanding of the Bible, the Mass or "Great Prayer" and fascinated them with a description of the black-robed men who foreswore wives and family to teach the faith. After many years his impassioned exhortations would inspire them to make a fateful decision.

In 1821 the North West Company merged with the HBC, and part of the expanded company's new charter enjoined it to look to the moral improvement and religious instruction of the native people which many critics believed had been harmed by competition between the two rivals. One of those responsible for seeing that this was done was George Simpson, an administrator of genius who succeeded in the improbable task of making the HBC efficient. Where the Company was concerned, he believed an educated native was a useless one, and he was not sanguine about the possibilities for evangelism among native groups, but he was mindful of the missions' practical advantages.

In 1822 he had Anglican Reverend John West sent to the Red River where he could minister to the colony's non-Catholics and develop a school sponsored by the London Missionary Society for its children. Simpson was directed to select suitable candidates for the school from groups he met during his inspection tours, and during a meeting with native leaders at Spokane House, a Company post at the confluence of the Spokane and Little Rivers, he chose two boys: one a Spokane, the other a Kutenai. Mindful, perhaps, of Yureerachen's prophecy, the headmen asked Simpson to send them a missionary, and one among them, Illim-Spokanee, made a brief speech.

> *You see, we have given you our children, not our servants, or our slaves, but our own. We have given you our hearts—our children are our hearts—but bring them back again before they become white men. We wish to see them once more Indians, and after that you can make them white men if you like. But let them not get sick or die. If they get sick, we get sick; if they die, we shall die. Take them; they are yours.*

Four days later Simpson, in his own words, baptized the two boys and gave them new names, each a combination of their group name and the name of a Company director: Coutenais Pelly and Spokan Garry.

At the Red River mission they were taught to speak, read and write English and they learned hymns, prayers and the fundamentals of Christian belief. Both returned to their people for a brief visit in 1829, but on his return to Red River, Pelly was thrown from his horse and killed. A year or two later, Spokan Garry returned to his people and took up work as the missionary they sought. Shortly thereafter, however, events occured further east whose effects would overwhelm Garry's peaceful work and radically affect the future of the region and its native peoples.

In the summer of 1831 the preaching of Old Ignace succeeded in inspiring the Flathead people to act. After much deliberation it was decided that a number of them would travel to St. Louis, whence Lewis and Clark and a host of trappers had come, and attempt to learn more about the white man's religion. In September, accompanied by at least one Nez Perce, they reached their goal. What happened afterward is still the subject of some debate.

William Clark, now a general and Superintendent of Indian Affairs for Missouri Territory, was headquartered at St. Louis, then a bustling frontier town of some 12,000 souls, the rough-hewn gateway to the West where the American Fur Company outfitted annual caravans heading into the Rocky Mountains. Native visitors, French and American settlers and Yankee traders jostled in streets that were dusty or mud-choked depending on the weather. Since 1827 it had been the Episcopal seat of Catholic Bishop Joseph Rosati, and it was the site of a Jesuit College.

Finding General Clark, the native men communicated their wishes to him in the universal sign language. Alerted perhaps by their making the Sign of the Cross, he directed them to the Catholic cathedral. By that time two had fallen ill from contagions in the settlement, and near death, they were baptized Narcisse and Paul by Jesuit priests. Shortly thereafter they died and were given Christian burial. The following spring the remaining two left for home, traveling up the Missouri on a steamboat where artist George Catlin painted their portraits and preserved their names for history: Hee-ob'ks-te-kin, "Rabbit skin-leggings," and H'co-a'cotes-min, "No Horns on his Head." That was the last of them; deep within enemy Blackfeet territory they disappeared, never returning to their expectant people.

According to Rosati, the four came looking for Blackrobes—the priests Old Ignace described—to take back with them to teach the white man's religion to their people. According to William Walker, an educated Wyandot-American trapper who happened to be in St. Louis at the time, they came looking for the Book of Heaven. A deeply religious man, Walker described the seekers and their mission in a letter to a friend, G.P. Disosway, a New York businessman and founder of the Missionary Society of the Methodist Episcopal Church, who had it published in an article in the *Christian Advocate and Journal* on March 1, 1833. The letter now appears to be a highly imaginative account of what happened, but it caused a furor of excitement among Protestant Church leaders.

To understand this, we must recount briefly how the Oregon Country and its native people had become so attractive to Americans. After the British obtained Fort Astoria during the War of 1812, the American presence on the Northwest mainland vanished for a time, and the HBC was left free to develop a great trading empire in the region, headquartered after 1825 at Fort Vancouver. The 1818 British-American treaty of joint occupancy and a subsequent treaty abrogating Spanish claims to the region were of little interest to most Americans who were busy settling the Ohio Valley and the old Northwest Territory. But the continental impulse that saw the Pacific Ocean rather than the Mississippi River as the nation's natural western boundary inspired visions in romantic minds.

One of these belonged to Hall Jackson Kelley, a New England Baptist, a school teacher and writer of textbooks. Well-educated, energetic and humorless, Kelley had become obsessed with the Northwest when few were even aware of its existence. Fevered with excitement after reading an account of the Lewis and Clark expedition, he claimed to have heard the voice of God command him to, "promote the propagation of Christianity in the dark and cruel places about the shores of the Pacific." Inspired, he devoted himself to this end, beginning in 1828 by bombarding Congress with memorials calling for the colonization of the Oregon Country, and by churning out articles and books describing it to the public. Religious enthusiasm and national expansion were wedded in his mind, and Kelley offered these as justifications for a national effort to claim this distant region. In 1829 he organized the "American Society for Encouraging the Settlement of the Oregon Territory," calling upon Americans to, "found, protect and cherish," a colony there, and extend to it, "the peculiar blessings of civil polity, and of the Christian religion."

Kelley's actual impact on events in the Oregon Country was slight, but he did a great deal to make it a household word. American churchmen shared his enthusiasm for national expansion, but their thoughts on native missions in the West were less vaunted. Several Protestant denominations had already made great efforts to develop native missions. In 1810 the Plan of Union among Presbyterians, Congregationalists and the Dutch Reformed Church enabled these denominations to pool their resources, and the formation of the American Board of Commissioners for Foreign Missions (ABCFM) gave them a powerful coordinating organizational tool.

The native missions produced mixed results however, and were sometimes disasters. The ABCFM missions among the Cherokee in Georgia, for example, seemed a brilliant success until the federal government forced them out of their homelands to locations west of the Mississippi. Several missionaries resisted the cruel expulsion, and suffered the consequences, seeing the work of many years destroyed. The experience taught a powerful lesson: for missions to succeed, they must be developed far from the press of white civilization.

In 1820 the ABCFM and the Methodists undertook missionary work in the Hawaiian Islands. While there, that they made contact with a native leader from the Northwest Coast, Skittegates, who asked that missionaries be sent to his people, a plea inspired possibly by the earlier work of the Spanish. But, although some churchmen back in the United States were interested in a mission to the Northwest Coast, they did not have the resources at hand to develop one. By 1833 they did, and the story of the native delegation to St. Louis inspired Dr. Wilbur Fisk, the most notable Methodist churchman in the Northeast and the president of Wesleyan University, to take action.

To Fisk, the plea of the St. Louis delegation was like the "Macedonian Cry" in Acts 16:10, where in a dream St. Paul heard the words, "Come across to Macedonia and help us." Once again the northwestern natives had called out, and this time the Church—the Methodist Episcopal Church, anyway—was ready. Fisk called upon the Board of the Church's Mission Society to organize a mission to the Flathead Nation, and he had a man to lead it, his most illustrious pupil at Wesleyan, Jason Lee. The Board agreed to his requests, and by mid-1833, made Lee the leader of the new mission.

Jason Lee founded the first Methodist Mission in the Pacific Northwest in 1834.

Courtesy Earl Howell Photo Collection, Pacific Northwest Methodist Annual Conference Archives United Methodist Church, University of Puget Sound, Tacoma, Washington.

In the meantime, the Reverend Samuel Parker, a Congregationalist minister teaching in an academy in Ithaca, New York, had read the same story in the *Christian Advocate and Journal* and had been similarly moved. He at once applied to the ABCFM for an appointment to establish a mission in the Oregon Country. In 1829 the Board had sent the Reverend Jonathan Green to the Hawaiian Islands with instructions to look for suitable mission sites in the Northwest, but bad weather off the Columbia River bar kept him from landing, and the only information he could gather came from HBC men who chanced to come aboard the vessel he was on. Unsatisfied, the Board decided to send Parker and two young assistants overland to Oregon on another reconnaissance.

Both groups headed for St. Louis in early 1834, hoping to join up with the American Fur Company caravan heading west. But the Methodists had the advantage, having earlier joined forces with Nathaniel Wyeth, a Boston businessman who had already been to the Oregon Country. Wyeth had been lured there by Hall Kelley's exhortations, and although the commercial venture he planned in the Northwest failed, he saw its potential for trade and resolved to try again. The notice of his return to Boston late in 1833 with two young native boys in his employ caught the attention of Lee who arranged a meeting with him. At it, it was agreed that the missionaries' supplies would be sent around the Horn to the Columbia on the *Mary Dacre,* a ship Wyeth had chartered for his second trip. Lee's party, which included his nephew, Daniel Lee, would travel overland with Wyeth and his band of trappers to Oregon. In addition, Wyeth loaned Lee the services of his two young charges, one of which had his head flattened in the style of some groups on the Northwest Coast. Just as bound feet would fascinate a later generation of missionaries headed for China, heads flattened to a high peak in infancy as a mark of nobility were eagerly accepted as signs of native's degradation and their need for salvation.

The Methodists departed Fort Independence with Wyeth and the fur caravan in late April, 1834, several weeks before Parker and his associates arrived. Without the caravan the trip west was impossible, so while the two men he had brought with him stayed to do missionary work among the Pawnee, Parker returned to New York to seek backing for another attempt and new assistants. Before the year was out he would have both: money contributed by congregations and applicants for his mission, among them a recent graduate from a medical school in Fairfield, New York, Marcus Whitman, and an attractive young woman named Narcissa Prentiss.

In July another plea for Blackrobes came out of the Oregon Country. This time it was made by a group of French Canadian and mixed blood settlers in the Willamette Valley, most of whom were retired HBC employees Chief Factor John McLoughlin let settle south of the Columbia River. It took many months for their petitions to reach Bishop Provencher at Red River, and then he could only promise to send priests when he found them.

Meanwhile, in August Jason Lee and his party were wending their way west across the arid wastes of the Snake River plain. On the anniversary of his departure from home, he was smitten by the recollection of family and loved ones, but in his journal he steeled his resolve.

I saw five brothers and four sisters, their husbands, their wives; nephews, nieces, friends and companions of my youth grouped together to take the parting hand with one whose face they had but the slightest expectation of seeing again. The parting hand was extended, it was grasped, tear after tear in quick succession dropped from the affected eye, followed by streams flowing down the sorrowful cheek. I turned my back upon the group and hurried me away, and for what? For riches? honor? power? fame? O, thou searcher of hearts, thou knowest. A year has passed, and I have not yet reached the field of my labors. O how I long to erect the standard of my master in these regions, which Satan has so long claimed for his own.

At this point, when native, mixed-blood and white were still sending out pleas for religious aid, and while the first American missionaries were still in transit, we should stand back and briefly examine the religious situation in what is now Washington State. In the summer of 1834, Spokan Garry was preaching and teaching a Christian message on a regular basis among the Spokane and their neighbors. Several HBC employees, notably Dr. John McLoughlin and his assistant James Douglas at Fort Vancouver, William Fraser Tolmie at Fort Nisqually and Pierre Chrysologue Pambrun at Fort Walla Walla offered prayer services on the Sabbath, and taught some doctrine, but it could be argued that they were joining in services as much as leading them since many native groups were already celebrating the Sabbath on their own.

HBC officials and other observers like Wyeth and the American explorer Benjamin Bonneville described native rites that appear to be amalgams of native and Christian forms. The Sabbath was considered a holy day during which many groups would not hunt, and when chiefs would lead their people in prayer and songs and give brief exhortations. Services sometimes culminated in a dance around a pole bearing a flag. Besides the Sabbath, Bonneville noted that the Cayuse observed the principle Catholic holy days.

Undoubtedly, there were many things at work here. The fact that native people were incorporating Christian forms and beliefs on their own into their cultures underscored their receptivity to new ideas as well as the respect they had for the religion of the technologically superior whites. We can wonder what the result might have been if they had been left alone to continue their spiritual revolution, but, tragically, this was not to be.

On September 17, Lee and his fellow Methodists arrived at Fort Vancouver. A week later he made his decision to locate the mission not in the country of the Flatheads whose call for aid had inspired his coming, but on the Willamette River. There appear to have been several reasons for the change. Jesuit historian Lawrence Pallidino argues that the Flatheads they encountered on their trip rejected them because they did not wear black robes, practice celibacy or carry crucifixes. Methodist historians claim Lee chose the Willamette Valley because it was closer to the sea, thus easier to supply, and more suited to agriculture. There were also numerous French Canadians who had settled there with their native wives, whose children needed educating and who could provide tuition. But weightier concerns may have been the intention of the HBC to keep the Americans south of the Columbia and the warnings given by Wyeth, McLoughlin and others familiar with the interior who claimed that it was too dangerous a place for a mission. The accuracy of their words would be born out in the years ahead.

On September 18, Lee began an inspection of the lower Willamette Valley. In October, he and his party moved up the Willamette River with supplies unloaded from the *Mary Dacre* and settled at French Prairie, upstream from the homes of the French Canadian settlement near present day Salem, the capital of Oregon. In November a log cabin eighteen by thirty-two feet was built, and the winter was spent preparing for the work ahead. In March, 1835, ground was broken for planting and fenced, and Cyrus Shepard was teaching children English lessons and religion in the new mission school.

In April, Parker and his new assistant, Marcus Whitman, were finally underway on their reconnaissance in the company of the fur caravan out of St. Louis. They reached the Green River in August, and while Whitman plied his medical skills on trappers at the rendezvous, Parker interviewed Nez Perce and Flatheads. They told him that Lee had passed by and repeated their desires to have missionaries among them. At this point, Whitman and Parker decided to part company, Whitman would return east to gather more recruits, and Parker would survey the region for mission sites.

Back east Whitman found his recruits. Two were Henry and Eliza Spalding, recently married. Another was Narcissa Prentiss whom Whitman married on February 18, 1836, only a few days before the party left for Oregon. They were accompanied by William Gray, a carpenter. The journey of this group with another fur caravan across the great heave of the continent was the prelude to the American westering epic. Narcissa Whitman and Eliza Spalding were the first white women to make the overland passage, and the Dearborn wagon driven by the Spaldings, dismembered piece by piece as the trip grew more difficult, was ultimately the first wheeled vehicle to cross it— the first of an endless train. The journey was a harbinger in other ways, too, for Marcus and Henry argued and fought over details of the trip for much of the distance, as would legions of harried emigrants after them. But where these later travelers would generally put enmity behind them once they arrived, the contention between the two men remained as aconstant irritant within the mission and it would play a major role in its dissolution.

On September 12, they arrived at Fort Vancouver where they were shocked to discover that Parker had not only failed to carry out his survey but had left for Hawaii only a few days before. So, while their wives remained at the fort as guests of John McLoughlin, the men hurried back up-river to find sites for their work. The Nez Perce led Spalding to Lapwai in what is now Idaho, but Whitman decided to settle among the Cayuse at a verdant spot along the Walla Walla River they called Waiilatpu, "place of the rye grass."

Back at the Fort, Eliza and Narcissa met the Anglican Reverend Herbert Beaver and his wife, Jane, another missionary couple who had arrived only a few weeks before them. Beaver had been sent by the HBC to serve as chaplain at the fort, but if his name seemed appropriate enough, his temperament was not suited to life at the post.

Ann Marie Pittman, first wife of Jason Lee; married 1837, died in childbirth in the first year of marriage as did her son.

Courtesy Earl Howell Photo Collection, Pacific Northwest Methodist Annual Conference Archives, United Methodist Church, University of Puget Sound, Tacoma, Washington.

He complained that his rooms were not carpeted; that those he came to serve were uncivilized or worse, Catholics. His preaching angered many when he condemned the taking of native or mixed-blood women to wife without benefit of marriage as sinful, and enraged McLoughlin when he refered to his mixed-blood wife, Marguerite as, "a female of notoriously loose character," and McLoughlin's "kept mistress." In the presence of Beaver's wife, the Chief Factor gave the Reverend a caning and threatened to kill him. Shaken and humiliated, the couple returned to England shortly thereafter.

By November, 1836, the Whitmans and Spaldings were settled at their stations and hard at work. On May 27, 1837, thirteen men and women sent by the Missionary Society at Lee's request arrived by sea to reinforce the Willamette mission. These included married couples like Dr. and Mrs. Elijah White as well as single women who had come to teach. On July 16, the little community was cheered by its first marriages. After Jason Lee married Susan Downing to Cyrus Shepard, he stepped into the congregation to take the hand of Anna Marie Pittman, and the two were married by Lee's nephew, Daniel.

These marriages affirmed not only the serious dedication of the missionaries to their calling in the new land, but also their desire to build a community in it. Their primary work was to evangelize, to spread the Word of God to those who would listen, convert them and baptize them into the Church. The theology of Protestantism required that belief must be based upon a thorough-going understanding of the Word of God as found in scripture. To preach or teach effectively, one had to learn the native languages, or, preferably, to teach the native people English. Thus, schools would be an integral part of the mission establishment. But long hours of study in school would not permit a nomadic way of life, and the missionaries believed it necessary to promote agriculture among their charges. Farming would provide the supplies necessary to support study, and the sedentary life of a farmer was thought more conducive to study and the formation of the virtues of hard work and thrift. To the missionaries it was obvious that if the native people were to succeed at becoming Christians, they must become civilized as well, and in the American style.

This would take time, and if they were to succeed in creating native Christian communities, the missionaries believed they must develop a white community to serve as a model as well as a source of stability and supply. From the beginning the Willamette was conceived as a colony, and if the other far-flung missions in the region were to succeed, the colony must thrive.

To insure that this happened, Lee returned east in 1838 with a request that the Mission Society support a greatly expanded mission. He also brought with him a petition drawn up by mission members and signed by thirty-six settlers requesting that the American government take formal possession of the Oregon Country and extend to it the laws of the United States. The petition was the first organized expression of national sentiment sponsored by Americans in Oregon.

It began by describing the rich land to which they had come and drew attention to its strategic importance as a trading entrepot for Asia and the Pacific basin. Then, it voiced the fears of the community about what would happen if the protective influence of the HBC should wane as the region developed and nothing take its place.

"By whom, then," it asked, "shall our country be populated? By the reckless and unprincipled adventurer, and not by the hardy and enterprising pioneer of the west. By the Botany Bay refugee, by the renegade of civilization from the Rocky Mountains, by the profligate, deserted seamen from Polynesia, and the unprincipled sharpers from South America." It was not all lurid fantasy: the "renegade of civilization from the Rocky Mountains," the Mountain men, were already there, and some, to the horror of missionary and HBC official alike, devoted their leisure hours to brewing rotgut whiskey for sale. If the region were to prosper peacefully, it was imperative that it have the protection of organized law and government.

Aside from its political importance, the petition had religious significance as well since it sounded a theme religious leaders would constantly repeat: what kind of society did people want here? In this first appeal the missionaries and their supporters voiced their hope that it would be made up of the "right" kind of people—presumably those most like themselves. Yet, in spite of its self-righteous tone, it was an important question. Without order the frontier community with its disparate and potentially antagonistic populations was defenseless against unprincipled sharpers whether they came from South America or New England.

Their call for an expanded American presence in the region seems at variance with the missionaries' earlier desire to develop native missions far from white settlement. Along with other observers, however, the missionaries appreciated the value of the land and understood that its settlement was inevitable. Understandably, they wanted to make the transition as orderly as possible, but their promotion of settlement may also have arisen from their disappointment with the native missions which had not prospered.

Generally, a missionary's first visit to a native group was met with enthusiasm inspired by the novelty of the experience as well as curiosity over the white's strange ways and their women. The Cayuse and Nez Perce were delighted when Narcissa Whitman and Eliza Spalding gave birth to their first children—both daughters—and took a very real interest in the children's welfare. But when it came time to hunt or fish, the missionaries found it next to impossible to maintain a congregation or keep students in school.

On almost every level cultural differences thwarted understanding. The curious demands of the missionaries for incessant labor at one location and to hoard supplies seemed perverse to a free-spirited people who had always trusted and shared the spontaneous bounty of nature. To pious whites the nudity, frank sexuality and the constant and often raucous socializing of the native people seemed scandalous and depraved. Many natives gave the missionaries credit for their virtues and initially overlooked their faults, but this tolerance was not returned. There was much each group could learn from the other, but the missionaries believed they were the ones to do the teaching.

In spite of these handicaps there were some successes and several opportunities that might have blossomed richly had fate been kinder. For example, William Brooks, a young Nez Perce convert Lee took back east with him, was an effective, even electrifying preacher, but he died before he could return to his people. Peopeomoxmox, "Yellow Serpent," a Walla Walla chief and one of the most influential native men in the Northwest at the time, met Jason Lee when he came west with Wyeth and invited him to set up his mission among his people. When Lee located on the Willamette, the chief brought his son to him and asked that he be educated. Lee renamed him Elijah Hedding, and the boy became an earnest convert. In 1837, however, the young man was murdered by a group of Americans at Sutter's Fort in California. While natives were routinely flogged for far lesser crimes, his murderers went unpunished. The experience had a profound effect upon Peopeomoxmox who came to see Lee and his fellow Americans as a threat to his people.

He was not alone, and the increasing tide of bitterness blunted the attempts of another powerful leader to forge a bond of friendship between his people and the encroaching white world. Shooktalcoosum, the "Broken Sun," was an extraordinary chief of the middle Columbia Salish peoples who succeeded in creating an alliance between several major groups along the river against the Blackfeet of the northern plains. A man of insight and uncommon ability, he saw advantages in the ways of the whites and introduced agriculture, stock raising, horticulture and even irrigation among his people. In 1837 Henry Spalding invited several native chiefs to send their sons to his school at Lapwai. Shooktalcoosum sent his favorite, Kwiltalahun, whom Spalding renamed Moses, signifying his presumption that the young man would lead his people out of their dark and savage ways into the light of Christian civilization. Moses was an indifferent student, but like Elijah Hedding, he became a sincere convert. He also became a shrewd observer of white hypocrisy, and like Spokan Garry, the familiarity with white ways he learned at the mission school enabled him to better defend his people when he became a powerful chief later on.

The missionaries' relations with the Catholic French Canadian and mixed blood population also turned sour. Initially, several couples sought to have their marriages regularized by the clergy; many attended Sabbath services, and a few were even baptized into the Church, but the bonhomie ended in 1838 with the arrival of the first Catholic priests.

Because the HBC wanted to discourage settlement in its fur-bearing lands, it resisted the coming of Catholic priests as much as it had Protestant missionaries. Their coming had also been resisted by the Reverend Beaver who maintained that his presence at Fort Vancouver and the Methodists on the Willamette was sufficient for the inhabitants spiritual needs however much they might wish otherwise. But the burgeoning American colony posed a threat to British claims in the region. Seeing the need to maintain the loyalty of its employees and ex-employees, the company sought to develop a colony north of the Columbia to offset the Americans south of it. To succeed, it needed to satisfy the call for priests.

By this time, Bishop Signay of Quebec had been forwarded the settlers' petition by Provencher, and two candidates had been selected: Fathers Frances Norbert Blanchet and Modeste Demers. At forty-six, the diminutive Blanchet had been toughened by years of missionary work among the settlers and native people of New Brunswick. Twenty years younger, Demers was more easygoing than his severe colleague, but he was well-suited to life in the Wild West. In February 1838, HBC Governor Simpson granted Signay's request for the two men's passage west at Company expense. In late November, after an adventurous journey across the continent, they arrived at Fort Vancouver. Immediately, they organized a mission among its Catholic inhabitants.

In the meantime, the Protestants expanded their missions. Early in 1837, Henry Spalding and William Gray the carpenter, who nursed missionary ambitions of his own, met Spokan Garry traveling through the Spokanes' country. Garry supplied them with potatoes and showed them the log schoolhouse where he taught and preached. They were astonished at what he had accomplished and determined to organize a mission to the Spokanes. With Spalding's approval, Gray headed east to persuade the ABCFM to support the new mission.

In a hurry to bring their proposal before the board, Gray decided not to wait upon the returning American Fur Company caravan and sought protection instead from a native party led by none other then Old Ignace, the Iroquois who had inspired the original "Macedonian Cry." He was leading a third native delegation to St. Louis to plead for Blackrobes (a second had met with Parker and Whitman at the Green River Rendezvous). On the trail they were attacked by a band of Sioux, and in a confused struggle for which he was widely blamed, Gray escaped with his life, while his native companions including Old Ignace were killed.

In the east, Gray succeeded in getting the board to support a new mission and reinforce those already in place. In the spring of 1838, he headed west with his new bride, Mary, and three other missionary couples: Asa and Sarah Smith, Cushing and Myra Eells and Elkanah and Mary Walker. The Smiths took up a new station among the Nez Perce at Kamiah, east of Lapwai, and the Eells and Walkers were sent to minister to the Spokanes at the mission site of Tshimakain, on Chemokane Creek, a tributary to the Spokane River. William Gray, whose egotism the rest had come to heartily dislike, joined the Spaldings at Lapwai with his wife.

While the Catholic fathers Blanchet and Demers were gripping the sides of their boats on the perilous descent of the Columbia in 1839, Lee was putting his requests for money and ministers for the Willamette mission before the Mission Society. The response was extraordinary: he received a $40,000 grant, and eventually fifty-one people, most of them married couples and their children, sailed for the Oregon Country on board the *Lausanne,* on the eve of Methodism's centennial. Among them was George Abernathy, the mission's business manager, who would become Oregon's first governor.

In the midst of his efforts, Lee did not neglect the political needs of the mission which were crucial to its success. In January of 1839, Senator Linn of Missouri introduced the petition to Congress that Lee had carried back with him. Although it was tabled, the work Lee and others did to popularize the idea of American expansion in the Oregon Country succeeded in inducing the government to assist the mission with a $5,000 grant.

By the summer of 1840, the missions appeared to be prospering. The ABCFM had four in the interior, two in what is now Washington State. The Methodists on the Willamette had missionaries at six stations, from the Umpqua River in southwest Oregon to the Dalles on the Columbia and at Fort Nisqually on Puget Sound. At this last location, Dr. John Richmond and his family had been sent to occupy the station prepared earlier for them by David Leslie and carpenter William Willson. Willson and Chloe Aurelia Clark, a teacher, accom-

Chloe Aurelia Clark came as a teacher to the Methodist's Nisqually Mission in 1841 and wed carpenter William Willson, the first American wedding in Puget Sound region.

Courtesy Earl Howell Photo Collection, Pacific Northwest Methodist Annual Conference Archives United Methodist Church, University of Puget Sound, Tacoma, Washington.

panied the Richmonds to the fort where they stayed as guests of Chief Trader William Kittson until Willson could finish their house. In between work, Willson found time to woo Miss Clark, and on August 16, they were married by Dr. Richmond, the first such wedding performed in what is now Washington. Eighteen months later, Francis Richmond, the first American child, was born Ine the Puget Sound country. The Nisqually mission appeared to be a germ of a new American colony growing in the heart of the HBC's dominion north of the Columbia.

In 1841 the United States Exploring Expedition commanded by Lieutenant Charles Wilkes anchored off Fort Nisqually. On July 5 (the 4th that year fell on a Sunday, and the religious Wilkes would not violate the Sabbath), an Independence Day celebration was held beside what has since become known as American Lake, a short distance from the fort, and Dr. Richmond was asked to make an oration. Echoing the sentiments contained in the 1838 petition, he prophesied:

The time will come, though you and I may not live to realize it, when these hills and valleys will have become peopled by our free and enterprising countrymen, when yonder towering mountains will look down upon magnificent cities, fertile farms, and smoking manufactures.

Describing the role religion was to play in this exuberant national effort, he added:

...it is undeniably true that the world's civilization today is indissolubly connected with the religion of Christ; and neither could survive the fall of the other. This permits me to say of our mission in this remote region that, by bringing these savage children of the wilderness the truths of Christianity, we encourage in them that future development of character which will fit them to act creditably their destined parts as citizens of the Republic.

The missions' effectiveness in this regard is still the subject of debate, but they had other, more palpable accomplishments to their credit. On the Willamette another gristmill and sawmill were put into operation, and Whitman built a gristmill on the Walla Walla. A temperance society, one of the first pioneer social organizations, was begun in the Willamette Valley, and a short while later the Columbia Maternal Association, the first pioneer woman's organization in the Northwest, was founded by Narcissa Whitman and Eliza Spalding to support one another after the birth of their children. In a move designed to make the sale of liquor less financially attractive, Jason Lee organized a cattle drive from California to the Northwest, greatly accelerating the development of the region's cattle industry. The missionaries pioneered the use of wheeled vehicles overland to the Oregon Country, and their perambulations around the country gave them a basic understanding of its geography which they readily passed on to immigrants.

Culturally, too, they made significant contributions. At Kamiah, in what is now Idaho, Asa Smith, a gifted linguist, succeeded in developing an alphabet for the Nez Perce language. Spalding used it to print a translation of the Gospel of Matthew on a printing press imported from the Hawaiian Islands—the first press and the first printed material in the Northwest. The first printing press in what is now Washington State was operated by the Catholic Oblates of Mary Immaculate in their mission on the Yakima River in the early 1840s. Both Catholic and Protestant missionaries did pioneering linguistic work in the area, producing grammars and lexicons for many of the native languages and the first translated works. They were first to develop an educational system in the region, and their organizational and administrative skills were crucially important in the development of the region's governing institutions.

In spite of these successes, however, the missions were threatened both from within and without. Among the American Board missions, the personal differences between the Whitmans and Spaldings grew ever more rancorous, and all except Spalding communicated their displeasures with one another and their concerns for the mission to the Prudential Committee of the ABCFM. Part of the problem was the missionary experience itself: the physical and emotional toll a rigorous and often terrible isolation among rude peoples exacted on high-strung individuals, none of which was noted for their sense of humor. One acute observer, the Astorian Alexander Ross, believed that much of the problem lay with the fact that the American missonaries were essentially greenhorns unable or unwilling to adapt to life among western peoples, and that they were trying to do too much too fast. In his account of the adventures of the first settlers in the region, he wrote:

> ...one of the greatest evils in the present [mission] system is, that men generally begin where they ought to end. They commence with religion before the heart is prepared to receive it. A thing easily got is thought but little of: religion must therefore be kept for some time,

as it were, at a distance from them; they must be taught to feel the
want of it; they must ask for it...

On February 25, 1842, the Prudential Committee acted. In a letter sent by corresponding secretary David Green, it ordered Spalding's recall, advised Gray and Smith to return home with their families, and ordered the Waiilatpu mission closed and the Whitmans to remove themselves to Tshimakain. By the time this was received, the Smiths had already left Kamiah, exhausted by their effort and alarmed by the growing disaffection of the Nez Perce, but the rest endorsed Whitman's plan to ride east and make a plea for the continuance of their missions, for the sake of their native charges and the American emigrants who had begun to move across the continent.

The Methodists, too, were plagued with dissension. The rigors of their widespread missions took their toll. Depressed by family illness and the bleak conditions of frontier life, the Richmonds left the Nisqually mission in 1842, on their way back home to Illinois, and the Willson's headed for Salem. Difficult conditions at the outlying stations were in contrast to the thriving farms and mercantile establishments on the Willamette, and many complained that Jason Lee was acting in a high-handed manner, spending too much time making his colony a commerical success rather than a source of spiritual strength.

The concern about the future of the missions deepened in the face of Catholic successes. In the Willamette Valley the native people the Methodists had chosen to proselytize were fast dying, and elsewhere the priests appeared to be making deep inroads, baptizing hundreds. Part of Catholicism's attractiveness to the native people derived from its close association with the HBC. It was easily the most respected western institution to operate in the Northwest, and many of its Catholic employees had married into native groups. Unencumbered by families and welcomed and provisioned at HBC forts and farms, Fathers Blanchet and Demers traveled widely, carrying out missions where large numbers of native people were regularly wont to gather.

The first efforts of the priests were directed to those to whom they were closest, the French Canadians. The mission carried out at Fort Vancouver for the benefit of its employees lasted four months and twenty days. A census was taken; marriages were regularized, and children and adults were baptized and taught their prayers and catechism. Since the French loved to sing, the priests taught a great many hymns, often having the men alternate singing verses with the women, and curious native people joined in freely. For those who had made an effort to keep up the practice of their religion, the mission was refreshing; for the rest it was unique, appealing in its novel rigor and a relief when it was over.

During this mission, Blanchet left to visit the Company farms on the Cowlitz River, to the home of Simon Plamondon, the patriarch who had authored the call for priests five years before, and from there to the French Canadian settlement on the Willamette. On this trip he set the pattern that was followed throughout the territory in the early days. Among the groups the priests visited, a leading individual, pious and well-informed, was selected as a catechist to lead the people in their prayers and instruct them when the priests were away.

Blanchet adapted this practice to native missions which commenced on his second visit to Cowlitz Farms in March, 1839. He was met there by a native delegation led by Tslalakum, a headman of a Whidbey Island village, who asked him to come to visit his people and instruct them. To prepare Tslalakum and his followers as catechists, Blanchet created the Sahale Stick (stick from heaven), a wooden mnemonic device that represented a simple history of Christianity in a way that could be easily understood.

Forty grooves on the bottom of a short length of wood represented the forty centuries from the beginning of the world to the birth of Christ. Thirty-three dots represented the years of Christ's life on earth. This was followed by a cross and then by eighteen more grooves and thirty-nine more dots, bringing the story to the present. With this device, the catechists could more easily recall the lessons Blanchet taught them, and having learned to make the Sign of the Cross, to sing several hymns and pray in the Chinook Jargon, they were sent back to their people to prepare the way.

The priests traveled more lightly than their Protestant competitors, and their expectations seemed to weigh less heavily upon the people they instructed. Other than conducting rigorous missions and teaching long hymns and complex prayers, they made few other demands on their native hosts. Children were baptized in large numbers, and adults were given the sacrament after they made a simple profession of faith. Taking the longer view, the priests did not require that their subjects experience a complete change of heart as Protestant ministers did, trusting that that would occur later after acculturation had taken effect. Colorful vestments caught the native's eyes, ritual fascinated them and the severe lives of the priests elicited admiration. Not surprisingly, the efforts of the two were often crowned with visible success.

This was bound to unnerve the Protestants who had labored so hard to win so few, and neither Blanchet or Demers made any attempts to conceal their triumphs. But the situation was made worse by the truculence with which the priests carried on their counter-reformation. Baptisims and marriages of French Canadians and mixed bloods that had been performed by Lee and others before the priests arrived were regarded as invalid, and couples so married were required to separate and take instruction before Blanchet or Demers would consent to remarry them. The insult was compounded by the Catholic Ladder, an elaboration of the Sahale Stick with which Blanchet sought to teach basic Catholic doctrines as well as some loaded church history. The Reformation was represented by a line leading off the mainstream of history and ending in the flames of Hell. The Protestants responded to this sectarian baiting by producing a "Protestant Ladder" which had mitered popes tumbling into the flames and by circulating among the Willamette Valley settlers copies of *Maria Monk,* a lurid anti-Catholic tract that just happened to be on hand.

While this lamentable fracas was astir, the Flatheads, whose original call had innocently set much of it in motion, sent a fourth delegation to St. Louis which included Young Ignace, the son of Old Ignace. On the way they stopped at Council Bluffs and met a young Flemish Jesuit priest, Pierre De Smet. A man of romantic temperament, De Smet spent hours in intense conversation—in French—with the Iroquois members of the party and enthusiastically offered to return with them to their homeland in the spring of 1840. The delegation continued to St. Louis carrying with it De Smet's offer which was delivered to Bishop Rosati. He gave his approval, and after a harrowing return through early spring snows that brought death to several in the group, they made their way home, and Young Ignace was finally able to announce that a Blackrobe was on his way.

De Smet kept his promise, and arrived at the beginning of summer with the American Fur Company caravan at the rendezvous in what is now Wyoming. There he met ten Flathead warriors sent to greet him and escort him to their country. Deeply moved by the historic occasion, he wrote: "Our meeting was not that of strangers, but of friends. I wept for joy in embracing them, and with tears in their eyes they welcomed me with tender words, with childlike simplicity." Arriving in their valley, he began his mission, and sent a letter to Blanchet, about whom he had been informed, telling him of his plan to return to St. Louis and come back the next spring with a caravan of missionaries.

In September of 1841, five Jesuits, three priests and three brothers led by De Smet and guided by veteran mountain man Thomas Fitzpatrick arrived in the Bitteroot Valley and founded the St. Mary's Mission in what is now Montana. With supplies purchased at Fort Colville, they wintered over, but the next spring, De Smet traveled to Fort Vancouver at Blanchet's request. In June the two of them and Demers planned the future of their church in Oregon. By this time Blanchet had gotten permission from the HBC to establish a mission south of the Columbia, and he made his headquarters at the community of St. Paul in the Willamette Valley that had grown up around the church the settlers had built.

It was determined that the base of Catholic operations would be along the Willamette River where the bulk of the Catholic population lived. Demers would be sent north into New Caledonia—present day British Columbia—to thwart whatever moves the ABCFM missionaries might make in that direction. The Canadian priests would also be responsible for work west of the Cascade Mountains, while the Jesuits would take up the burden to the east. Near the end of summer, Blanchet welcomed two new priests who had arrived by sea. Demers headed up the Columbia into the wilds of New Caledonia, and De Smet, after stopping briefly at St. Mary's Mission, journeyed on to St. Louis and across the United States and the Atlantic to Europe to recruit more missionaries and gather some teaching sisters.

The growth of "popery" in the Oregon Country alarmed the Protestants. "Romanism," Narcissa Whitman wrote in 1844, "stalks abroad on our right hand and on our left, and with daring effrontery, boasts that she is to prevail and possess the land. I ask, must it be so?" The many instances of McLoughlin's generosity toward the Americans did little to dampen suspicions that the HBC was somehow in league with the Catholic Church, a charge that would have horrified Governor Simpson. The Catholic Church paid for the supplies it received from the Company, but it paid for them in London or Montreal, out of the

American's sight. The fact that the bulk of its employees and that traders like Pambrun at Fort Walla Walla were Catholics seemed evidence of collusion. If more proof were needed, the conversion of Chief Trader Kittson to Catholicism at Fort Nisqually in December, 1841, and John McLoughlin's dramatic return to the faith of his birth in November, 1842, receiving communion from Blanchet at a high mass at Fort Vancouver, appeared to supply it.

The Americans' anxieties expressed a deep-seated xenophobia. The HBC represented the interests of Great Britain—the historic nemesis of the Republic—in the Oregon Country, and memories of the War of 1812; the burning of the national capital and the rampages of Britain's native allies on the frontier were still fresh. The HBC, known derisively as "Here Before Christ," was viewed by most Americans in Oregon as a foreign institution representing a foreign power on American land. The religion of its employees and its Chief Factor was a mark of its foreigness. It even sounded foreign. The priests spoke to their French Canadian congregations in French, and when they spoke English, they did so with a heavy French accent.

The hubris that enabled late-coming Americans to view French Canadian settlers as foreigners in the Oregon Country saw the success of the Catholic fathers as part of an anti-American plot, strengthening the native's resistance to the triumphal tide of American settlement. This sentiment was compounded by the prevalent racism of the period. Many were quick to dismiss native Americans as a depraved and savage race and regarded intermarriage with them as degrading to whites, an opinion not generally shared by the French Canadians. The Americans looked upon their emigration into the Northwest as the advance of social and moral progress into the new land, before which the native people and their patrons must yield. When relations between them and the Americans went to blood, it was easy to see the HBC, the French Canadians and mixed-bloods and their priests as conspirators if not the outright villains of the piece. No less a figure than Henry Spalding had carved on his wife's tombstone the belief that the Jesuits were behind all the violence.

It can be argued that the HBC was using the Catholic Church to further its ambition to keep the land north of the Columbia under its control, but it is equally likely that Blanchet would have liked nothing more than to see the Company and the Catholic settlers maintain their predominance in the region. Although he did not voice his bias, his brother, Augustine Magliore Blanchet, who came west in 1847, was open in his dislike of Americans and their institutions. As French Canadians, many remembered too well the insults to their religion suffered at the hands of American troops in Montreal during the war of 1812, and many nursed an antipathy toward what they regarded as a nation of heretics no less virulent than what many Americans cultivated against them. Inevitably, tragically, because religious figures played such important roles in the events of the time, the political issues of the day developed strong religious overtones, and lines were being drawn in the sand.

In 1840 another petition, authored by the Reverend David Leslie, was sent to the Congress where it suffered the same fate as the first. But late in 1841, the death of wealthy pioneer Ewing Young presented the settlers with the problem of finding a legal way to dispose of his estate. Normally, the HBC would have settled affairs, but on Jason Lee's suggestion, a committee was formed to devise laws and set up a government south of the Columbia. His desire to organize a full-blown provisional government did not succeed, largely because the French Candians and some Americans suspected the missionaries wanted to run it. Another committee was formed; Lee prevailed upon Blanchet to head it in an attempt to secure French Canadian support, but when the time came for the committee to make its report, Blanchet informed the settlers that it had not met. He excused himself by saying he wished first to discuss the issue of provisional government with the American naval commander Charles Wilkes, who was shortly to arrive in the territory, but Blanchet was accused of flummoxing the drive for self-government. Wilkes himself thought the idea premature and unnecessary, but in the eyes of the priest's critics, Blanchet's delay was seen as one more proof that he and his co-religionists were on the side of the British.

All this contention dismayed the native people. The competition between Protestants and Catholics for the natives' souls and the obvious rancor between them was injurious to all. It may have begun when Samuel Parker scandalized a native gathering by plucking a wooden crucifix he regarded as idolatrous from a grave and smashing it to bits. Both sides excoriated each other, claiming they alone were the true faith, and each made impossible demands by threatening damnation to those who chose "wrongly." In the narrative of his naval expedition, Lieutenant Wilkes wrote:

> Such difficulties are very much to be deprecated, as they cannot but injure the general cause of Christianity in the eyes of the natives; and it is to be wished that they could be settled among the different sects without giving them such publicity; for the natives seldom fail to take advantage of these circumstances, and to draw conclusions unfavorable to both parties.

The native people were more alarmed, however, by the Americans' lust for their lands. The missionaries had been among the loudest to call for emigration to the Oregon Country, and they were instrumental in creating a political consciousness among the settlers that led to the creation of a provisional government in 1843 by which they claimed the right to possess the whole region.

By then, the conflict within the Methodist mission had resulted in Lee's removal. In 1848 Whitman brought this news back with him from the east where he had succeeded in getting the American Board to maintain its own mission. The next year, Lee returned east, defending himself successfully against his critics, but haggard and ill, he died a short time later. That same year his replacement, George Gary, took up his office, and after examining the mission's affairs, decided to close it and sell its property. In spite of this setback, most of the missionary families remained. They had become settlers now, and as the "mission party," they continued to exercise a powerful role in the Provisional Government, succeeding in getting George Abernathy elected first governor of Oregon Territory in 1845.

As time passed, emigration increased. British attempts to induce settlement by Canadians could not compare with efforts of Elijah White, who had come west with his wife on the *Lausanne,* and Marcus Whitman who beat the drums for settlement of the Oregon Country. When Whitman returned in 1843, he preceeded a caravan of a thousand people and had Waiilatpu stocked to provision them when they arrived.

As the pioneers kept coming, resentment among the native people increased. The emigrants generally settled where they pleased regardless of native claims to the land, and rarely felt obliged to treat native people with the same respect they demanded. The situation grew critical among the volatile Cayuse where the Whitmans became the focus of complaint. They resented him welcoming whites into their lands, and the fact that he could cure whites of their diseases but could not—or, as some believed, would not—cure them increased their hostility. In November of 1847 an outbreak of measles brought in by an emigrant train ravaged the native's encampments. Scores died in spite of Whitman's efforts to save them. Early in the morning of the 29th, a group of Cayuse led by Tilaukait, a chief whose son had died only hours before, attacked the mission, killed Marcus and Narcissa Whitman and twelve others and took forty hostages. When word of the massacre got out a wave of horror swept the Oregon settlers. The Provisional Government declared war on the Cayuse and once again it petitioned Congress to extend the laws and protection of the United States to the embattled region. Spurred by reports of the disaster, the government acted, and on August 14, 1848, Oregon was made a Territory of the United States. What the missionaries had failed to accomplish in life, they succeeded at in death.

The death of the Whitmans also succeeded in closing the ABCFM missions in the interior. The Spaldings escaped shortly after the massacre with the help of the Nez Perce, and they were followed to the Tualatin Valley in the spring by the Walkers and the Eells. With the Protestants virtually abandoning the native missions for the time being, the work of evangelizing fell to the Catholic orders, the Jesuits and the Oblates of Mary Immaculate in particular, whose missions in the area persisted and in some cases prospered. Although other missions would eventually be organized in the area, they would never play so important a role in the region's history, nor would the missionaries so dominate the historic stage. Having acted as midwives at the political birth of the region, they were caught up with the rest in the surge of events that followed and were carried forward by the current. As church leaders, their ambitions to shape society never lessened, but they would be but one group among many seeking to mold the character of the commonwealth.

In the meantime, the fate of the native people the missionaries had come to rescue from darkness became darker still. The Cayuse War was only the opening phase of a conflict that flared intermittently for thirty years until the native peoples had been thoroughly subdued and penned up in remote reservations. There, interest in religion grew stronger as sufferings increased.

The ferment that had marked the development of their religious activity in the time leading up to white settlement intensified during the time of war and incarceration. The most significant developments included a return to traditional beliefs and a continuing synthesis of native American and western religious ideas and practices.

Spokan Garry was one example of those who had become disillusioned and embittered by whites and who sought to return to their traditional beliefs. But Garry knew whites too well to ignore them. During the Yakima War of 1855-56 and all the subsequent wars, he counseled peace, and his command of the English language enabled him to plead his people's case skillfully. But even he could not forestall the inevitable. In 1858 the Spokanes were crushed by Colonel Wright in a military campaign, and the subsequent influx of settlers pushed them out of their lands and reduced them to miserable poverty. During the 1870s, Garry attempted to alleviate some of their suffering by resuming his teaching and preaching, seeking to lift them out of their despair through moral reform and temperance. He attacked white injustice at every opportunity, but could not prevent his own land from being taken from him, and he died in poverty. Although he never lost his faith in the Christian God, the blessings of Christian civilization promised his people had become more of a curse.

In this dire time there arose individuals who offered spiritual guidance and comfort. A few may have been charlatans like the figure who gained prominence among the Suquamish on Puget Sound in the 1830s. He seemed able to produce wealth by magic until it was discovered that he got his blankets and other goods by looting graves. Most were genuine, however, and drawing from their experiences, they affirmed the worth of native traditions and gave hope to those in despair. Among these were prophets who proclaimed their messages after having undergone intense visionary experiences. They called upon the people to reform their lives, and many introduced new dances and ceremonies. The messages were often apocalyptic, warning of the approach of a great turning-over of the world when the white tormenters would be swept away and the dead would return. One of these prophets, Ha-hei-balth, also known as "Johnny Stick" preached a message of world renewal along the Skagit River in the late 1860s. Another, a shadowy figure called Father Woods, had a large following around the Dalles. But the most influential of Washington's native prophets was the Wanapam religious leader, Smohalla.

Beginning in the 1860s, Smohalla called upon his people to honor the religious practices of their ancestors, to celebrate the return of the salmon and the ripening of roots. They were to shun white ways, to stop wearing the white's clothing and to keep their blood pure by not intermarrying with them. The religion he preached was called the Washani, although whites called it the Dreamer Religion because of the trances its adherents experienced during ceremonials. Something of its spirit was recorded by major J.W. MacMurray in the 1880s when the army was rounding up native bands and escorting them under arms to the reservations where they were to be "civilized." MacMurray had been sent to Priest Rapids on the Columbia to bring in Smohalla and his followers, but instead he received a stinging rebuke.

You ask me to plow the ground! Shall I take a knife and tear my mother's bosom? Then when I die she will not take me to her bosom to rest.

You ask me to dig for stone! Shall I dig under her skin for her bones? Then when I die I cannot enter her body to be born again.

You ask me to cut grass and make hay and sell it, and be rich like white men! But how dare I cut off my mother's hair.

Smohalla formalized the old Washani religion and developed and organized its ceremonial structure. He reinvested the ancient symbols of the sun, moon and the north star with meaning and used them as symbols on ceremonial clothes and paraphernalia. He devised a calendar that enumerated the year's ceremonial seasons and set aside every seventh day for the celebration of the Washat, the dance he had been taught in a vision. This was done in a large mat lodge measuring seventy-five by twenty-five feet that he had built at Priest Rapids. It was surrounded by a white picket fence, and within the enclosed space stood a flagpole. On the days of the Washat the pole was topped with the wooden image of a sacred bird, apparently an oriole, who called the salmon to spawn, and it flew a flag which bore a five-pointed star and a red circle on a white, yellow and blue background. The ceremonies were accompanied by the drumming of seven drums, and by the ringing of a brass bell to keep time and show Nami Piap, the creator god, that the Washat was being performed.

At the beginning of services, Smohalla led his followers, divided into two groups of men and women wearing traditional clothing, into the lodge where they enjoyed a ceremonial feast and gave thanks. Then, led by the rhythmic ringing of the bell, the people danced and some experienced visions. At the end they filed out holding eagle or swan feathers symbolizing their heavenly journey and ultimate goal. Smohalla's followers were told to reform their lives, to return to their native traditions and to celebrate the Washat every seventh day so that when the great catastrophe ended the world, they might be saved. At that time the whites would be destroyed, the world would be rejuvenated and the blessed would live among the returned dead.

Arising similarly out of native tradition but bearing a much stronger imprint of Christianity was the native Shaker Religion that appeared on Puget Sound in 1889. John Slocum's experience of death, the heavenly message he received and his return to life inspired him to make an impassioned call for his people to reform their lives, and subsequent events provided his followers with a means of curing spiritual and physical ills through prayer and the invocation of the Holy Spirit whose presence was believed to be heralded by fits of shaking. The Indian Shaker Church as it was formally titled combined native American and Christian religious ideas and used many Catholic practices, and in a relatively short time gained adherents in native communities throughout Washington and along the entire West Coast.

The emergence of these congregations was evidence of the native people's determination to exist as culturally distinct groups in the face of tremendous pressure to assimilate into American society. We will return to them when we examine the role of the ethnic churches, but we are getting ahead of our story. As important and interesting as these movements are, they nevertheless represent side currents of the mainstream of Washington's religious history.

The westward movement the American missionaries had helped lead into the region at a stately walk soon turned into a headlong rush. The high hopes that attended their first efforts lay in ashes at Waiilatpu, but there was little time to grieve and no inclination to retreat. The frontier had materialized on the shores of the Pacific, and the work of building an American commonwealth in the Northwest consumed the participants' attention. Like the rest, church leaders were eager to grasp the opportunities the frontier offered, but there were many problems that had to be faced.

Pierre Chrysologue Pambrun: The First Sunday School Teacher?

arly explorers of the Pacific Northwest would occasionally be surprised to meet an Indian inhabitant who seemed to have basic familiarity with Christian dogma. Who taught them? Where did these religious encounters take place? It was frequently presumed that trappers and hunters—usually of French origin—were the cause of this pre-missionary phenomenon.

In some instances such rudimentary religious "lessons" might have been taught by members of a ship's crew to native prisoners or traders. The confused but fascinated Indian student of these rare experiences must have been impressed. Imagine a white-faced, probably hirsute stranger, garbed in folds of colorful cloth, aboard a great water craft with wings. This exotic human was adorned with metal objects and created loud noises from a stick. When he asked an awe-struck Indian to recite the catechism—or anything else—it's not difficult to gauge the response. Great spirits and spells were already a fundamental sinew of native life.

One pre-missionary religious instruction story, however, can be traced. Pierre Pambrun was born in Quebec on December 17, 1792. With some education, and experience as a British lieutenant in the War of 1812, he had no difficulty adapting to a primitive, but rewarding life in the backcountry. He may also have been the first Caucasian Sunday school teacher of record within the present-day boundaries of Washington State.

Joining the Hudson's Bay Company in 1815, Pambrun found himself roaming the Great Lakes area as a soldier, rather than commercial trader, on behalf of his employer. North West Company employees attacked a Hudson's Bay outpost near what is now Winnipeg. Taken prisoner, Pambrun witnessed a brutal massacre at the Battle of Seven Oaks and was later called as witness in a lengthy trial.

Upon his return to duty, he married a half-Indian woman named Catherine Humpherville. For the next twelve years Pierre Pambrun served as manager, clerk and trader at several Alberta posts. In 1832 he was transferred to the first Fort Walla Walla at the confluence of the Columbia and Walla Walla rivers. Although the fort had been in

Old Fort Walla Walla, Hudson's Bay Company Post supervised by Pierre Chrysologue Pambrun.

Courtesy Special Collections Division, University of Washington Libraries Negative #4169, Seattle, Washington.

existence for a decade its previous occupants came and went, leaving few records for posterity. Indian trails and white visitors soon found their way through Pambrun's neighborhood. Explorers Nathaniel J. Wyeth, David Douglas and B.J.E. Bonneville described Pambrun and his wife as ideal hosts—although the American Bonneville was told by Pambrun that, as a Hudson Bay employee (British), he could not sell goods to an American.

Soon after taking over Fort Walla Walla Pierre Pambrun held Sunday Catholic services for Indians. Transients commented on the curious fact that local Nez Perces understood Catholicism. In fact, one account points out that, after Pambrun's teachings, they refused to hunt on Sundays. Several also gave up theft, believing it to be a sin.

Without Pierre Pambrun, it's probable that Marcus and Narcissa Whitman would have had difficulty settling at Waiilatpu. Pambrun accompanied the Protestant Whitmans and Spauldings on several trips, and later, Catherine Pambrun assisted at the birth of Narcissa's daughter, Alice Clarissa.

On May 11, 1841, Pierre Pambrun died from injuries suffered in a Walla Walla Valley horse-back riding accident. His crude but genial quarters, and apparent tolerance of diverse faiths, made an impression on travellers. Most reports at that time commented on the affection he showed for white and Indian alike.

Pierre Pambrun rarely missed conducting Sunday services. His Indian pupils, in turn, listened carefully to lessons based on an early French-Canadian upbringing—a religious background that would play an important part in Washington history.

Marcus Whitman:
"Long Ride and Frozen Limbs"

Thomas Jefferson's prescience in sending Meriwether Lewis and William Clark to the little known Pacific Northwest in 1805-6 certainly helped further U.S. claims to Oregon, already established by Captain Robert Gary's voyages and discovery of the Columbia River in 1792. Marcus Whitman's life as missionary and doctor among the Cayuse Indians in what is now southeast Washington also contributed to America's eventual possession of the vast Oregon Country.

In the 1830s the Boston-based American Board of Commissioners for Foreign Missions was a joint agency of the Congregational, Presbyterian and Dutch Reformed churches. Four Indians who had befriended the Lewis and Clark party visited St. Louis and asked for information about "the White Man's Book of Heaven." On this incident, and a Protestant revival called the Second Great Awakening, a western missionary activity of extraordinary dimensions was undertaken.

Massachusetts-bred 30-year-old Whitman, graduate of the Fairfield Medical Institute, and committed Presbyterian elder (although a former Congregationalist), offered himself to the Board of Foreign Missions as "physician, teacher or agriculturalist." His application was accepted. The winds of fate would allow Whitman to practice all three professions—and more—at Waiilatpu (place of rye grass) in the shadow of the Blue Mountains. Narcissa and Marcus Whitman, and Eliza and Henry Spalding, accompanied by teamster William Gray and two Indians named Richard Tak-ah-too-ah-tis and John Aits, began a transcontinental journey in 1836 that would help promote westward settlement.

Whitman has been described as physically robust, about 5'10" in height, with dark brown hair streaked with white. Narcissa was light haired, with a "form full and round." Taciturn Marcus was encouraged to sing by the presumably more cheerful Narcissa. One can imagine them warbling hymns at the stars as they trudged across the Continental Divide.

The Whitman's wagon and mules upended in the Snake River. Tenderfoot Eliza Spalding recovered from a fever after eating dried kamas root biscuit prepared by Indians. Stringy dry buffalo meat was a diet staple, and the breaking and repair of wagon axles were common experiences. Experts of that day, including the famed artist George Catlin, said it was impossible to take women cross-country into Oregon. Despite the danger, Whitman's party made it. They were feted at trails end—Fort Vancouver—by old John McLoughlin, factor for the Hudson's Bay Company and ironically, a supporter of Catholic missionary activity in Oregon. The Whitman transcontinental trek, in fact, was the first ever made by white women.

Narcissa Whitman, wife of Marcus Whitman, pioneer missionary, teacher and mother at Waiilatpu (1836-47).

Courtesy of National Park Service, Whitman Mission National Historic Site, Walla Walla, Washington. Sketch by Canadian artist Paul Kane, circa 1846.

Marcus Whitman, A.B.C.F.M. missionary at Waiilatpu (1836-47); sketch by Canadian artist Paul Kane, circa 1846 — believed by several scholars to be the only known likeness of Marcus Whitman.

Courtesy of National Park Service, Whitman Mission National Historic Site, Walla Walla, Washington.

The Whitmans bore one child, Alice Clarissa. In June of 1839, when she was just over two years old, Alice Clarissa drowned in the Walla Walla River. This bright little girl had sung songs—like her mother— in the Nez Perce (Cayuse) dialect and was a favorite of the Indians. Her death, at least one source said, estranged the Indians from the mission. Dr. McLoughlin had also warned Whitman that his neighbors were restless and suspicious of white "medicine." Their daughter's tragic death, however, and the unfriendly demeanor of the Cayuse, seemed to reinvigorate Marcus and Narcissa. They pledged, with God's help, to carry on.

Mission work consisted of religious services, administering medical aid, running a tiny school and never-ending gardening and general maintenance. It also included embryonic political strategy. Differences among the Protestant missionaries frequently arose, as did misunderstandings between the missionaries and their New England Board. The arrival at Fort Walla Walla of Catholic priests Francois N. Blanchet and Modeste Demers in November 1838 was another annoyance. Narcissa wrote in 1839: "A Catholic priest has recently been at Walla Walla...and used (his) influence to draw all the people away from us...the conflict has begun; what trials await us we know not."

Abraham Lincoln, in 1864, invited each state to send to the United States Capitol two statues of persons to be honored "for their historical renown or for distinguished service."

In May 1953 Marcus Whitman's statue was placed in Statuary Hall, Washington, D.C., as Washington State's first representative. On May 1, 1980 the statue of Mother Joseph was presented in ceremonies of dedication to fill our state's second niche.

Duplicates of these two statues have been created for installation at our State capital and the Mother Joseph Foundation cordially invites you to attend the ceremonies of dedication on October 9, 1980 at 2 p.m. on the steps of the Legislative Building, Olympia, Washington. A reception will follow.

Whitman/Joseph statues, Olympia, Washington, 1980 dedication.

Courtesy Dan Peterson, Pacific Northwest Clipping and Ephemera Collection, Seattle Central Community College, Seattle, Washington.

Historically, the unsurprising conflict between individual missionaries was relatively tame compared to Whitman's famous "Ride to Save Oregon." Briefly, Oregon settlers had occasionally come together to discuss common problems, including mutual defense against predator wild animals. Larger civil defense issues also were introduced at these meetings which tended to pit American against British settlers. Oregon, it was feared by the Americans, including the Whitmans, was in danger of being lost to the British by treaty. Although mission business was the reason for Whitman's arduous 1842-1843 trip to Washington, D.C. and Boston, a visit with President

John Tyler became the source of historical controversy over whether Marcus Whitman had indeed "saved Oregon." At that meeting the President was reported to have said: "Dr. Whitman, your long ride and frozen limbs speak for your courage and patriotism." Thus, a legend—and controversy—burgeoned.

Despite his relentless efforts to provide Christianity, industry and medicine to the natives, Whitman also collected enemies. On November 29 and 30, 1847, Marcus, Narcissa, and twelve others were murdered by Indians in a slaughter that would reverberate across the country and into American history. Blame for the tragedy has never been completely established, although Dr. Whitman's "poison" (i.e., medicines), Catholic-Protestant missionary quarrels, the encroachment of whites on Indian lands, and recurrent illness linked to the many Oregon Trail travellers, are usually listed as significant ingredients leading to the massacre.

In recognition of the Whitmans' legacy and the American presence in the then disputed Oregon Country, a distinguished college, an agriculturally-rich county, and many streets, businesses and schools bear the name Whitman.

At 2:00 p.m. on May 22, 1953, in the Rotunda of the U.S. Capitol in Washington, D.C., a statue of Dr. Marcus Whitman was unveiled by two collateral descendants of Whitman—both named Marcus Whitman. The dedication address was given by Associate Supreme Court Justice William O. Douglas, a graduate of Walla Walla's Whitman College.

Mother Joseph (Esther Pariseau): Good Health and Gum-Syrup

Mother Joseph, (1823-1902) Sisters of Providence, officially recognized for her distinguished humanitarian services by 1980 U.S. Senate Concurrent Resolution.

Courtesy of Sisters of Providence Archives, Seattle, Washington.

In late 1856 young (33) Sister Joseph of the Sacred Heart sat down to write a letter. She and five colleagues from the French Candian "Providence Asile," or asylum for women, had just completed a harrowing journey of six thousand miles over a period of five weeks.

En route to the Oregon Country these innocent, cloistered women had seen the rough streets of New York City, witnessed the perfumed Port of Kingston, Jamaica through a tropical downpour, bumped across the Isthmus of Panama in a narrow-gauge railcar among chattering monkeys, and been mercifully revived by the Sisters of Mercy at St.

Mary's Hospital, San Francisco, California. Again aboard ship, the little group of sisters looked for death as an answer to unrelenting seasickness and wild weather. Crossing the feared Columbia River bar was an inch-by-inch adventure. Reaching Ft. Vancouver's calm, green shores and the Diocese of Nisqually brought thanksgiving and relief. In a letter to Mother Caron in Montreal dated 21 December 1856, a few days after her arrival, Sister Joseph described the voyage hardships, noting how brave the other sisters had been. "As for myself, dear Mother, (I did) not possess...sufficient courage to leave my cabin..."

Such humility and self-effacement, throughout a long pioneering stewardship in the Pacific Northwest, would characterize the religious and professional lives of a woman once known as Esther Pariseau. In 1823 baby Esther arrived as the third child of Joseph and Francoise Pariseau, a farming couple near the village of St. Elzear, Quebec. Before her death from a brain tumor in 1902 Mother Joseph helped establish a legacy of twenty-nine hospitals, schools, orphanages, retirement homes, shelters for the mentally ill and Indian schools. Many of these facilities would rest within the present-day boundaries of Washington State. Quebec's Esther Pariseau had made the Pacific Northwest her own.

A resourceful clear-eyed woman, Mother Joseph (the title "Mother" was given Sister Joseph in 1864 when her Oregon domain achieved provincial status) successfully combined religious duties with nononsense business acumen and industry. Handy with tools, drawing board and pencil, she took the time to describe in letters and chronicles the personalities and problems of her stewardship. A year after her Oregon arrival, in a letter to Bishop Larocque, she noted that, "Sister Blandine labors indefatigably...and admits her antipathy for me..." "Sister Mary...shows ennui at times." "Sister Vincent de Paul...continues...in her progress in perfection." Perhaps to see if the Bishop was paying attention, and as an expression of contrition for her candid remarks about others, she complained that "I am the one who deserves pity...I am incapable of doing any good..."

Converting an old Hudson's Bay building into a church was an early test of Sister Joseph's budding carpentry skills. Other examples would follow, many on a grand scale. The name Providence is incorporated into shelters, schools and hospitals across the state, a reminder of Sister

Fort Vancouver, Washington Territory, circa 1856. As Mother Joseph would have seen it.
Courtesy Special Collections Division, University of Washington Libraries Negative #4171.

Joseph's first rough hammer and saw.

Mother Joseph marvelled at, and gave thanks for, the sympathy and generosity of "even infidels and Protestants." Her "begging tours" as she blandly described them, followed backcountry routes through Idaho, Montana, Oregon and Washington. Stagecoach, horseback, river craft or on foot, she saw the Real West. Relaxing around an evening campfire, her French background required crepes for dinner. Never mind the barbecue. In a letter to Mother Vicar dated February 10, 1877, Mother Joseph wrote: "I consulted Bishop Bourget to know if we…must ride a man's saddle into town, transgressing a propriety not allowed women…his lordship…answered: NO!"

Post Civil War days brought a migration of ambitious, rough characters to the west. Mining, railroads and land speculation followed. As the white settlers intruded, the Indians either took cover, were confined to reservations, or fought back. The Whitman massacre had occurred in 1847, and the Sioux uprising and General George A. Custer's legendary death in 1876. Indian missions were organized by the Sisters of Providence as a response to this turmoil. Tulalip was established in 1868, followed by Colville. Selstice, chief of the Coeur d'Alenes, was grateful to Mother Joseph and her colleagues, referring to them as the "women blackrobes."

Mother Joseph wrote Sister Vicar in August 1876 that "a bilious attack forced me to lose a stage on return...a good dose of blue mass and a few sedlits plus quinine have revived me." This powerful combination of medicines might have revived—or flattened—anyone. Later that year, after her recovery, Mother Joseph returned to work and described the establishment of agencies to market "gum-syrup," an apparent patent medicine and commercial alternative to "begging tours."

Sizing up the 1895 Providence Hospital situation in Seattle, Mother Joseph found that politics and religious animosities were making life difficult for her staff. "Happily," she wrote, "the better class of Seattle people have only contempt for that impious newspaper which is not only against the hospital, but against all things Catholic." Her letters were signed in a variety of ways, like the many tasks she undertook: "Your imperfect;" "Your humble daughter;" "Yours devotedly in Jesus' Sacred Heart."

U.S. Senate Concurrent Resolution No. 48, 1 April 1980, accepting the gift of Mother Joseph's statue, states: "The statue of Mother Joseph of the Sisters of Providence, presented by the State of Washington for the National Statuary Hall collection...(commemorates) one of its most eminent personages, illustrious for her distinguished humanitarian services." Mother Joseph, a Catholic medical missionary to the Oregon country is one of two Washington State representatives in Statuary Hall. The other is Marcus Whitman, Protestant medical missionary who died within sight of the Blue Mountains less than ten years before seasick Esther Pariseau, Sister Joseph, crossed the Columbia Bar.

William Keil's Perfect World

Religious fervor, salted with utopian ideals, inspired a German immigrant to found a mystical colony near the head of Willapa Bay. Dr. William Keil was part of a nineteenth century tradition spawned by theological controversies of the Reformation. Religious persecution drove many of these splinter groups into communal practices. North American examples of this phenomenon were Brook Farm in Massachusetts, New York's Oneida Community, and the Mormons. Later, Marxists, Edward Bellamy followers, single-tax advocates, anarchists, and populists each contributed ideas to this frantic search for heaven on earth.

Born in 1812, Prussian Keil emigrated to New York, continued his tailor's trade and practiced Lutheranism. He tried Methodism for a time, and then found his spiritual plan in the Acts of the Apostles: "All that believed were together, and had all things common." This meant the embracing of a muddled pre-Marxist communist Christianity. Today this sounds like a contradiction, but to William Keil it was the answer.

William Keil sold 23,000 acres near Bethal, Missouri, the site of his first community, to finance a trip to the promise of a new life in the West. On November 1, 1855, Keil and 250 followers arrived at Willapa, a few miles southeast of today's Raymond, Washington. The small scouting party he had dispatched two years before had cleared land, planted crops and constructed log houses through the gentle valley. Before deciding that the Willapa site was not perfect—probably due to lack of markets for his product—he buried his nineteen-year-old son. Willie's body had been transported from Missouri, 2,000 miles in a sealed alcohol-filled lead casket. Young Willie Keil's resting place is today a modest tourist attraction beside State Highway 6 in Pacific County. Further up the road German-Swiss names on mailboxes, and neatly tended properties in the villages of Menlo, Lebam and Frances, testify to the probable influences of Keil's Willapa pioneers. German hymns were sung at the evening ceremony for Willie, perhaps a precursor to the rich musical and academic traditions that would survive in Keil's future settlement at Aurora, Oregon.

And Dr. William Keil? There is no record that he had any scientific training. He practiced medicine, however, and the title "Dr." struck. His authoritarian personality tended to overshadow the religious and social principles of his colony. He described his group as "one family." Collective ownership, discipline, celibacy and a "law of love" were Keil's standards. For about twenty-five years, or until his 1877 death in Oregon, the force of Keil's personality held the industrious, cooperative colony together.

"Equal service, equal obligations and equal rewards" as applied to Keil's followers, but not always to the ruling Keil family, was a maxim adopted by a string of Washington State utopias up to the first world war. Dr. William Keil's sect was, however, the first successful example of a Washington State communal living experiment shaped by religiosity.

Elder Van Horn's Tent

Issac D. Van Horn carried a fifty-foot tent when he traveled. That great canopy was paid for by fellow Seventh-day Adventists at a May 7, 1871, state convention in Santa Rosa, California. He, his wife and the tent arrived in the Walla Walla Valley during April 1874.

Before Van Horn's trek to the Pacific Northwest, however, California Seventh-day Adventist converts had been won since 1859 by Dr. Merritt G. Kellogg. Kellogg asked for help — and a large tent. His appeal was answered by two church evangelists who took a steamer from New York to San Francisco. They, in turn, were in touch with settlers in Milton, Oregon, and Walla Walla, Washington. During 1871,

Isaac D. Van Horn, Seventh-day Adventist elder who brought his church tent to the Walla Walla Valley in the 1870s.

Courtesy of Lee Johnson and Ellwood L. Mabley, Walla Walla College Archives, College Place, Washington.

the year of the Santa Rosa Convention, three families, who would comprise the core of early Washington church activity, moved into the Walla Walla Valley from California. Offerings were sent to the California headquarters along with the call for a missionary. Now eight Valley families, including over a dozen children, meant that a real spiritual and missionary effort should be undertaken.

I.D. Van Horn, who had served in Michigan and Minnesota, accepted that faraway call and packed up his tent. Mrs. Van Horn, the former Adelia Patton, was related to a West Coast family already active in the Church. After raising tent and travel money ($550), the Van Horns left San Francisco by steamer. At Portland they transferred to river transport and arrived in Walla Walla on April 8, 1874. Within days the great tent was pitched and ready for business on a vacant lot at Fourth and Birch Streets, Walla Walla. The first meeting under canvas was held on April 22nd.

Seventh-day Adventism, a relatively young faith (1840s), originally known as Millerism, had troubled beginnings. Apparently a date for the second coming — or advent — of Jesus was set by founder William Miller. When the millenium came and went without incident, and the group lost members and suffered ridicule by outsiders, Seventh-day Adventist founders, without necessarily criticizing the Millerites, succeeded in re-establishing the movement as an evangelistic Christian faith. For example, I.D. Van Horn's tent meetings in Walla Walla had no difficulty drawing a crowd. There were few unfilled seats and no record of horseplay or ridicule by passersby. Within twenty-five years the Millerites/Seventh-day Adventists had become a main-line pioneer religion.

Adelia Van Horn described an August 1874 meeting which included: a sermon by her husband based on the words of Revelation; the baptism of six members in Mill Creek; hymn-singing and prayer. "We saw the man of gray hairs, the middle aged, and the youth unite in the solemn ordinance (baptism) and the Church was much pleased to receive them," she wrote.

Bearded, handsome Elder Van Horn kept moving, at first with his protective, weathered tent, and later into permanent church buildings. He presided over meetings in Salem, Oregon City, Weston, The Dalles, Milton, La Grande and Pendleton, Oregon. In Washington Territory, Waitsburg, Dayton, and hamlets of the Palouse were sites of Van Horn services. Mrs. Van Horn, sometimes in poor health, usually remained in Walla Walla.

Baptisms, ministering to the ill, comforting the J.F. Wood family which had lost three of their seven children to diphtheria, counseling the family of a man who had apparently lost his mind after falling from a fruit tree (but then miraculously recovered): these duties comprised the rural beat of a western missionary. Elder Van Horn also found time to serve as president of the church's 1880 North Pacific Conference in Salem.

By 1880, Seventh-day Adventist activity had taken root in the Oregon country. Churches were thriving from Vancouver to Cheney. Milton Academy (1887) would grow from the missionary seeds of Van Horn and others. The hope of establishing other regional schools such as Walla Walla College (1891) found inspiration in Van Horn's emphasis upon religious education.

Missionary work is by definition the act of sending and establishing. In 1881, after seven years in the Territories of Washington and Oregon, Elder Van Horn relinquished his role of president of the North Pacific Conference. He packed up, leaving the remains of his fifty-foot tent behind, and returned to the East Coast.

Arthur Davies:
Reincarnation On A Hill

William W. Davies was born at Denbigh, Wales, in 1833. A convert to Mormonism, he migrated to Utah. Shortly after his arrival Davies joined another group called the Morrisites which was headed by self-proclaimed prophet Joseph Morris who had been excommunicated from the Mormon Church. When Morris' predicted dates of the second coming of Christ came and went without incident several converts to this new sect decided to withdraw the property they had "consecrated to the common fund." Morris and his stalwarts imprisoned the dissenters, which led to a bloody battle between the Morrisites and the territorial militia near South Weaver, Utah, at which time Joseph Morris was killed. Davies was horrified.

DAVID.

ARTHUR.

WILLIAM W. DAVIES.

William W. Davies and his sons David and Arthur, the latter the "Walla Walla Jesus."

Courtesy of Penrose Memorial Library, Eells N.W. Collection, Whitman College, Walla Walla, Washington.

Believing himself a true mystic having direct communion with God, Davies attracted his own band of about forty followers and began a trek through Montana and Idaho, eventually arriving at Walla Walla, Washington in 1867. On February 11, 1868, Davies and his wife produced a son, Arthur. Davies announced to his followers that Arthur was the reincarnation of Jesus. In 1869 his second son was proclaimed the Spirit of God and the Father made Manifest.

Davies' commune was designed as a religious utopia. It was called the Davisite Kingdom of Heaven, with all administrative and economic matters resting in the hands of William Davies. Money was apparently raised locally and through printed leaflets and missionary endeavors as far away as San Francisco.

It was said that Davies and his two sons represented the Holy Trinity in human form. There was no dissent from members for many years. The Davisite Kingdom relied on the good health and deportment of the Davies family. However, in 1880 matters began to fall apart.

Mrs. Davies died of diphtheria, followed by the youngest son. Within a week of that tragedy, Arthur, the Messiah, passed away. During the following year the kingdom was shaken by disagreements, threats, and legal suits. A root issue to unhappy members of the commune was property. Walla Walla County, acting on a court order, finally sold the communes' eighty acres, including sixteen head of horses, cows, sheep and farm implements.

Moving to property on Mill Creek, Davies tried to re-build his kingdom with the help of a few followers. Upon re-marrying in 1881, Davies again used reincarnation — the basic tenet of his sect — as an excuse. The second Mrs. Davies, formerly known as "Miss Perkins", was, he claimed, the reincarnation of his first wife. At this point his "new" kingdom collapsed. Davies himself disappeared. It was rumored that he had gone to California and joined an Orthodox faith.

Arthur Davies, the deceased Messiah, would later be referred to as "the Walla Walla Jesus". Apparently Arthur was a handsome, bright boy. His early death, and the mystical heavy-handed beliefs of his father, consigned the Davisite Kingdom of Heaven to an historical footnote.

A Temporary Pulpit
For David and Catherine Blaine

Rev. David E. Blaine, first Protestant minister in Seattle, held services in Bachelors Hall from 1853 until the "Little White Church" was opened in 1855. Wife Catherine taught school in the same Bachelors Hall.

Courtesy Special Collections Division, University of Washington Libraries Negative #1886, Seattle Washington.

Young Methodists David and Catherine Blaine arrived on Puget Sound soon after the pioneer Denny party had left a rain-drenched beach at Alki Point to found the city of Seattle. Similar to Marcus and Narcissa Whitman, who had been murdered by Cayuse Indians in Eastern Washington five years earlier (1847), the Blaines were part of a major New England evangelical movement.

Considered eastern effetes by many, the Blaines were offended by the rowdy nature of early Puget Sound residents. Reverend Blaine's disillusionment, however, did not prevent him from establishing Seattle's first church in 1855, called the "White Church," (Reverend Daniel H. Bagley built Seattle's second church, called the "Brown Church," a few years later) nor from profitably investing in a string of local business deals, including choice real estate.

No sooner had the White Church (Methodist-Episcopal) opened its doors, than the Battle of Seattle occurred on January 26, 1856. Taking refuge with their three-day-old baby on the U.S. Sloop of War, *Decatur,* the Blaines apparently had second thoughts about devoting most of their time to converting local Indians. A ragged, infidel, white population presented, they concluded, a very long day's work.

Through folksy, erudite letters from the Blaines — especially Catherine — to eastern relatives and friends, a clear picture of their views and trials is evident. David referred to the Indians as a "poor degraded race" which would "soon disappear." Catherine compared the "stupidity and awkwardness" of the Indians to the Irish. Further, they complained about the native's laziness, foul smell, and lack of intellect. When territorial Governor Isaac I. Stevens proposed removal of the Indians and the sale of their lands, David wrote what "a blessing" such action would be to all concerned. In return, Catherine's parents counseled a more charitable (they apparently did not say "Christian") view of their flock. David wrote back a crisp letter which in effect said that they — Catherine's folks — didn't know what they were talking about.

Catherine and David Blaine were not alone in their view that "removal" of the Indians would solve a "problem." Their attitude raised a crucial question about the Christian missionary effort. Methodists believed that proclaiming the gospel of Jesus would inevitably have "civilizing" effects. Stark experience with the Indians — and tough white pioneers — by sensitive Easterners such as the Blaines called evangelical plans into question.

Credited with growing the first apples in Seattle (by seeds brought from Seneca Falls, New York) and establishing the city's first school in 1854, Catherine Blaine tried to make a life for herself. Her husband's first sermon, for example, was reportedly a disaster. He assumed his listeners were uneducated ruffians and proceeded to oversimplistically describe a Saviour who had died to save them. Catherine quickly apprised David to upgrade the content of his sermons. He did so. Puget Sound frontier life, especially after the Battle of Seattle, was not comfortable for the Blaine family. By 1857 they left for missionary duties in Portland — presumably a calmer venue. Many years later, the Blaines returned to Seattle in retirement.

The White Church was closed briefly, then re-opened as a church, gambling hall, saloon, restaurant and vaudeville house. The Indians, in time, gained some measure of respect, and in several instances were honored by successive generations of Seattle residents. The city of Seattle and the Blaines' good reputations, seemed to survive those early raw years, despite harrowing experiences.

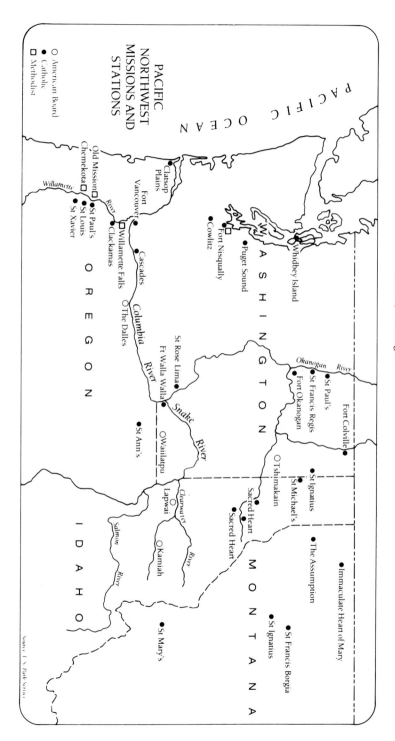

PACIFIC NORTHWEST MISSIONS AND STATIONS

○ American Board
● Catholic
□ Methodist

PACIFIC OCEAN

Clatsop Plains
Fort Vancouver
Old Mission □ St Paul's
Chemekota □
□ Willamette Falls
St Paul's
St Louis
St Xavier
Clackamas
Cascades
Cowlitz
Fort Nisqually
Puget Sound
Whidbey Island
Willamette River
Columbia River
The Dalles
St Rose Lima
Ft Walla Walla
Snake River
St Ann's
Wailatpu
Lapwai
Kamiah
Clearwater River
Salmon River
St Mary's
Okanogan River
St Paul's
St Francis Regis
Fort Okanogan
Fort Colville
Tshimakain
St Michael's
St Ignatius
Sacred Heart
Sacred Heart
Immaculate Heart of Mary
The Assumption
St Francis Borgia
St Ignatius

WASHINGTON
OREGON
IDAHO
MONTANA

Source: U.S. Park Service

Pacific Northwest Missions—1830s-50s, map prepared by Larry Cort, Rainier Mapping, Tacoma, Washington.

85

Between the Rock
and a Hard Place

Escorted by territorial troops, the ABCFM missionaries left their stations for the security of western Oregon, bringing an epic chapter to a close. By 1853 even the Methodists had abandoned the field, only nineteen years after their labors were begun. The historian of their missions, the Reverend Harvey Kimball Hines, sought to find a larger meaning in their failure to convert the native peoples.

They did their best to save the melancholy remnants of that fated race, but Providence and destiny were stronger than they. It can not be profane to believe that God had larger and better uses for the wonderful land that these tribes had cumbered so long. Its position on the map of the world predetermined its vast relations to the purpose of God in the history that was so soon to be wrought out on the American continent. As the Indian tribes were incompetent for the intellectual and moral work that must needs be done on that shore to fit it for the part it was necessary it should take in the world's evangelization, nothing could follow but their annihilation. This is God's historic order in leading the march of the ages upwards toward himself.

However fatuous and cruel Hines' remarks read today, their strident tone expressed the genuine bewilderment attending the missions' failure. It was more comforting to ascribe the reverse to God's providence than to human blundering. To do so also made it possible to blame the native peoples for their own oppression, leaving church leaders free to address the affairs of the growing pioneer community with single-minded zeal. Such confidence enabled them to produce great works, but left them vulnerable to self-delusion.

Another sad result of the closure of the missions was the exacerbation of the conflict between Protestants and Catholics, for while Protestant missionaries left the interior, many Catholic missionaries remained, heightening the suspicion with which many regarded them.

The Oblates briefly left their mission of St. Rose of Lima on the Yakima River, founded on land given them by Chief Peopeomoxmox, and then returned, over the objections of the territorial army. Believing their Rocky Mountain missions to be outside the war zone, the Jesuits objected strenuously when the territorial legislature forbade delivery of firearms to native groups. Father Joseph Joset, who had replaced De Smet as head of the Jesuit missions, traveled to Oregon City to demand the ban be lifted, and expecting that this would be forthcoming, had the shipment of arms just arrived at Fort

Vancouver—1,080 pounds of powder, 1,500 of balls, 300 of buckshot and thirty-six guns—sent inland. It was intercepted at the Dalles by a Lieutenant Rodgers who announced loudly that it was to be used by hostile groups to slaughter Americans. Joset argued that the arms were needed by the Jesuits' charges for hunting and to protect themselves against the Blackfeet, but Rodgers kept them all. Shortly thereafter, a petition calling for the expulsion of all Catholic clergy in the territory was introduced in the legislature, but cool heads prevailed, and it was rejected by a two-thirds vote.

The Catholic missions did not come through the Cayuse War unscathed. The St. Ann Mission on the Umatilla River, founded by Father Pascal Ricard in 1843, was burned in 1850. In that same year, Augustine Magliore Blanchet, who had been made Bishop of the Diocese of Walla Walla when his brother became Archbishop of Oregon City, was transferred to the new Nesqually Diocese on the safer west side of the mountains with its seat at Fort Vancouver. In spite of these reverses, the Oblates founded several more missions in the eastern foothills of the Cascades as well as St. Joseph's at Newmarket, the future site of Olympia.

The animosity continued when Congress created Washington Territory in 1853 and appointed Isaac Stevens its first governor. Stevens was also made Superintendent of Indian Affairs, and as soon as he arrived, he set about preparing treaties for the various native groups in order to extinguish their title to the land and open it for settlement. In his rush to get the treaties accepted, he invited—in some cases ordered—priests to attend the treaty councils and convince the chiefs to sign. When the situation exploded in the Yakima War, there were some who blamed the priests as they had during the Cayuse War. Several settlers in Olympia demanded the Oblates in the Yakima county be hanged, and when troops arrived in the Yakima Valley, they razed the Ahtanum Mission on the Yakima River and St. Michael's Mission on the Wenatchee, dancing about in looted vestments as the latter's buildings burned. To deflect criticism from his bungled treaty-making, Stevens accused the Catholic mixed-blood settlers in Thurston and Pierce counties of aiding hostile groups, and had them arrested and incarcerated at Fort Steilacoom. Many pioneers expressed outrage, but Stevens remained popular enough to be elected territorial delegate to Congress after his term as governor expired.

There would be official apologies, but no remuneration, for the burnt missions, and like Stevens, army officers made use of priests like Joset and especially De Smet to pacify the rebellious tribes. But Joset's presence among the attacking force during the Army's debacle at Steptoe Butte in 1858 was branded by many as one more example of Catholic collusion with hostile natives, even though Joset was at the battle scene to parley peace.

The effect of all this was to create a siege mentality among Catholics not unlike that experienced by their co-religionists in the east. Along with their non-Catholic kin, native Catholics were thoroughly oppressed by white officials on and off reservations, and the French Canadians, mixed-bloods and the immigrant Irish soldiers that made up the bulk of the non-native Catholics refrained from participating fully in the emerging frontier society partly out of fear. In the late 1850s, Army surveyor A.N. Armstrong would write, "The French are not liked at all by the other citizens of Oregon. They speak their own language, and have no more manners than the Indians—care nothing for schools—and are kept in ignorance by their Romish priesthood." Like the banishment of the native peoples to their reservations, this isolation of a religious congregation was a tragic loss to the healthy growth of the commonwealth.

In spite of these debilities, however, the commonwealth did grow, and the major Protestant denominations that were present at its birth: the Methodists, Presbyterians and Congregationalists, were intimately involved with its development. After the Cayuse war ended there were no white ministers to serve the small native congregations in what is now Washington, and no white congregations at all, but in the troubled peace that followed, plans were made to return to the field.

Since the boundary settlement of 1846, Oregon had ceased to be considered a foreign mission field, and appeals were made from churchmen already here for missionaries to serve the growing American community. In response, the domestic counterpart of the ABCFM, the American Home Missionary Society (AHMS), sent Congregationalist minister George Atkinson to Oregon in 1848. Atkinson had been born in Newburyport, Massachusetts, in 1819 and had studied for the ministry at the Andover Theological Seminary in Vermont, hoping to be sent to the ABCFM mission to the Zulus. But the ship for Capetown sailed before he could be ordained, and apprised of this development, the AHMS asked him if he and his new wife Mary would undertake work in Oregon instead.

When he arrived in the Northwest he found church work woefully undersupported. Many ministers had come west as itinerants, supporting themselves from their own labor and adding their individualistic preachings to the confusing stew of sectarianism. The trek west had exhausted their own resources, and there was little help to be gotten from the pioneers. The slow pace of economic development before the appearance of the railroads kept contributions to a minimum. Atkinson observed that a pioneer who saw a preacher support himself with his own labor felt little need to provide him with an independent income. Most of the pioneers came from the rural Midwest where churches were spare to begin with, and the leveling process of the frontier reduced their expectations even further. Camp meetings sufficed. Myron Eells, the son of Cushing and Myra Eells, told how an excited participant in an Oregon camp meeting explained his enthusiasm for them by saying, "I tell you, it takes a great deal of religion to do me a year." "This was the idea," Eells wrote, "to go to a camp meeting, and there to get about enough religion to last a whole year..." In this setting it was not surprising that denominational lines blurred as people listened to the preachers who pleased them the most and inconvenienced them the least. Church schools faced the same problem: a little schooling was deemed a luxury, and the choice of one denomination over another was not thought important.

The difficulty in establishing regular churches in this environment became even more extreme when news of the California gold rush reached the settlements in August of 1849. The country emptied as men flocked to the gold fields, and those who remained to make their fortune exporting produce and lumber to the ravenous California market were not easily diverted by religion. In spite of this, the optimistic Atkinson saw a silver lining among the clouds. In an 1850 issue of the *Home Missionary* he wrote:

> "Why was not this gold discovered until now? How will it affect the Kingdom of Christ? Already we see a check on papal influence. By its wealth in this territory, it was holding men in bondage, but money has made them independent and free."

We can imagine that even dour Archbishop Blanchet, scraping about in his diminutive clapboard cathedral, would have been amused by the reference to his church's wealth.

Adding to the difficulty of building any kind of community organization in Oregon was the enactment of the Donation Land Law by Congress in 1850. This granted large tracts of land—as much as half a square mile—to settlers if they would live on it and make improvements. A large part of the remaining population was thus spread thinly over the land as settlers took up their claims, and the growth of towns and the economy was slowed even further. Since married couples received more land than single men, there was a rush to marry available women, and girls as young as thirteen became brides. Churches and schools that had lost most of their men to gold fever now lost many women as newly-married couples took up residence in their isolated shanties.

North of the Columbia River, the country was settled even more slowly. There was not the great expanse of open land here as there was in the Willamette Valley, and the two largest prairies, Cowlitz Prairie and the Nisqually Plains, were already occupied by the HBC and its employees. By 1850 about 1000 whites lived north of the river. In 1852 they petitioned Congress for separation from Oregon, and in March, 1853, President Millard Fillmore signed the bill creating Washington Territory. By then their numbers had risen to almost 4000, virtually all living west of the Cascades in farmsteads and a sprinkling of towns along the Columbia and the margins of the Sound.

The first to enter this new region were the Methodists who sent circuit riders to Fort Vancouver and Cowlitz Prairie. In 1852 the Methodist Episcopal ministers James Wilbur and William Roberts visited the new town of Olympia where Wilbur attracted a crowd by setting off the town's cannon.

Shortly after Washington Territory was created, Bishop E.R. Ames of the Oregon Conference of the M.E. Church appointed the Reverend Benjamin Close Presiding Elder of the Puget Sound District and the Reverend W.B. Morse as his associate. At the time, the district encompassed all of western Washington, and Close sent Morse to what appeared to be a promising settlement on Whidbey Island, while he made his residence at Olympia, the territorial capital, drolly characterized by one observer as ''a flourishing city of ten or twelve houses.''

While there, Close acted on the recommendations of Bishop Ames and appointed Reverend John DeVore to Olympia and Reverend David Blaine to the new community of Steilacoom. Neither man would reach his appointed post, and their stories highlight the important position of the church in Washington's frontier society.

Born in 1817 in Kentucky, DeVore and his family came by ship to the Northwest via the Isthmus of Panama in 1853, stopping briefly at Portland to confer with Bishop Ames before heading north by sea to Olympia. Shortly afterwards, Lafayette Balch, an enterprising promoter, heard that a minister was about to take up residence in the territorial capital. Three years before, Balch had run a store in Olympia but grew tired of competition from other merchants and sailed north about twenty miles where he set up a prefabricated house on his claim and advertised lots in the new town of Steilacoom. Any advantage a budding town could gain over its rivals was eagerly coveted. Having a minister was a real plus, a sign that a town had a future, since no minister would settle where he could not be assured of a congregation. His presence would, therefore, attract settlers and increase the value of real estate. With this in mind, Balch made plans. He knew the ship carrying DeVore would stop at the tiny settlement of Alki on its way up sound, and he and several other proprietors hired native men to paddle them there in a canoe. They intercepted the ship off Alki Point and succeeded in convincing DeVore to stop at their town. Olympia already had a minister they told him, and anyway, there was a plague going on there now and the place was on its last legs—unlike their booming metropolis. DeVore agreed to visit their town, but not until he passed around a subscription list to determine just how much the townsmen were going to contribute toward his new church. It was better to have his own church rather than assist Close, and shortly after he landed at Steilacoom, he had one, the first Protestant church built in Washington, which put him one up on Close who conducted services in a house.

David Blaine and his wife Catherine had expected to go to Steilacoom when their ship arrived in the Sound in November, but by then, DeVore was there. Fortunately, several Methodist settlers from Illinois had settled on the east shore of Elliott Bay—a few miles north of Steilacoom—and expressed a strong desire to have a minister settle among them. The Blaines were agreeable and were soon settled in the little town of Seattle. The settlers' desires for a minister were similar to Balch's and prompted Catherine Blaine to write in a letter home:

> There are, as I wrote before two or three town proprietors here, and there exists between them a jealous spirit, which affects us rather unfavorably in the effort to build a church. Each is afraid that the other will have some preference shown him or will derive more than his share of the benefit from the locality of the church.

These ministers entered Washington after the California gold rush had transformed the economy of the West, and the role their churches played here was far different from that played when Methodism first entered Oregon. There, they provided a nucleus for an American pioneer community; here they helped promote towns. The rural phase of development had given way to the urban.

It would be erroneous, however, to characterize the townfolk's desire for churches as purely monetary. Many of the pioneers who came across the continent in covered wagons did so as families, and the single men among them eagerly sought wives for reasons other than property. In antebellum America, family life was intimately bound up with religion, its progress marked by the ministerial acts of baptism, marriage and funerals. In spite of the fact that civil marriages were common and that Masonic orders provided funerals for their members, there were few pioneer families that did not admit to at least a nominal association with some church, and the harrowing experience of the trek west and of pioneering itself underscored the role of religion as a source of consolation and social cohesion.

Once they arrived at their destinations, pioneer families attempted to recreate as far as possible the world they remembered. For many it was important that the Sabbath be honored in the proper way, with prayer, singing and preaching if a preacher could be found. For women in their isolated homesteads, church going was especially important since it was one of the very few acceptable ways for them to socialize outside of their homes.

So we see the first settlers in Seattle assembling in the cookhouse of Henry Yesler's sawmill to hear a Catholic priest, Modeste Demers, deliver the first sermon in town, something it is doubtful they would have done back in the Midwest. Alone and vulnerable in the wilderness, the words and the moment were especially meaningful. In her book *Four Wagons West*, Roberta Frye Watt records their recollection by Lenora Denny, who was only five years old at the time.

"I was a very little girl when I heard this sermon—the first I remember. But the speaker's earnestness impressed me deeply as he repeated his text in a deep, sonorous voice, often saying 'Charity, my friends, charity.'"

In this way the thread of communal life could be respun in a new world and the old familiar pattern of life rewoven in a new setting. It satisfied the yearning for the things of the spirit in a raw, rough and sometimes hostile land and for the things that had been and that might be again.

The Methodists were not alone in their work. On a March Sunday in 1853, the Reverend George Whitworth preached a sermon in Olympia, the first Presbyterian minister to do so in Western Washington. Born in England in 1816 but raised in the Midwest, Whitworth planned a Presbyterian colony on Puget Sound and promoted it in the Ohio Valley shortly after he was ordained in 1848. In the summer of 1851, fifty families had agreed to join the colony, but by the time Whitworth led his wagons out of St. Joseph, Missouri, the eastern terminus of the Oregon Trail, fear of hostile natives, measles and smallpox had reduced their number to fifteen. By the time he and his wife Mary, their four children and his 70 year-old grandmother reached The Dalles, they were alone. But Whitworth was not daunted by the collapse of his dream. After wintering over in Portland, he traveled north to Olympia by steamer and canoe. He filed a claim shortly after he arrived and brought his family into the new Territory. On November 12, 1854, he and seven others met in a cooperage and organized the First Presbyterian Church of Olympia. This was the first of as many as twenty churches Whitworth organized during his long and energetic career in the Northwest, one that earned him the title: "Father of Presbyterianism in Washington."

Other denominations made their presence known. The Disciples of Christ organized a congregation at Castle Rock on the Cowlitz River in the middle '50s and another at Dixie, northeast of Walla Walla a year later. In Oregon since 1848, the Baptists organized their first congregation in Washington territory at Mound Prairie near the Chehalis River in 1859, and within a few years other Baptist churches sprouted nearby. Episcopal missionaries had held services north of the Columbia River as early as 1851, and in 1860, the Reverend John D. McCarthy, D.D., organized St. John's Church in Olympia, the first Episcopal church in the Territory. Shortly afterwards, St. Paul's Church was organized in Port Townsend and Trinity Church in Seattle. In the early 1850s George Atkinson canvassed the territory to prepare for the development of Congregationalist churches, believing there was great potential, but the Home Missionary Board thought otherwise. Although Congregationalists were involved in several religious ventures in the territory, it was not until 1870 that their first church was organized, in Seattle.

As the land slowly filled with settlers, other groups such as the United Brethren, Universalists, Unitarians, Lutherans and Seventh-day Adventists appeared, and after the transcontinental railroad was completed to Puget Sound in 1883, hardly a year passed that a new denomination did not raise a church.

In the early days of settlement, ministers of different sects often assisted one another in their work. At the first formal dedication of a Protestant church building in Oregon, Methodist, Congregationalist, Presbyterian, Baptist and Episcopal ministers all participated in the service. When George Whitworth entered Seattle in 1866 to assume

1869   First Catholic Church in Seattle   1904

Seattle's First Catholic Church built by Father Prefontaine in 1869 and dedicated in 1870.
Courtesy Special Collections Division, University of Washington Libraries, Negative #5383, Seattle, Washington.

his duties as President of the territorial university, he inaugurated Presbyterian services in Daniel Bagley's Methodist Protestant church, and he and Bagley agreed to preach on alternate Sundays. Methodists and Presbyterians also joined in prayer meetings and Sabbath schools, and elsewhere they and other sects shared buildings, pulpits and even pastors. This fact was remarkable to Father Louis Rossi, the priest Archbishop Blanchet sent north to Olympia to serve white Catholics in the archdiocese's Puget Sound District. In his book, *Six Years on the Northwest Coast of America,* he wrote:

"I must say that Americans have a pronounced leaning towards religious ideas and they have no equal, perhaps, in their zeal for building churches and listening to preaching. You never ask in vain, especially when it is a question of erecting a meeting-house or a school.

*For the six churches I built during my missionary period, nearly half
of the money was given by American Protestants."*

But the cooperation demanded by frontier life did not entirely dispel
sectarian disputes. In 1859 Methodist Protestant minister Daniel Bagley
arrived in Seattle after having served an Oregon congregation for eight
years. The M.E. Church in Seattle had had no assigned pastor, since
the departure of the Blaines in 1856 during the Yakima War. With
the permission of presiding elder Nehemiah Doane, Bagley held services in the "White Church" Blaine had built. In 1863, however, Doane
became pastor of the Seattle church. Bagley suggested that since the
town was too small to support two congregations, they share the pulpit,
but Doane refused. In response, the popular Bagley and his followers
left and built the "Brown Church" a few blocks away, a move that
left Doane virtually without a congregation.

The debate in American Methodism that produced the split between
the Methodist Protestant and Methodist Episcopal churches in 1830
was over the power of the bishops. A generation later, the issue was
still potent enough to cause discord in Seattle. On occasion, voices
were also raised against controversial sects like the Unitarians, when
they came to Olympia in the 1870s, the Mormons and, of course, the
Catholics, but even among the more well-established denominations,
contention was not unknown. Rossi was giving voice to more than
his own prejudice when he wrote:

*"...I've met Episcopalians, Presbyterians, Mormons, Universalists,
Unitarians, Methodists, Baptists, and many others. But, with the exception of the last two sects, I have always found politeness, generosity,
and a taste for learning...*

*As for the Baptists and the Methodists, that's a different story; the
first comer can be a clergyman. They have only a nominal heirarchy,
and all their religious educational establishments would never be able
to produce the infinite number of clergymen abounding in this country. All the other sects detest them because of their exclusiveness and
their truly Pharisaical hypocrisy."*

Sometimes, too, there was discord over the slender resources of the
country. In one instance, a Methodist minister sent to the pioneer community of Snohomish caused the local Presbyterians to protest his
presence as being unfairly competitive.

Generally, however, the number of churchmen was small enough
and the task before them daunting enough to prevent the expenditure

of much energy on the luxury of strife. As the territory developed, the principal of comity was observed in which ministers respected the integrity of churches already established. By extending the privilege of preaching from one another's pulpits—which carried with it the right to take up a collection—the churches supported one another in what they regarded as the higher work of salvation.

Saving souls could be a risky business, especially when ministers visited scattered and far-flung congregations. Historically, the Methodists provided the model followed by other denominations in evangelizing the frontier. Elected in regional conferences, bishops identified the circuits their pastors would ride and selected the towns in which they would reside. This gave the church an organization flexible enough for it to respond quickly to the needs of the people who often organized prayer meetings on their own, keeping their faith alive in isolated communities.

The circuits ridden by pioneering pastors carried them where roads were nonexistent, and travel on trails or in tippy canoes on turbulent rivers could be treacherous. Methodist historian Earl Howell opined that most circuit riders were rather circuit walkers or paddlers. It could take many days to reach a destination, and shelter on the way could be no more than a canoe turned up on a windswept beach. The Reverend William McMillan, whose circuit extended far up the Skagit River, observed wryly that he had often prayed that God would send him where no other preacher would want to go, but he had no idea that God would answer his prayer so literally.

The difficulty in getting around the territory persisted even after the railroad arrived. The Reverend A.J. McNemee, "Brother Mack," described the difficulty of traveling his circuit in King County in 1885.

"It took me three weeks to go around the circuit afoot as there were scarcely any roads, only a sled road or a pack trail and often only a blazed path, sometimes not even that, to follow. Often when going down the Snoqualmie River bottoms I followed the bear trails in preference to crawling through the brush."

It was no less daunting elsewhere. Presbyterian Reverend Herbert Course took his nickname, the "Jack Rabbit Missionary" from his ministry among followers in the Okanagon country where he made monthly journeys of fifty to 250 miles through the hills on foot. The hallmark of pioneer Baptist preacher B.N.L. Davis was a tall walking staff which he used to measure the depth of the innumerable tidal streams he had to cross on the Skagit River delta, and to vault the narrower ones.

Indeed, the labor exerted by these men was no less taxing than that of the earlier missionaries to the native peoples. The comparison occurred to Rossi who wrote of the work to which Blanchet had assigned him on Puget Sound.

"So it was to this mission that he sent me, making me priest to the Whites and vicar to the Indians, while the Oblates were priests to the Indians and vicars to the Whites. I must say, however, that they had sometimes more work as my vicars than I had as their priest."

Life in the West, particularly in its vast interior reaches, was often marked with an emotional barreness that mirrored the emptiness of the land itself. In this numbing environment, the powerful words of an intinerant preacher could have profound effects. The Reverend G.W. Kennedy preserved this account of a cowboy's encounter with a circuit rider in the sagebrush wastes east of the Cascades.

"One day we saw a man riding across the prairies singing 'Jesus Lover of my Soul.' He came to the ranch, got down and said, 'Boys I want you to put my pony up and feed him. I am a Methodist circuit rider and have come out here to stay with you.' I looked at him and loved him, but I was afraid to get close to him. My heart would not beat right. I was afraid to ride his horse to water for fear it would fall down and kill me. Brother, his horse was religious. His saddlebags would put you under conviction. When we sat down to eat and went to help ourselves as usual, he said, 'Wait men, I'm going to ask a blessing.'

Everything was as still as death. When he turned loose my mind went back to my boyhood when I heard the old father ask a blessing at home.

The boys began to eat and before they were through he said, 'Now men, don't leave here until we have prayers.' I was afraid to go. After supper he took his Bible and sat down to read a chapter with a good deal of Hell in it. He read as long as he wanted to. He was boss of the devil. He got down on his knees and prayed just as loud as a man could. He shook us over the pit. I saw billows of Hell. My heart went awful fast. Then it would seem to stop dead. It seemed like I was going to die. He told God about everything we had ever done, all the stealing, lying, fighting, and cursing. When prayers were over we were just barely able to walk out but we got out as quickly as possible.

The next morning the preacher asked the blessing again and said, 'Don't you boys go out until we have had prayers, then I will have to leave you, but I will be back in about a month.' After breakfast he prayed until it nearly broke our hearts and then he got on his pony and rode away. About a month rolled around and we got sort of anxious to see the man again. He came again and acted about as he had the other time, but some of us didn't do just as we did before.

When he was through with the evening prayer I went out with the boys and told them that prayer had been down on my nerves for a month. I couldn't beat it any longer, that I would quit then and there the blasphemous life I was living. Then I went into the bushes and told it all to God. I tell you, before the next day dawned I was a changed man."

The terrible loneliness of the frontier sometimes produced interesting aberrations. In his book, *Glimpse of Pioneer Life on Puget Sound,* the Reverend A. Atwood wrote how the Methodist church on Whidbey Island begun with such great hopes by Morse and DeVore disintegrated. In the early 1870s its pastor had a vision which led him to the premise that dancing, which the Methodists condemned, was rather a boon to living. "Thereupon," wrote the horrified Atwood, "the young people and some of the older people quit praying and went to dancing. They exchanged the church for the ball-room, the songs of Zion for the revelry of the dance."

Elsewhere work that had been begun with great enthusiasm came to naught, especially during times of economic distress. Ministers who could no longer gain a livelihood from impoverished congregations found other work or left the area. In the 1880s, booms that went bust left many abandoned church buildings in the Puget Sound region, and several denominations noted reductions in rolls and finances. Part of the problem was the nature of the region's economy, based on extractive industries like lumber and mining which were the first to suffer from an economic downturn. To flourish, the region had to develop, and because of their education and position in the community, churchmen led efforts to build up and improve society.

Probably their single most important contribution to the community was their work in education. Many of the first schools in Washington were run by church women: Chloe Aurelia Clark at Fort Nisqually, Catherine Blaine who opened a subscription school in Seattle in 1854, and Mary Whitworth who in 1855 taught in the school she and her husband opened in Olympia. These able and educated women formed a Protestant "sisterhood" in some ways the equivalent of the Catholic teaching sisters such as the Sisters of Notre Dame de Namur that DeSmet introduced into Oregon in 1844, and the Sisters of Providence who arrived in Blanchet's archdiocese in 1857, led by the redoubtable Mother Joseph. So important were teaching women regarded that Protestant congregations often chose to support a married pastor rather than a single one if his wife could teach.

Besides organizing many of the territory's first primary schools, the churches also organized its first secondary schools, then known as seminaries or academies. In 1856 the first were opened by the Methodists and the Catholics. The Puget Sound Wesleyan Institute opened its doors in Olympia with the Reverend Isaac Dillon serving as principal. In November Archbishop Blanchet opened Holy Angels College in Vancouver, a boys school which had one lay teacher. Both endured a precarious existence and succumbed after a few decades, but between their opening and the time of statehood (1889), at least twenty-eight denominational academies were opened in what is now Washington. By way of comparison, at the time of statehood, there were only five territorial high schools. Of the denominational schools, Catholics founded fifteen, Methodists four, Baptists, Congregationalists, Episcopalians and Presbyterians two each, and United Brethern, one. Two of these that still continue today as secondary schools are the Holy Names Academy, founded in Seattle in 1881, and Annie Wright Seminary, founded in Tacoma in 1884.

Beyond their own schools, Protestant church leaders were instrumental in promoting and supporting the territory's public school system. Historically, they had been in the vanguard of the development of the nation's common schools where sectarian differences were muted. Education was deemed the "handmaid of religion" and churchmen lobbied for the provision in the land ordinances that devoted a section in every township for the benefit of a public school.

In 1854 the territorial legislature enacted a common school law and appointed temporary superintendents in the counties that had been organized, but since there was little money to support schools, tuitions were charged and education was left largely in the hands of church people. George Whitworth was elected superintendent of the common schools of Thurston County in 1854 and re-elected in 1857. While serving in that capacity, he and his wife continued to run their private school. East of the mountains the Methodists ran a primary school in Walla Walla until local government could support it on its own. This partnership between church and government was not uncommon on the frontier where the parsonage was one of the few sources of educated men and women. Whitworth took the lead in writing a new common school law for the territory in 1876 and was nominated to be the first territorial superintendent of public instruction. Later, historian Edmond Meany would write that he had more to do with school law enactments in the territory than any other person.

It was assumed that the public schools would be nominally Christian and so reflect the character of society. In 1859 the Congregational Association of Oregon and Washington Territory resolved in its annual meeting that Christian teachers should be employed in the common schools, "laymen, if possible, ministers, if need be," and that the reading of the Bible should be a regular school exercise, a position the Methodists conferees echoed in their 1866 statement declaring that:

> "While we should deprecate any diversion of the common school to sectarian purposes, yet regarding the Bible as the source of civil and religious liberty, we trust it will continue to be read in all our schools without note or comment."

During the time the churches dominated education in the territory, these views held considerable sway.

Beyond the nominal Christianity taught in the schools, the churches were concerned that children and adults receive instruction in the more specific tenets of their faiths, and to satisfy this need, Sunday schools were organized and supported. Introduced from England toward the end of the eighteenth century, Sunday schools appeared first in Philadelphia, and by 1824, widespread support led to the formation of the American Sunday School Union. Sunday school work began in the Northwest in the 1850s, and as government assumed the capacity to run the common schools, the churches came to depend on Sunday schools as the primary vehicle for early religious education.

As the need for higher education became more apparent, several of the church-run academies developed college-level curriculums, and in time some of these schools expanded to become universities. Ironically the first of these colleges appeared in the relatively unpopulated interior, barely a year after the military reopened the land to settlement. Among the miners and farmers that reentered the region was the old missionary Cushing Eells, making a poignant pilgrimage to the site of the Waiilatpu mission, desolate now after being abandoned for more than ten years. Standing above the mass grave, it occurred to him that the most fitting memorial to those who died would be a school to carry out the work begun here more than two decades before.

The Congregational Association approved his plans for a memorial high school on the spot along with his desire to serve as a home missionary in the Walla Walla Valley. In 1859 the Whitman Seminary opened with a faculty of three, a student body of two and a library of fourteen books and fifteen pamphlets. It was organized as a non-sectarian school, but until 1908 it received most of its financial aid from the American College and Education Society. This was run and supported by Congregationalists who required that the school president and the majority of its trustees be Congregationalists. In 1860 the territorial legislature granted the seminary a charter, and on November 17 of that year, the first board of trustees elected Eells its president, a position he held for thirty-two years. For years Whitman remained little more than a glorified high school, but in time it emerged from these humble beginnings to become one of the foremost private colleges in the Northwest and the nation.

In time it was followed by other more specifically denominational schools. George Whitworth resumed efforts toward his earlier dream, and in 1880 filed articles of incorporation with the territory for his "Washington Colony and Academy." A short time later he dropped his plan for the colony and concentrated his energies on the school. In 1883 the town of Sumner was chosen as its site; work moved forward, and in January of 1884 the doors of the Sumner Academy opened to its first twelve students, under the care of the Presbytery of Puget Sound. In 1890 the Academy was incorporated as Whitworth College and began its perambulations, first to Tacoma in 1899 and then to Spokane, its present home, in 1914.

In 1883 the Methodist Episcopal Church announced plans for, "... an institution of learning which, by example and facilities and able administration, will command the respect and patronage of Methodist people within the territory." Groups in Port Townsend and Tacoma invited the Puget Sound Conference to build the school in their towns.

Tacoma was selected, and in September of 1890, Puget Sound University (now called the University of Puget Sound) opened its doors to a student body of seventeen.

The Catholics followed closely. Of the many colleges and academies founded by orders in the territory, three survived to become colleges in the modern sense of the term: the Jesuits' Gonzaga College in Spokane and Seattle College in Seattle, opened respectively in 1887 and 1894, and St. Martin's College, opened by the Benedictines at Lacey, near Olympia, in 1895.

Behind the two Jesuit schools stands the figure of Father Joseph Mary Cataldo, one of the most remarkable Catholic personalities in Northwest history. Born in Sicily in 1835, Cataldo was ordained a Jesuit priest at the relatively young age of twenty-five. Shortly afterwards, he was sent to Boston in the United States where he studied theology and English.

In 1856 he was assigned to the Rocky Mountain Mission which oversaw stations in what is now Washington, Idaho and Montana. Although of frail build, Cataldo was possessed of abundant energy and a keen mind, and during his stay at the Coeur d'Alene mission in what is now Idaho, he became proficient in several native languages. In 1866, he and Jesuit Father Paschal Tosi founded St. Michael's Mission among the Spokanes, but responsibilities elsewhere kept him away from them for many years. Not the least of these was his effort after being made Superior General of the Rocky Mountain Mission to keep Catholic tribes such as the Coeur d'Alene from joining with Nez Perce warriors during Chief Joseph's War.

Nevertheless, his affection for the Spokanes and his fascination with the area around Spokane Falls remained active. As the Northern Pacific Railroad built its tracks toward the area, Cataldo determined to purchase land near the falls for a mission headquarters and, "a central school for Indians and perhaps for whites." Out of this endeavor came Gonzaga College, today a University, which became one of the foremost institutions of learning in the Northwest as well as an important cornerstone of the growth of the city of Spokane.

In 1891, Cataldo sent Father Leopold Van Gorp to purchase property in Seattle for a Jesuit school in that growing city. In 1891, the Jesuits took over a parish boy's school which they reincorporated as the School of the Immaculate Conception. This soon became known as Seattle College, the ancestor of today's Seattle University.

Three other denominations that opened colleges in the last years of the nineteenth century that are still extant were the Lutherans, the Seventh-day Adventists and the Free Methodists. Institutionally, Lutherism was late in establishing itself in the Northwest, and it did so primarily among German and Scandinavian immigrants. In 1890 the Norwegian Synod founded Pacific Lutheran College in Tacoma, the ancestor of today's Pacific Lutheran University. Two years later the Adventists opened Walla Walla College, and in 1893 the Free Methodists opened Seattle Pacific College, today Seattle Pacific University.

Aside from their own schools, church leaders played a crucial role in siting and organizing the paramount center of higher learning in the region, the University of Washington. It was Daniel Bagley who was responsible for locating it in Seattle, and he labored mightily to bring it into being. His son, the historian Clarence Bagley, later wrote: "Bagley worked like a Turk on that job a built the university within a year. He handled the whole business, and if the university has got a father, his name is Daniel Bagley." He was president of its Board of Commissioners when it opened in 1861. In 1866, when it was near bankruptcy, the old warhorse George Whitworth was called to its presidency to put things right, but the regents closed the school before he could act, and it did not open again until 1869.

The major problem facing territorial institutions like the university was lack of money. Church schools faced the same problem, but their denominations at least had access to funds outside the region. Catholic schools had the added advantage of being run by able men and women religious who received essentially no wages, living off the tuitions they collected. The only state school ever to be funded from outside was the Benjamin P. Cheney Academy, founded in 1882, by a director of the Northern Pacific Railroad. In 1890 the Academy was deeded to the state for a normal school, the ancestor of today's Eastern Washington University. In spite of their advantages, however, some academies that attempted to become colleges, such as the Baptist's Colfax Academy, failed.

The churches were by no means rich, except in able and dedicated individuals. The labor in creating these schools was prodigious, and the benefits they supplied the community were and continue to be enormous. The churches' constant and unflagging support of education kept it before the public mind, and even after the state and local schools became well-established, the church schools provided an intellectual competition that kept their secular counterparts to a higher level of competence than they might have attained otherwise.

More ambiguous results attended the churches' resumption of missionary work among the native peoples. While Cushing Eells was welcoming the first students at Whitman, none other than Henry Spalding was living on the Touchet River, a short distance to the northwest. James Wilbur had been appointed presiding elder of the M.E. Church's Walla Walla District, and together, Spalding and Wilbur sought to continue the work that had come to a bloody end in 1847.

Spalding had been making repeated requests to return to the Nez Perce, but his old colleagues and critics, Eells and Walker, had advised against it. Nevertheless, in 1857 the American Home Mission Society, (A.H.M.S.) appointed Spalding a missionary in Oregon with a salary of $500 a year. In mid-August of 1859, a Nez Perce delegation met Spalding at his daughter-in-law's claim on the Touchet River. In an emotional reunion, they begged him to return. However, he had to wait four years for an appointment as interpreter at the Lapwai Agency. As always, he was convinced that his difficulties were the result of some collusion between U.S. officials and the perfidious Catholics.

Although many Catholic missions had been burned during the Indian Wars, several including the Jesuits' St. Paul mission on the Colville River had continued to operate even after the interior had been closed to white settlements. In 1859 St. Patrick's mission was organized at the American military post of Fort Walla Walla, and in 1861, St. Peter's mission church at the Dalles was rebuilt from the ashes of war.

In the meantime, Wilbur had been visiting points in his district including the military post among the Yakimas, Fort Simcoe, where he had been appointed pastor. He taught there in the Indian school until he was dismissed by the Agent-in-Charge, B.F. Kendall, who accused him of bribing students to attend his Sunday school classes, of giving his wife and relatives jobs and of harassing those who were not Methodists. In spite of these charges Wilbur was able to get Kendall dismissed and have himself made Agent-in-Charge in Kendall's place, a position he retained for the better part of twenty-seven years. A forceful personality, Wilbur's penchant for unorthdox methods produced his share of critics, but also won a following that referred to him affectionately as "Father Wilbur."

Wilbur's 1879 Indian Methodist Episcopal Church,
Yakima Indian Reservation.

Courtesy Earl Howell Photo Collection, Pacific Northwest Methodist Annual
Conference Archives, United Methodist Church, University of Puget Sound,
Tacoma, Washington.

Wilbur's tenure as agent occurred at a critical period in the reservation's history. Throughout the West, bands uprooted from their homelands were herded onto reservations where they were expected to die out quietly or learn to live like whites. On the Yakima Reservation there were besides the native Yakima bands remnants of the Palus and Cayuse as well as Paiutes and Bannocks from southeastern Oregon. It was an impossible situation, and that the reservation did not explode in chaos was due in part to the shock and grief of its benumbed residents as well as their desire to survive as best as they could in a world transformed. There was not much overt resistance—

Wilbur traveled through the reservation unarmed—and the peace over which he presided enabled him to produce tangible results, at least among a few. In his 1877 report to his superiors, he wrote:

"Many of the good results are apparent in their personal cleanliness, their dress, houses, schools, and churches. This class of Indians are exerting a salutary influence upon the Yakima Nation, and teaching them in a language they cannot misunderstand, the advantage they have gained in abandoning their roving habits, making themselves farms and homes, enriching themselves with stock and products of the soil."

As a minister, he was after a change of heart in his charges as well as a change of living.

"The first condition of improvement in the outside manner of life of my people is the improvement of the heart. Here is the place to begin the work of reform among the Indians. If I fail to give moral character to an Indian I can give him nothing that does him permanent good. If I can succeed in giving him moral character, so that he is no more a liar, a thief, a drunkard, a profane person, a polygamist or a gambler but a man of integrity, industry, sobriety and purity, then he no longer needs the gifts of government or the charities of anybody. He then becomes a man like any other man and can take care of himself."

To produce this paradigm, Wilbur needed absolute control of affairs, and he determined to get it by eliminating any competition for his charges' attention. He witheld supplies and support from those he considered recalcitrant or a threat, and high on his list were the followers of Smohalla who had no place on his reservation while Wilbur was in charge. Other targets were the Catholics who were attempting to reorganize their interior missions. In 1865 the St. Ann mission on the Umatilla was rebuilt, and year later Cataldo and Tosi founded St. Michael's mission among the Spokanes, much to the displeasure of Spokan Garry. In 1867, Father Louis St. Onge reestablished the St. Joseph mission to the Yakima on Ahtanum Creek, right next to Wilbur's domain, and the contest was on. In 1871 Bishop Blanchet had intended to turn this mission over to the Jesuits, but that was the year President Grant's Peace Policy for Indian reservations went into effect. This divided reservations among several religious denominations who had the right to nominate their own agents. Initially the policy was hailed by both Catholics and Protestants, but conflict arose once the reservations were alloted. This was to be done according to certain criteria, for example, who first proselytized among a group. Catholics believed they would receive forty reservations, but they received only seven, and the Yakimas were not among them.

Wilbur used this decision to keep Catholic missionaries out of the reservation, and to keep those residing on it from attending Catholic services. It became a cause celebre among Catholics who hammered away at Wilbur in the *Catholic Sentinel* printed in Portland and kept a steady stream of protests flowing to Washington, D.C.

Wilbur was not particularly upset by any of this. Those enrolled on the reservation voted Joseph Stwire, also known as White Swan, Chief to assist him in his duties. Stwire was a Methodist and a brother

/. THOMAS PEARNE.   CHIEF WHITE SWAN.   REV. GEO. WATERS.

Cut the courtesy Pacific Christian Advocate, Portland, Oregon.

Some of "Father" Wilbur's Native American converts on the Yakima Reservation. The Reverend George Waters was a missionary to the Nez Perce with Spalding.

Courtesy Earl Howell Photo Collection, Pacific Northwest Methodist Annual Conference Archives, United Methodist Church, University of Puget Sound, Tacoma, Washington.

of George Waters who had studied at the Jason Lee Missionary School near Salem, Oregon. In 1869 Wilbur presented Waters to the Annual Conference, and he was appointed to serve on the Simcoe Circuit. Shortly afterwards, he left the reservation with three other Yakimas and began preaching among the Nez Perce.

The Nez Perce had been troubled by factional disputes that pitted Christian converts led by chiefs Timothy and Jude against non-Christians. Spalding had resided among them for several years, moving from his position as interpreter up to Agent-in-Charge, but in 1865 he was dismissed as the result of yet another feud with his superiors. Shortly after they arrived, Waters and his Yakima associates organized a highly successful revival, and there was great religious enthusiasm. When Spalding returned in 1870, a spiritual revolution was in progress, and he helped bring it to fruition. Whatever his failings in his relationships with whites, he was extraordinarily effective as a missionary among the Nez Perce, and with the help of another missionary, the Reverend Henry Cowley at Kamiah, he succeeded in baptizing over 1000 people and laying the foundations for six Presbyterian churches. In 1873 Spalding was invited by Spokan Garry to come and preach to the Spokanes which he did with similar success, helping organize two churches among them. Finally, the harvest for which he and others had labored so long seemed ready to bring in.

Elsewhere, other churchmen also appeared to be making progress. In spite of harassment, Catholic missionaries counted their successes. In 1860 Oblate father Casimir Chirouse founded the St. Francis Xavier Mission on the Tulalip Reservation near the mouth of the Snohomish River. There, in a scene reminiscent of earlier missionary triumphs in dark age Europe, native converts piled religious artifacts at his feet during Mass. A year later he founded St. Joachim's Mission among the Lummi and St. Peter's Mission at Suquamish where Chief Seattle had served as one of Demers' original catechists.

Their Protestant rivals west of the mountains were equally busy. Methodist missions on the Quinault and Neah Bay reservations supported schools and churches where services were held in English and Chinook Jargon. In 1871, Edwin Eells, another of Cushing Eells' sons, was appointed agent of the Skokomish Reservation on Hood Canal where he was joined by his father and brother, Myron, who became pastor on the reservation in 1876. Among the Nooksacks near the Canadian border, there were many converts, among them Chief Lynden Jim, converted at a revival organized by two men from LaConner, Jimmy Adams and William George, who had themselves been converted at a Methodist camp meeting in Chilliwack, British Columbia.

This heightening of religious interest preceded the ferment that occurred among the Skokomish people in 1881 when John Slocum's vision and call for moral reform inspired the formation of the Indian Shaker Church. His message received wide hearing throughout the Puget Sound region and was helped not a little by the antagonistic attitude of reservation missionaries, Protestant and Catholic alike. At first they tried to ignore the phenomenon, but when it continued to grow, they took harsher measures. When Big John, a Skokomish man who preached the new religion in defiance of Myron Eells' ban, proclaimed himself the Christ and rode through the streets of Olympia at the head of some fifty followers with his arms outstretched, Eells had him arrested and imprisoned. When other Shakers sought to cure a sick woman through their ecstatic ritual, Edwin Eells had them arrested and imprisoned for seven weeks, cumbered with balls and chains. But such tactics proved fruitless; the church gained legal status, and the missionaries were forced to accept it, although some like the Presbyterian missionary at Neah Bay, Helen Clark, worked to suppress it by enjoining the agent to severely regulate its services.

Where the formation of a native congregation reflected the peoples' own desires, and where they participated in its functioning in meaningful ways, the churches took root and survived. But where inspiration and authority were the prerogatives of whites, the churches did not long outlive whoever brought them into being. After Wilbur retired in 1882, for example, the size of his reservation church, which counted 502 members and probationers, shrank dramatically.

The squabbles between Catholics and Protestants over which native groups were "theirs" was symptomatic of a paternalism that threatened to crush its subjects in its overbearing embrace. The effects could be observed in the reservation schools where church and state labored to recreate the native personality. Children separated from their families were dressed in uniforms and regimented with military thoroughness. There were some positive results: students learned to read and write and some schoolmasters encouraged them to help run the school and join organizations like the Good Templars, a temperance group that gave them responsibility and the opportunity to travel. There were sports teams and brass bands. But the schools also broke the generational link that had kept the native heritage alive. Native customs and religions were ridiculed, and native languages were suppressed despite the earlier efforts of churchmen to commit them to writing. In some cases children who persisted in speaking their own language were beaten or had their tongues placed against frozen pipes. Whatever the intentions of these punishments were, their effects were disastrous. Teachers and administrators, both Protestant and Catholic lamented that their students who were so bright, energetic and well-mannered when young grew sullen and dull in mid-adolescence. By then the young had begun to sense the scale of the disaster that had befallen their people.

The desire for moral reform, to make the way straight and lead the sinner back to God was at the heart of Christian practice, as it is of virtually all religions, but the desire to impose reform from without rather than encourage it from within reflected the arrogance of the time. With few defenses, the native peoples could only submit to the ordeal, but when the churches attempted to impose reform on the population at large, the results were considerably different.

The three great crusades of nineteenth century American Protestantism were missionary endeavor, humanitarian reform and moral renewal. Missionary endeavor had brought the churches west, and much of their energies for humanitarian reform had been consumed, for the time being, in the fight to abolish slavery. Moral reform, however, was alive and well in the West.

Ministers preached on several moral issues. Miscegnation, in this case, the cohabiting of white men with native women, horrified many like the Blaines who believed it threatened the well-being of white society. In one letter home, Catherine wrote:

"...you have no idea of the degredation men bring on themselves by their intercourse with the squaws. These squaws are lower and more degraded than you can imagine, but little better than hogs in human shape, and when men so debase themselves as to live with them they lose all self respect, shun the society of virtuous people, in fact, all white society except it be that of those equally debased, must be given up. This one sin is the greatest drawback to reform which we find and it is by no means confined to a few."

A dearth of white women was a perennial problem on the frontier which many pioneers solved practically enough by marrying or living with native women. An attempt at a solution to this dilemma that many churchmen supported was the scheme of Seattle's Asa Mercer to import boatloads of marriagable women from the East, but in spite of his herculean efforts, only a few came west. Although settlers poured into the region, men continued to outnumber women until this century. As the numbers of native women shrank proportionally, the ministers' moral outrage was turned from miscegnation to the more general problem of prostitution, a growth industry in the Northwest.

An argument churchmen rolled out against the issue of women's suffrage when it first arose was that the body of enfranchised women would include numbers of "fallen women." But this reservation was dismissed when it was understood that women's votes might make possible the great goal of moral reform, the banishment of alcohol.

Temperance had been a part of territorial politics since the days of the HBC. Jason Lee had organized the first temperance society in Oregon with Dr. McLoughlin's blessing, and churches were always in the van of drives to restrict drinking. The corrosive effects of alcohol on society were not hard to see. It inflamed the antipathies that had grown up between native and white, and many blamed the violent breakdown in relations between them upon the liquor trade that accompanied settlers into the region. Without question, the desperate condition of native people on and off the reservation was made worse by unscrupulous liquor dealers who plied territorial waters in their whiskey boats and hauled kegs of spirits over primitive trails. White society hardly suffered less. The death of one of Washington's ablest legislators, George McConaha, was blamed on his drinking, and no less a figure than Isaac Stevens was accused of being drunk during important treaty councils. Then as now, wives and children were the common victims of drunken husbands, and in many communities it was not at all difficult for children to have drinks served them in local saloons.

The majority of the white population, however, were young, single working men, who enjoyed a drink in the convivial atmosphere of the saloon, the "poor man's club," and many if not most were opposed to an infringement upon their pleasure. A bill modeled after the Maine Liquor Law, the first statewide prohibition law, was introduced during the first session of the territorial legislature by Arthur Denny, a staunch Methodist, temperance man and supporter of women's suffrage, but it was defeated by one vote.

Undeterred, temperance workers kept up their efforts and lobbied for the extension of suffrage. In 1883 their efforts bore fruit when the territorial supreme court granted women the vote in territorial elections. In the larger communities of the territory, reform movements were organized to ensure that laws restricting the sale of liquor were enforced and to enact new ones to restrict it even further. These movements drew much of their leadership and support from churches as well as national organizations like the Women's Christian Temperance Union (WCTU) which sought to make Washington an example for the rest of the nation.

In Seattle, the largest city in the territory, a reform group called the Law and Order League appealed to women for support of its slate of candidates in municipal and county elections. At Plymouth Congregational Church all the women attending a mass meeting called by the League rose as one in a dramatic assent to their plea. The reformist candidates triumphed at the polls, and one immediate result was the strict enforcement of the Sunday closure law which banned the sale of liquor on the one day workers had off. Not unexpectedly, many went elsewhere to get a drink and took with them the money they normally spent on their free day for supplies.

The loss of the saloon trade coincided with the severe effects of a national depression that struck the Northwest in 1885 and 1886. Candidates supported by the business community blamed the reformers for the economic troubles and succeeded in defeating them in the 1885 municipal election. Rankled by their defeat, many women threw their support behind anti-business groups, particularly those organized by labor leaders who gained prominence by their involvement in the anti-Chinese riots. In the municipal election of 1886, the People's Party defeated the businessmen's candidate for mayor and chief of police, and so disturbed the business community in Seattle and elsewhere that their friends in government succeeded the next year in nullifying the legal decision that had given women the vote. Suffrage was taken back by the judiciary that had granted it, and it was not returned until 1910. In 1887 the businessmen's candidates were once again in control of municipal affairs, and the saloon trade was booming.

This foray into territorial politics cost church leaders the voting block they had looked to for support, but their zeal for reform remained undiminished, and they resumed their efforts on behalf of both temperance and women's suffrage. They would eventually triumph, but the lesson of 1887, of how dangerous it was to impose a particular moral point of view on an unwilling populace, went unlearned. Ultimately, that ignorance would lead to disaster.

The Moving Pen and Pencil of Charles Hiram Mattoon

New Prospect at Mound Prairie, Washington, was the first Baptist church organized in Washington Territory (1859). A small group of worshippers — most of them had emigrated from the Willamette Valley — met at the Scatter Creek schoolhouse under the leadership of rail-thin, ascetic, Brother Thomas J. Harper. Harper hailed from Tennessee and had served eighteen years as a lay preacher before his ordination. When he stepped forth to "exercise his gifts" he converted a number of followers, including his son, P.J. Harper. The son would, in turn, take his conversion seriously, leading several Pacific Northwest Baptist congregations in the late 1800s.

T.J. Harper, the first Washington Baptist preacher, was, ironically, one of the few characters overlooked by scribbler Charles H. Mattoon (although he mentions son P.J.). His two-volume *Baptist Annals of Oregon,* and his editorship of the anti-slavery, pro-temperance *Religious Expositer* placed him in the forefront of early western religious chroniclers. Although Catholics, Methodists and Congregationalists seemed to produce inveterate amateur historians, C.H. Mattoon held the pen high for his fellow Baptists. The *Expositor* lasted for only twenty-six issues, but Mattoon couldn't stop recording everything and anything he saw within the Baptist family. Canastota, New York was Mattoon's birthplace. He attended a Presbyterian institution, Central College, in Ohio, but at a youthful nineteen years he embraced the Baptist faith. Like many of his Eastern brethren who heard the call, he crossed the plains in 1851 and joined a growing Baptist membership in the fertile, bustling Willamette Valley.

After bringing his Ohio sweetheart west in 1860, he married and was ordained ten years later. At this point his busy pencil began to record statistics and historical data from every Baptist source within reach. Referred to in later years as the "Baptist historian of the Upper Coast" Mattoon jotted down quaint details of churches stretching from Alaska to Washington to Utah. Showing no sign of writer's pride, he loaned his notebooks to anyone. His church mini-histories, coupled with personal, and sometimes colorful, descriptions of men, women and events, garnered him a reputation.

Mattoon wrote: "The early Baptists were an enthusiastic, emotional people...shouting and noisy demonstrations were not uncommon." He described the preaching themes of pioneer ministers as "The Cross, God's Abhorrence of Sin, Christ's Atonement, Divine Love, The Sinner's Desperate Condition, and The Judgement Bar."

Struggling with his newspaper, the *Religious Expositor,* Mattoon aimed to "harmonize...discordant materials of which our churches are composed." He paid scant attention to his own firm, sometimes righteous, views which may have contributed to occasional Baptist disharmony. The *Expositor* would, he hoped, enrich the mind and elevate moral character. Mattoon saw his paper as presenting "the Way, the Truth, and the Life."

At $3.50 a year the *Expositor* was expensive. Eventually eastern, secular publications stole his market. It was estimated that subscribers to the *Expositor* did not exceed 375 persons — although pioneers tended to liberally pass around reading material, a precious commodity and diversion. When the burgeoning *Oregonian* accused Mattoon of plagiarism, it couldn't resist reminding the *Expositor's* editor of the commandment, "Thou shalt not steal." After this set-to, Mattoon quickly diverted his literary and forensic abilities to another battlefield: temperance.

When the *Expositor* expired in 1856, Mattoon continued his statistical note-taking, eventually turning those jottings into the *Baptist Annals of Oregon,* Volumes 1 and 2 (despite the ambitious title, Vol. 2 was never published). In the introduction to Volume 1, W. Carey Johnson, an Oregon attorney and son of the famous Baptist missionary, Hezekiah Johnson, wrote that Mattoon had "the patience and faith necessary for this duty (the *Annals*)." Mattoon preserved and gathered journals, minutes, documents, lists, reminiscences, registers, tall tales, and used his own considerable powers of observation when writing everything down. Mattoon, in his 1905 preface to Volume 1, only asked his readers to "exercise kindness and leniency" towards his "hitherto untrodden" effort.

Known as a Landmark, or high-Baptist, Mattoon believed that his church was *the* church of Christ — part of an unbroken succession from the apostles. He wrote about and engaged in public debates to support his Landmarker views. When in 1893 a church leader referred to Landmarkers as "sneaks and traitors," C.H. Mattoon replied that the anti-Landmarkers were "trying to split the denomination."

In the 1890s Mattoon criticized "city" preachers: "Christ," he wrote, "preached comparatively but little in the towns, and what few churches the apostles planted in the large cities, became...corrupt...and it has ever been so."

C.H. Mattoon liked to write. He was in fact, indefatigable. His talents, also stretched to oratory, theology, and education. For years he served as Professor of Mathematics at Oregon's tiny McMinnville College. When the Oregon State Educational Association was formed in 1858, Charles H. Mattoon was a charter member of the board.

Mattoon died in 1915. His *Annals* became a basic source for church historians. He wrote that "revival followed revival in many parts of the (Oregon) Territory, and Zion, which had languished, now began to bud and blossom." History buffs and curious Baptists will not languish, however, thanks to the incessant scribbling of Charles Hiram Mattoon.

"Grandpa"
William M. Stewart's Inferno

Boom was the right word for British Columbia's Fraser River Gold Rush in 1858. Just south of the Fraser in today's Whatcom County, settlements at Sehome, Semiahmoo and California Creek were then bustling centers of gold fever. Commercial activity, families and churches appeared.

"Grandpa" William Stewart, eighty-year-old patriarch of a local pioneer family, took his preaching seriously. He knew the Lord and he understood damnation. Beginning in 1876 the log church at California Creek used to shake with vibrations from Rev. Stewart's pulpit. His son, William Stewart, Jr., a respected deacon of the little church, had the unfortunate propensity to doze off in the first pew during his father's fire and brimstone orations.

One memorable Sunday "Grandpa" Stewart, voice rising and arms flailing, had the devil cornered. With a crescendo he described the enemy's inferno as "Fire! Fire!" His son the deacon lurched awake, jumped to his feet, and answered "Where? Where?" Without missing a beat the venerable preacher looked past his son and yelled "In Hell! in Hell!"

The congregation got its money's worth that day in California Creek.

The Muscular Arms of
James H. Wilbur

James Harvey Wilbur was over six feet tall. In his prime he weighed almost 300 lbs. That imposing physique could plow fields, calm crowds and preach the gospel with equal ease.

Wilbur must have had a stubborn mind to match his large frame, for his initial journey to Oregon territory was a feat in itself. Aboard the bark *Whiton,* Wilbur and his new wife Lucretia sailed from New York's Battery to the Cape Verde Islands off the coast of Africa. From there they sailed southward around the tip of South America, and then to Monterey, California. After a stop at Astoria, they disembarked in the village of Portland, Oregon, on June 27, 1847.

Methodist pioneer trail blazer Jason Lee had begun his Oregon work thirteen years before Wilbur's arrival. Wilbur built on Lee's work, extending it to eastern Washington. He also became the Indians' friend. Watching his great strength behind a plow or while falling trees, an awed Indian claimed that "he is not all man...he is part bear." After displaying prodigious physical efforts, Wilbur would hold church services, weeping his way through the sermon.

"Father" was the title given to the broad-shouldered Wilbur. He was not offended by the obvious borrowing of that word from Catholic priests. "Father" seemed to fit the large-boned, genial preacher.

Wilbur used Fort Simcoe as an Indian refuge, resting and learning place, where Indian needs came first. He had built churches in Portland, and helped set up religious activity in Walla Walla and the Dalles, but Fort Simcoe and the Yakima Indians would get to know Father Wilbur best.

In 1860, Reverend and Mrs. James H. Wilbur established a weekday secular school, while preaching Sunday Christianity amidst the local white settlers and Indians. The Indian Agency School included Bible readings alongside texts of the 1860s—Sander's Primer, Sargent's Readers, and Cornell's Primary Geography. This idyllic period was suddenly shattered in 1862 with the abrupt dismissal of Wilbur as Fort Simcoe Superintendent of Instruction. Benjamin F. Kendall, Superintendent of Indian Affairs, not only fired Wilbur, who volunteered to stay on without pay, but Kendall also dismissed several other ex-

The Reverend James Wilbur, Methodist Missionary on the Yakima Reservation 1855-1882.

Courtesy Earl Howell Photo Collection, Pacific Northwest Methodist Annual Conference Archives, United Methodist Church, University of Puget Sound, Tacoma, Washington.

perienced hands. Opposition to Kendall's action spread, resulting in his own dismissal, and the return of Wilbur. (Kendall, by the way, ended his days as a Steilacoom newspaper editor and lawyer. He died of gunshot wounds inflicted by an irate victim of one of his editorials.)

The 1870s saw the last outbreak of Indian wars in the Pacific Northwest. Wilbur's friendship with the Yakimas and neighboring tribes is credited with mitigating what could have been anti-white massacres. Federal troops were briefly called back to Fort Simcoe, which had been under civilian jurisdiction for many years. Immediately after that period of martial law, a belligerent Paiute chief began threatening violence against the whites. At a council called by Wilbur to hear the dissident Paiute's grievances, the Indian chief's remarks grew into a tirade. When he wouldn't calm down, a white observer described what happened: "Father Wilbur stepped quickly to the chief's side, ran his powerful right hand under the heavy braid...clamped his fingers over the back of the chief's head and marched him through his circle of warriors to the jail..." No one budged. Wilbur's faith—and muscular arms—beat the odds.

Stories were told of Father Wilbur physically subduing Indian and white men alike. Liquor had brought troubles, and the local police, both Indian and white, had occasionally retreated from confronting particularly obstreperous drunks. Wilbur had reputedly lifted two quarelling Indians by their hair. On another occasion he flattened a pistol-wielding German immigrant with a ham-fisted blow to the head.

Wilbur encouraged church attendance. When an Indian farmer declined his invitation to attend services because of an unplowed field, Wilbur dismounted and helped the farmer finish his work. The surprised Indian must have known that Father Wilbur's eyes would be scanning the congregation to see if his generosity paid off.

Coupled with fearsome physical strength and religious devotion was another trait: a canny sense of business. Andrew J. McNemee, later known as "Brother Mack," describes a 1869 encounter with Wilbur: "I hired out to Reverend J.H. Wilbur for $2.50 per day (to clear land)...when he learned that I wanted to go to college, he said that he held a scholarship in the Willamette University that was good for $50 a year, and that he would sell it to me for $25...After I paid him for the scholarship, he cut my wages to $2.25 per day and the next week he made another cut to $2.00 and I quit." Wilbur made profitable investments along the way, especially in Walla Walla. Upon his death in October 1887 (Lucretia died four weeks earlier) he left an estate appraised at $55,000—a veritable fortune. Methodist churches, libraries, and Willamette University received the bulk of those monies.

Although Father Wilbur's physical traits were legendary, his signal devotion to the Indians of eastern Washington may be his greatest gift to our history.

Brother Mack's "Tale of Woe"

What do we say about a self-made, tough, backcountry reverend who was described as follows by a presiding elder at a 1866 Methodist Church council? "He didn't claim to be a great preacher...(but)...he knew how to "rustle."

Andrew J. McNemee was raised in the 1850s among Indians, wild bear and hellfire religion near the mouth of the Columbia River. "Brother Mack" as he was later called, hit what was known as the sawdust trail. A circuit-riding, homespun Methodist preacher who boiled blue-jays for dinner and slept on the floor of his bush patrons' cabins, Brother Mack once explained to a suspicious farmer that he was preaching in the neighborhood "for want of a better man."

Camp meetings were Brother Mack's specialty. Rousing customers throughout Oregon and Washington, he sold his boots to buy food, strapped himself to a tree's topmast to escape wolves, and was told at age thirty-four that the Bishop was opposed to sending out "old men" on the circuit.

Brother Mack's friend and mentor, Reverend John N. Denison, was threatened by vigilantes during the Seattle anti-Chinese riots of 1885. When brother Mack arrived on the scene by foot from his temporary base in Squak Valley (Issaquah), Denison greeted him with these encouraging words: "don't...leave me...the mob has threatened to kill me and burn up my church. If they do, I want you here with me." Brother Mack stayed and the mob dispersed.

Living off the hospitality of strangers, an occasional odd job, and a dollar or two offered by generous hands, Brother Mack hiked his Pacific Northwest preacher circuit for thirty-three years. In 1888 he was officially complimented on his "good work," but it was noted that his district needed a preacher "who has a wife that can play the organ." Brother Mack declined both the wife and, presumably, organ lessons.

Brother Mack worked all the little towns: Langley, Blaine, Chimacum, Ferndale, Kalama, Cherry Valley (Duvall), and every hamlet in between. When he sermonized that the saloons in Friday Harbor should be closed — buttressed with a series of fire and brimstone temperance lectures, his life was threatened by imbibers at Edison, his next stop.

Perhaps the most remarkable footnote to the life of Brother Mack is that he tried to write it all down. His primitive journal, festooned with yarns, charming misspellings and earnest, original syntax, ended on August 1, 1924. On April 25, 1936, age 88, Andrew Jackson McNemee died on Whidbey Island. He finally ended, as he put it, his "endless tale of woe." Today, however, that rustic story of a circuit preacher reads like an exuberant odyssey through a formative period of Washington State history.

Tom Gourley's Pentecostal Island

Sir Thomas More's 1516 description of Utopia has for centuries, like the fabled Fountain of Youth, attracted wise, unwise, and desperate characters. Washington Territory, and later the state, also flirted with religious and secular utopias.

Edward Bellamy's 1888 novel *Looking Backward,* and the Bellamy clubs, may have inspired some of that 19th century social experimentation, but the end-of-the-road character and temperate climate of Washington seemed to be attractive nurturing ground for this activity. Charles P. LeWarne, in his fascinating book *Utopias on Puget Sound 1885-1915* (UW, Seattle, 1975) noted that our region's versions of utopia had the following characteristics: small, isolated, strong leadership, a sense of cooperation and visionary ideals. Utopian adherents, LeWarne noted, often professed "a religious fervor, which afforded unusual insight into the problems of society and their solutions." That same fervor, usually directed by a single leader, frequently doomed the experiment. In fact every local utopia from the Puget Sound Cooperative Colony to Walla Walla's Davisite Kingdom of Heaven was short-lived and marked by strife and confusion.

Kansan Thomas Hampton Gourley arrived in Seattle after the demise of several well-known Pacific Northwest utopias. His Pentecostal paradise, however, was going to be different. In 1908 he organized a mission in downtown Seattle. After neighbors complained about the noise — services were noted for their loud praying and singing — Gourley decamped with his followers to the newly annexed town of Ballard in the northwest corner of Seattle.

Gourley's tabernacle aboard an offshore float was financially supported by dedicated members of his colony. Those members also held "outside" jobs as fishermen, teachers, printers and carpenters. The inevitable conflicts with non-members came sooner rather than later. On March 16, 1911, approximately 150 members of Gourley's colony, after settling their bills in Ballard, boarded assorted watercraft for a journey to the true promised land: Lopez Island in the scenic San Juan group.

After erecting buildings and planting vegetables near Sperry's Point on the idyllic 12-mile-long island, disaster struck. Their spring water proved contaminated. A number of colonists died; everyone became sick. Several members packed up and left. When the colony tried another site at Hunter Bay, it had more success. A school was built, cordial relations with neighbors developed, and the colony's Christian fundamentalist beliefs were given full expression.

Although Gourley's sect was called Pentecostal it apparently had no direct connection with the Church of the Nazarene or similar groups. At various stages it had been labeled "Apostolic Church of Jesus Christ," the "'Tongue Mission" (because its members spoke in tongues), "Holy Rollers," "Come Outers" (from the biblical source to "come out from among the many and be separate"), "Gourley Camp," "Hunter Bay Camp," or "Gourleylites." Perhaps its basic tenet came from the Book of Acts: "And all that believed were together and had all things common; and sold their possessions and goods, and parted them to all men as every man had need."

Gourley's teaching of a millennium and second coming of Jesus was not unlike other fundamentalist sects. When, as promised, these events did not occur, dissension arose within the colony. Perhaps Gourley's well-meaning but vociferous preaching against America's entry into the Great War, 1918, was also a turning point. Charged with violating the Wartime Espionage Act, Gourley's trial was held in Bellingham. A deadlocked jury did not free Gourley from the taint of being a traitor, however, and things began to fall apart.

Leadership is a fragile quality and Gourley's firm hand was challenged from within. Rumors persisted that the Gourley family always had abundant groceries when other colonists could barely feed their children. Murmurings of funds mismanagement and who-told-what-to-whom peppered local gossip. In 1920 Tom Gourley and his family left Lopez Island. Within months bickering and disillusionment caused the final breakup. Sale of the colony's farm equipment allowed each remaining family to take $175. Later, squatters and Prohibition rum runners from nearby Canada occasionally used the abandoned buildings. A small cemetery plot is today's only evidence that a utopia once prospered on that site.

Tom Gourley took up evangelism in St. Louis, Missouri. On the 26th of February, 1923, returning from Macon, Georgia, and while trying to jump from a train involved in a rail accident, Gourley was decapitated.

John C. Kimball
and the Templar's Hall Debates

Real estate speculation and raw adventure pulled a number of pioneers to the Pacific Northwest. Missionary fervor, especially out of the denominational cross-currents of New England, brought others. Pioneering was not everyone's favorite game, however. After gallant effort, and some embarrassing failures, a small percentage of these trekkers gave up and returned to their eastern home towns.

Missionaries usually came fully packed and for the duration. Creature comforts held less attraction for the godly than they did for business speculators with families. Reverend and Mrs. John C. Kimball, representing the New England Unitarian Missionary Association, arrived in the Territory of Washington in June of 1871. After touching base with a fledgling Unitarian group in Portland, Oregon, minister-at-large Kimball settled in Olympia, unpacked his bags and immediately began a series of packed house Sunday afternoon sermons in the Old Templar's Hall at Fourth and Columbia Streets. Those rousing, reasoned talks brought forth counterstatements that would stir several territorial communities. After a year and a half, Reverend and Mrs. Kimball packed their bags and accepted a call to Hartford, Connecticut. Here's a glimpse of what John Kimball left behind.

Organized in 1825, a small Boston meeting of laymen and young congregational ministers, established the American Unitarian Association. Promotion of "Pure Christianity," that is without adherence to the Holy Trinity, i.e., their title "Unitarian," was the goal of this group. Fellow Unitarians drifted westward to San Francisco and later to Portland.

Several eminent Washington pioneers adopted Unitarianism. Ezra Meeker and his brothers, for example, arrived in Washington Territory in covered wagons. Meeker not only embraced Unitarianism, but would profit in commerce, write rough but readable memoirs, and become famous as a long-lived professional pioneer and Oregon Trail enthusiast. Family members of Washington's first Territorial Governor, Isaac I. Stevens, including son Hazard and daughter Kate, were active Unitarians. Early Seattle's wily sawmill operator and real estate speculator Henry L. Yesler lent his support and all-purpose cookhouse to a tiny band of Unitarian followers. Rev. John C. Kimball's presence was therefore preceded by a sympathetic audience, small in number, but well placed.

Olympia's Hall of Good Templar's hosted sermons, entertainments and civic gatherings in the late 1800s. Kimball's Sunday afternoon talks were popular and duly reported in Olympia's *Daily Pacific Tribune.* A June 1871 Kimball sermon titled "Man's Relation to God" was described as "very interesting and eloquent." Quoting from Ecclesiastes, "Lo, only this have I found, that God hath made man upright; but they have sought out many inventions," the *Tribune* lauded Rev. Kimball's warm presence and appealing delivery. "Mr. Kimball," stated the Tribune, "is a ready speaker, and his services were conducted with impressive fervor. He has succeeded in awakening considerable interest in the community."

That "considerable interest" was aptly applied to both Kimball's fans and detractors. Such sermons as "The Unitarian Idea of Man" and "Christianity in Everyday Life" might have caused passing interest, but perhaps the text of his talk "Is God a Christian?" created a stir. Conversations within the community began to take place. Kimball's—and the Unitarian's—views were debated. There was nothing new about Christian denominations differing over which path leads directly to heaven, but the intellectually-oriented, newcomer Unitarian point of view was a special challenge. Kimball roamed from Seattle to Port Gamble to Vancouver, B.C., his road show filled the halls everywhere. The debate followed.

Within Reverend Kimball's sermons were strong opinions about the Deep South and slavery. Only six years after the cessation of North-South hostilities, passions were still high. Also, a large number of Southerners had emigrated to the Pacific Northwest to escape the privation and humiliation of Reconstruction. Looking for a clean slate and new challenges, these southern citizens, including their orthodox ministers, ran smack into the eloquence of Reverend John C. Kimball. Kimball's religious views, including a New England accent, didn't help his cause among conservative settlers.

The Washington Standard of March 23, 1872, printed the following letter: "The remarks of the lecturer (Kimball) who professes to preach the gospel of peace, has already stirred up strife in our community …it has come to our knowledge that two gentlemen who had always been friends had a quarrel and came to blows…the writer warns the readers not to take *ipse dixit* (an unproven assertion) of every missionary from New England as the law and gospel."

Kimball responded through a reporter on March 29. Claiming that the critical letter was, in fact, a compliment, he described the sociability and good reading available at Unitarian meetings and decried "sectional prejudices." Kimball was quoted: " 'Hail Columbia, all good and all ours,' that is the *ipse dixit* of a New England missionary." The *Standard* and other papers encouraged the debate.

The Templar's Hall debates, at least in newspaper pages, continued into the 1880s. Walla Walla, another Unitarian stronghold, also found Kimball's message provocative. Seattle audiences and readers joined the fray. Kimball had left for Hartford by 1873 but other Unitarian ministers, notably Reverend David Utter, carried on the "debates." A close look at the Unitarian pulpits and sermons in Washington State today suggest that Reverend Kimball's style, and in some cases his sermon topics, are alive and well.

Missionary Profile:
The Douglas Corprons of Yakima

"The missionaries who labored... certainly had uphill work. Not only had they to combat with the opposing elements in the Indian, but with unprincipled and bad white men, who appeared resolved to undo what the missionaries had done."
Andrew Dominique Pambrun, 1822-1895, *Sixty Years on the Frontier in the Pacific Northwest.*

Propagation of the faith to far-flung lands remains a core duty of many religious organizations. The early 1800s saw a dramatic rise in Pacific Northwest missionary activity, some of it from the Catholic traditions in Quebec and other examples out of Boston

Mr. and Mrs. Douglas Corpron, son Douglas O., on his right his sister Ruth, on his left his sister Mary, and in the middle a Chinese orphan the family helped raise.

Courtesy Francis A. Hare, Archivist of Yakima Valley Museum and Historical Association and the Dr. Douglas Corpron family, Yakima, Washington.

1948 Anniversary Celebration of one of the Christian Hospitals the Corprons helped develop in China.

Courtesy Francis A. Hare, Archivist of Yakima Valley Museum and Historical Association and the Dr. Douglas Corpron family, Yakima, Washington.

on behalf of the (Protestant) American Board of Commissioners for Foreign Missions.

Not everyone agreed with missionary purposes. In fact, the occasional mistake in judgment was made by neophyte religionists, resulting in disagreements, broken promises, even violence. At about the time American western—and international—missionary efforts were reaching a 19th-century crest, Samuel Wilberforce, Bishop of Oxford, wrote the following stanza:

"If I were a Cassowary
On the plains of Timbuctoo,
I would eat a missionary,
Coat and bands and hymnbook, too."

A strong missionary tradition remains implanted in our state. Fledgling small-town and big city churches, some barely able to support their tiny congregations, made (and still make) financial contributions to missionary work. Much of that effort today is directed "overseas," just as an earlier missionary program targeted "foreign missions," which included the Oregon Territory.

To illustrate the nature of our state's strong missionary tradition, here is the story of the Corprons, who were affiliated with the First

Christian Church of Yakima. Douglas Corpron moved to Yakima from Minnesota in 1907. His boyhood hikes around the hills of Yakima were frequently in the company of William O. Douglas, later a member of the U.S. Supreme Court. While taking an undergraduate degree at the University of Oregon, Eugene, Corpron pledged himself to a career as a medical missionary. After receiving his medical degree from the University of Cincinnati, and after his wife Grace (who had been his childhood sweetheart) completed a teaching certificate at the University of Minnesota, the young couple spent time in missionary training. In the fall of 1923 the Corprons sailed for China and the Luchowfu (Hofei) Hospital.

Forced to leave China because of antiforeign riots in 1927, the Corprons moved to the Philippines. While Douglas worked at the hospital at Vigan, tragedy intervened. Both the Corpron children, Billie and Phyllis, died from dysentery within a few days of each other. Following postgraduate work in New York City, and an opportunity to recover from their personal loss, the Corprons returned to China, where they raised three more children. Dr. Corpron treated thousands of patients and helped establish rural clinics. Grace ran the Sunday school, supervised a playground, taught cooking, sewing and dietetics, and operated a baby clinic. Despite obvious hardships, letters from the Corprons described the satisfaction and joy of their work.

While on much-deserved leave in the United States, the Japan-China war broke out in 1937. As this was a prelude to the Second World War, the Corprons gave up plans to return to China — but not for long. After working among Southwest United States Indians, they returned to China in 1939 and again in 1947. The war forced them out, and Douglas and Grace found a calmer life while semiretired in Yakima.

During their late years Dr. Corpron practiced medicine and became a charter member of the local chapter of the American Association of General Practitioners. Their missionary spirits kept them active in local church and civic affairs for many years.

Minnie "Ma" Kennedy
and the Monticello Porch

Minnie Pierce was born in 1871. Her Canadian upbringing included a "shouting Methodist" mother and a childhood commitment to the Salvation Army. At fifteen, a child bride, she married 48-year-old James Kennedy. The Salvation Army's hallelujahs, however, seemed more important than her marriage. Pedaling

The Monticello Hotel in Longview where Ma Kennedy rode her white horse across the porch.

Courtesy Special Collections Division, University of Washington Libraries, Negative #4464, Seattle, Washington.

or walking the five miles to the Army's Sunday School in Ingersoll, Ontario, she eventually earned the rank of Junior Sergeant Major.

According to Minnie's recollection the biblical tale of Hannah's barren marriage inspired her to fervent prayer. The result, she claimed, was the October 9, 1890 birth of a baby girl. That child was named Aimee Elizabeth—briefly called Betty—and would cause a sensation in America's raucous 1920s as the evangelist Aimee Semple McPherson. Little Betty was bombarded by Minnie with Bible stories and hymns. She learned to clutch a Salvation Army tambourine in her tiny hands. Minnie took Betty everywhere, including Pentecostal free-for-alls where "Holy Rollers" performed and "speaking in tongues" was demonstrated.

At age seventeen Betty—now known as Aimee—married a 6'2" tall firebrand preacher named Robert Semple. Their wedding trip included a year in China as missionaries. "Look to Jesus" Aimee said to Minnie as the train pulled away from Ingersoll. Semple would die in China, leaving Aimee with a babe-in-arms.

Next, Minnie watched her daughter try marriage to a wholesale grocer named Harold S. McPherson. After suffering neurotic breakdowns and dizzy spells, Aimee left everything and everyone behind for a road tour as an itinerant evangelist.

Minnie intermittently accompanied her daughter in the gospel car, banging drums in Tulsa, Oklahoma, or passing the plate in Denver, Colorado. Aimee would sometimes leave Minnie behind and preach in such exotic places as Dayton, Washington. Minnie's fundamentalist religious beliefs also found their outlet, sometimes in original ways and byways.

Watching Aimee and the hard-earned church funds became Minnie's fulltime job. Both the money and her daughter's personal and evangelical antics proved an ordeal. Litigation, disappearances, sexual innuendos, mother-daughter estrangements, wild publicity and financial irregularities turned Minnie into a first-rate stage manager, publicist, and critic.

Banished to "the field" by her daughter, Minnie undertook "missionary" work. She travelled to Portland, Oregon, and then Seattle, Washington, in her chauffeur-driven, blue limousine. Minnie's revival meetings in Seattle, Longview, Kelso and other Puget Sound cities became famous. Although Seattle was Minnie's official headquarters her happiest Pacific Northwest days appeared to have been at Longview's old Monticello Hotel, where she occasionally rode her white horse Billy Sunday across the front porch. Her success in Washington State was apparent, with a following that caused Los Angeles-based Aimee to wonder. In 1929 a curious Aimee accompanied her mother on a tour of Minnie's Pacific Northwest bastions.

About this time Minnie was labeled "Ma" by the newspapers. Reporters also tried to find answers to why both Aimee and Ma had been hospitalized at the same time. Had Ma broken her nose? Was it true that Aimee has undergone plastic facial surgery? Apparently Aimee and her daughter fell to blows. Ma's broken nose was the result of a straight punch by the Angelus Temple evangelist. A battered nose, however, did not prevent Ma from attending a dedication ceremony in Olympia, Washington. Later, she spent four hours climbing Mt. Rainier. It was not reported whether Ma reached that earthly summit.

On June 28, 1931, in Longview, Washington, Minnie "Ma" Kennedy married Guy Edward Hudson. Ma was sixty years old. The slender, dark-haired bridegroom was "somewhat younger" according to local sources. When the honeymooning couple were discovered eating in a Seattle coffee shop, Ma referred to her husband as "what a man!" That moniker stuck: "Whataman" Hudson was big news.

Celebrating their marriage in Longview, Ma dressed up in a powdered wig and "Lord Chesterfield" costume. Whataman disguised himself as a be-whiskered cowboy. Longview citizens put on a banquet for the newlyweds that was talked about for years.

During a trip to southern California, Ma and Whataman were the subject of more probing by the press. At least three women claimed to be Hudson's wife. It was also asserted that an earlier Hudson divorce had occurred in Bellingham, Washington. The district attorney of Cowlitz County charged Whataman with bigamy. Daughter Aimee, who was in Seattle at that time, told a reporter that "Mr. Hudson is just a newspaper headline to me." As if this confusion was not enough, Ma petitioned for an annulment and then found her mental competency challenged by the Los Angeles Lunacy Commission. Someone from Aimee's Angelus Temple, it was rumored, had instigated the latter indignity. Further complicating this fracas was a refusal by the governor of Washington to sign an extradition warrant to bring Whataman back on bigamy charges. "A couple of careless performers" was the governor's laconic remark.

Comedy—or was it clever press clippings?—soon cluttered Ma's and Whataman's lives. Waving IOU's at photographers Ma claimed that her husband wouldn't go to work. She wanted a divorce. Whataman countered with the charge that his employment status had nothing to do with anything. "Ma's got a sweetie", he said. "One of those Salvation Army Officers". This was too much for Ma who pointed out all she had done for her man. "I even bought him hair tonic for his bald spot".

The wrangling never ceased. Three generations of the Kennedy family fought, testified against each other in court, and disagreed about money for the next twenty years. Aimee died of mysterious circumstances in September, 1944. She left the bulk of her estate to her son Rolf. Ma, who started it all, was bequeathed ten dollars.

Minnie "Ma" Kennedy remained interested in the Salvation Army. Obscurity closed in. When she died in 1947 the Reverend J.G.Gay of Kelso, Washington, who had married her to Whataman Hudson, officiated at her Los Angeles funeral.

4

Challenges and Opportunities

T he tumult of the 1880s signaled the onset of profound changes in the Northwest as rural frontier society became increasingly urban and industrial. In 1889, Washington Territory became a state. Tied firmly to the rest of the nation by the political bonds of statehood and the more palpable cords of railroads and telegraph lines, Washington's opportunities and problems now more nearly resembled those of the rest of the country. With the gradual disappearance of the frontier, the region entered a period of accelerating and often unsettling change.

Religious groups adapted themselves to the changing conditions in order to survive, but they also sought to affect, even direct the change. Some of the more romantic attempts at this involved the creation of model communities where individuals might live happily and in harmony with one another, free of what their participants regarded as the corrupting influences of society, and where they might serve as a beacon of hope. In a sense, this had been the goal of Jason Lee and his followers, but their failure did not dampen the ardor of others who sought to realize their own visions.

The middle decades of the 19th century witnessed the brief appearance of William Keil's religious colony on Willapa Bay and the Davisite Kingdom of Heaven near Walla Walla. In the 1890s, several members of the Progressive Brethren Church, known also as the Dunkards, organized the Christian Cooperative Colony in the Yakima Valley, platted the town of Sunnyside, and sold lots to those who vowed to forego the pleasures of drink, gambling and whoremongering. Perhaps because these pleasures were available in quantity across the river in Toppenish, the proprietors of Sunnyside—known by wry locals as the "Holy City"—eventually gave up seeking the Kingdom and settled for profits from land sales.

Later attempts to create model communities, the so-called "Utopias," derived their inspiration less from Christianity than from the secular philosophies of anarchism, Socialism and Fourierism. Some, however, like the Burley Colony on Puget Sound's Henderson Bay, entertained a kind of theism, and theosophical ideas influenced such colony founders as Burley's Cyrus Field Willard and the Puget Sound Cooperative Colony's George Venable Smith.

These model communities were successors in a long and much esteemed tradition of communitarian experiments like Brook Farm, Oneida Community and New Harmony. But only one of these antebellum movements, the Church of Jesus Christ of Latter-day Saints—the Mormons—survived to become a potent force in the West.

Mormon missionary work in the Oregon Country began as early as 1850, barely four years after the first groups of Latter-day Saints entered the Great Salt Lake Valley on their epic journey from the Midwest. By 1855, enough Mormons had settled in Washington Territory's Clark County to form a branch of the church.

Few in number, the Mormons kept to themselves, hounded by notoriety stemming from their religious and historical beliefs, the persecutions they endured and the attachment of some of them to the institution of polygamy. This last issue helped kindle a debate among Mormons over the election of Brigham Young as the leader of the Church after the death of its founder, Joseph Smith. This led to a schism and the formation of the Reorganized Church of Jesus Christ of Latter-day Saints headquartered at Independence, Missouri.

Little therefore was heard from the Mormons in Washington until the 1890s when representatives of the Northern States Mission carried out work in the eastern part of the state. By 1904, 536 Mormons and their forty-two ministers occupied several branches and districts in the Northwest. But not until 1938 was the first Northwestern Stake of Zion, a congregational unit comparable to a diocese, organized in western Washington.

Even so, the elaborate, tightly knit social structure characteristic of Mormon Society was already present. Bred in a tougher clime, the Saints flourished in a harsh landscape and spread throughout the arid West, carrying with them their skills at irrigation and the basis for much of the region's water law. That they did so while other communitarian experiments failed amid the gentler confines of the Puget lowland may reflect the discipline that is more naturally a part of religion than it is the romanticism of communal philosophy.

Against the impulse to be separate, to build a society outside the mainstream, was the desire manifested by the major denominations to build and reform society from within. This took many forms, but one of the most notable and important was their effort to perform the Christian works of mercy, specifically to heal the sick. And, as they had done in the field of education, the churches' efforts in this regard provided the model and much of the content for the present state-wide system of hospitals and health care.

Rudimentary care had been provided by HBC officials like Dr.

McLoughlin and William Fraser Tolmie, who had been trained in medicine, and by American military doctors at frontier forts. But the bulk of the settlers shifted for themselves or tried their luck with itinerant doctors who treated patients out of their saddlebags or their offices in town.

A number of Jesuits boasted medical skills, and it will be remembered that Marcus Whitman spent time doctoring mountain men, immigrants and native people alike. He and Narcissa cared for the sick at their mission and were doing so at the time of their deaths. But most missionary doctors went off to serve in the overseas missions, and most of the doctors that served in the West were secular. Nevertheless, as the churches became established, they followed the dictates of scripture and conscience and devoted a considerable amount of their energies and resources to the care of the sick.

The first hospital in Washington, indeed the entire Northwest, was St. Joseph's in Vancouver, solemnly dedicated by Bishop Blanchet on June 7, 1858. This was the work of the Sisters of Providence led by Mother Joseph who directed the workmen roofing the small 16 by 20 foot structure. The call for the hospital and most of its initial support came from a women's group, the Vancouver Ladies of Charity, made up principally of Catholics but including also Methodists, Episcopalians and Jews. The group's first president was Mrs. William Rogers, a Methodist whose ties to the Vancouver establishment invited wide community support for the hospital.

Staffed by Providence nuns and administered by Mother Joseph, the hospital grew rapidly, moving to larger quarters at several successive locations. Although not without its problems, this success led to an offer of land and money in 1874 from the Portland St. Vincent de Paul Society for the construction of a hospital in that booming town. St. Vincent Hospital's opening a year later, inaugurated a period of expansion that saw hospitals popping up like mushrooms throughout the Northwest. In Washington, The Sisters of Providence took over the operation of the King County poor farm in 1877 and transformed it into Providence Hospital. When it opened in its new Seattle quarters in 1882, it was the largest in the territory. In the years following, the Sisters founded St. Mary's Hospital in Walla Walla, St. Peter's Hospital in Olympia, the St. Ignatius Hospital in Colfax and St. Elizabeth's Hospital in Yakima. They were not the only women religious active at the time—in 1891 the Sisters of St. Joseph of Peace opened St.

Joseph's Hospital in Whatcom (Bellingham)—but the achievement of the Sisters of Providence was unsurpassed.

The number of Catholic hospitals in combination with other Catholic institutions in the state was remarkable given the fact that in 1890 there were probably not 20,000 Catholics in Washington, most of whom were poor. When Holy Names Academy opened in Seattle in 1880, it was the second Catholic institution after the parish church in a town whose Catholic population did not exceed 100. The abilities of the orders to build and maintain so many institutions rested upon the great need they satisfied as well as on the fact that the dedicated and often well-educated women who ran them were willing, indeed often committed, to work for virtually nothing. The money to operate hospitals came from contributions, patient fees and government service contracts. Public expenditures for hospitals existed in the form of specific rates of payment per patient. Contracts were bid on competitively, but few could underbid members of religious orders who took a vow of poverty.

Catholic orders were also in the forefront of the effort to develop orphanages. In the Northwest, children who had lost their parents were at a special disadvantage since the nearest kin were often thousands of miles away. With few resources to devote to their care, the region relied on the churches to do the work as they had done in the fields of education and health care. The first orphanages in the Northwest were built by the Sisters of Providence and were followed by others built by the Sisters of St. Francis, the Missionary sisters of the Sacred Heart and the Brothers of Our Lady of Lourdes.

Prior to the enactment of child labor laws, orphaned boys were quickly absorbed into the largely male workforce, but employment opportunities for orphaned girls were limited. In many cases, destitute young women found it necessary to sell themselves on the street. To provide a haven for them and to rescue others from prostitution, the Sisters of the Good Shepherd opened St. Euphrasia's Home in Seattle in 1890 and another home in Spokane in 1905. The Young Women's Christian Association's dormitories served a similar purpose by providing safe havens for young women who left home in the 1880s and 1890s to work in the larger towns.

The only other religious groups that built and maintained hospitals and orphanages on a scale comparable to the Catholics at this time were the Episcopalians and the Methodists. Between 1881 and 1894 the Episcopal Church in Washington built five hospitals: the Fannie Paddock Memorial Hospital in Tacoma, Grace Hospital in Seattle, St. Elizabeth's Hospital in Sedro, St. Luke's Hospital in New Whatcom and St. David's Hospital in Hoquiam, as well as a nursery and orphanage, Sheltering Arms, in Tacoma. All of this is remarkable in light of the fact that in 1890 the Episcopalians counted only 1700 communicants. However, many of these were in the highest echelons of society and, like Tacoma's Charles Wright, practiced a generous philanthropy. Sadly, however, this noble effort could not be sustained, and by 1912 all but one of their hospitals had been sold or closed.

The first graduating class of nurses, 1897, standing with superintendent Dr. Charles McCutchean in front of the Episcopalian Fannie Paddock Memorial Hospital, Tacoma, Washington.
Courtesy Washington State Historical Society photo collection, Tacoma, Washington.

The Methodists enjoyed a longer-lived success, opening the Marie Beard Deaconess Hospital in Spokane in 1897 and the Central Washington Deaconess Hospital in Wenatchee in 1915. They also sponsored the Deaconess Orphanage in Everett and the Deaconess Home in Seattle. In 1906 they assumed the administration of the Washington Children's Home Society, an affiliate of the national association that had begun work in the state in 1896. In 1900 the Puget Sound Conference Deaconess Association took over Seattle General Hospital, but the effort proved too expensive, and eventually the Conference withdrew its support.

Pioneering another field, many denominations invested in the development of homes for the aged, especially after their congregations became established and members grew older. The Catholic and Methodist churches took the lead here as well, but rest homes were something in which more denominations could afford to invest. Two of the better known early examples were the Lutheran Martha and Mary Home, begun as an orphanage in 1891 by the energetic pastor, Ingebrigt Tollefsen, and the Kenney Presbyterian Home, built in West Seattle in 1901.

Churches oftentimes pooled their resources to support nondenominational institutions just as they had earlier shared pastors and church buildings. This was also true of Masonic lodges and fraternal orders which helped fund hospitals and provided members with life insurance. Service clubs and organizations like the Y.M.C.A. and the Y.W.C.A. also attracted support from the major denominations with the exception of the Catholics who, as they had done in other areas, chose to develop their own parallel institutions. Neutral grounds for other cooperative efforts were provided by relief societies organized in towns as their citizens confronted the increasing challenges of urban life. Most of these, like the Vancouver Ladies of Charity, were founded by middle class women active in their churches. One of the foundresses of Seattle's Ladies' Relief Society was Babette Gatzert, wife of Seattle's first Jewish mayor, Bailey Gatzert, who had helped organize Temple de Hirsch in 1899. She was joined, among others, by Abby Hanford of Seattle's First Baptist Church, Mary Leary of Trinity Episcopal Church and Caroline Sanderson of Plymouth Congregational Church.

Another of the crucial roles the churches played during this period of rapid growth was to provide incoming ethnic groups with a central point around which they could develop a sense of community. This is no more true than it was among the Northwest's black populations. Blacks had accompanied white discoverers and settlers into the region from the earliest days, but it was not until the transcontinental railroads were completed that they came in any sizeable numbers. In the 1880s Bishop Abraham Grant of the African Methodist

Colored Baptist Mission.

The colored Baptists of the city have established a mission, which will hold services every Sunday at 11 o'clock a. m. and 8 o'clock p. m. The meetings will be held in the Young Naturalists' hall in the old university grounds.

By 1895 a major depression had set in and the small struggling church became a mission that year.

The Panic of 1893 hurt all of Seattle and as this newspaper clipping shows, a mission was opened in rented quarters several years after the panic.
Courtesy of Esther Mumford's The Black Victorians.

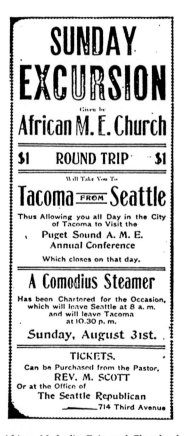

SUNDAY EXCURSION

Given by

African M. E. Church

$1   ROUND TRIP $1

Will Take You To

Tacoma FROM Seattle

Thus Allowing you all Day in the City of Tacoma to Visit the

Puget Sound A. M. E. Annual Conference

Which closes on that day.

A Comodius Steamer

Has been Chartered for the Occasion, which will leave Seattle at 8 a. m. and will leave Tacoma at 10.30 p. m.

Sunday, August 31st.

TICKETS.

Can be Purchased from the Pastor,

REV. M. SCOTT

Or at the Office of

The Seattle Republican

714 Third Avenue

Seattle's African Methodist-Episcopal Church advertised Puget Sound A.M.E. Annual Conference excursion in the Seattle Republican *newspaper.*
Courtesy of Ester Mumford, Seattle's Black Victorians.

Episcopal (AME) Church sent a missionary to Seattle to determine the feasibility of organizing a church. Led by Seaborn J. Collins, local blacks began holding prayer meetings in private homes, and in 1886 a Sunday School was organized. Early in 1890, the Reverend A.M. Taylor completed the organization of the church, the first in the town and the state, and shortly afterward, he organized the Allen AME Church in Tacoma. In that same year black families in Spokane organized Calvary Baptist Church. In 1891 Tacoma blacks organized a Pentecostal Full Gospel Church, and shortly thereafter, black churches appeared in Roslyn, Franklin, Newcastle, Kennydale, Everett and Yakima.

Although blacks continued to worship at other predominantly white churches, the AME or the Baptist churches, or both, became the hubs of black communities. They often represented the community's single greatest financial investment and were among the few places blacks could gather without enduring the scorn and hostility of white society. Black churches celebrated and fostered black culture, instilled a respect for black history and served as major forums for the discussion of regional and national concerns. As such, they provided leadership and hope in the black community.

Jews entered the Northwest primarily as merchants, especially after the California gold rush stimulated the regional economy. The first Jewish community organization in the Northwest was Portland's Mount Sinai Association, which provided Jewish burials. It briefly antedated the founding of Portland's Congregation Beth Israel in 1858, which built the region's first synagogue. In 1880, there were about 150 Jews in Washington Territory, perhaps fifty in Seattle, engaged mostly in selling clothing, merchandise and tools. Jewish families gathered to celebrate the Sabbath and High Holy days, but it was not until 1889 that they formed Havra Bikur Cholim. This was an Orthodox Ashkenazic (Germanic) congregation. Ten years later, its more liberal members organized the Reform Temple de Hirsch.

Besides theological and social differences, Northwest Jews were divided ethnically and linguistically. German Jews had founded Congregation Beth Israel in Portland, and later Polish Jews organized Congregation Ahavai Shalom and Russian Jews the Congregation Shaarei Torah. A wave of Sephardic immigrants in the early 1900s led to the organization in Seattle of Congregation Ezra Bessaroth, made up of Jews from the Island of Rhodes, and Congregation Sephardic Bikur

Holim, made up of Jews from Turkey. In Spokane, Russian Jews organized Congregation Keneseth Israel. In an effort to modernize and Americanize their members, Temple de Hirsch in Seattle and Temple Beth El in Boise offered services in English.

Linguistic and cultural divisions also worked to divide Washington's Orthodox Christian community. Orthodoxy has a long history in the Northwest beginning in the 1760s when Russian settlers in Alaska formed parishes and began to convert its native peoples. In 1794 Orthodox missionaries founded the first of several missions in southern Alaska. An attempt to colonize Oregon in 1808 failed, but Russian and Aleut employees of the Russian American Company succeeded in 1812 in founding Fort Ross on the California coast, and organizing a parish, St. Helen's, there fifty miles north of San Francisco Bay.

During the 1849 gold rush, Russians and other Eastern Europeans immigrated to California, and in 1868 several of them in San Francisco organized a Greek-Russian-Slavonic Church. It was supported by the Tsarist government, but in 1870, the Holy Synod of Orthodox bishops in St. Petersburg created the Diocese of the Aleutian Islands and Alaska whose see would be San Francisco. This was to be an American Orthodox Church, and in 1891, Bishop Nicholas of San Francisco sent missionaries out to organize parishes among the Orthodox in the West. Father Sebastian Dabovich helped organize the first in Washington, St. Spiridon's in Seattle, and this was soon followed by St. Saava's in Johnson, near the Idaho border, Holy Trinity Church in Wilkeson and the Church of the Resurrection in Cle Elum. In Seattle, the Orthodox Church was predominantly Greek but included Russians, Serbians, Ruthenians, Bulgarians, Syrians and Gypsies. In 1916 the Greek element in the congregation broke away to form St. Demetrius Greek Orthodox Church. This happened to pan-Orthodox parishes throughout the West, and breaks also occurred when Russian church members engaged in theological and political disputes following the Russian Revolution.

Ethnic and theological divisions were even more pronounced among Washington's Lutherans. Lutheranism was established in the Northwest in 1867 when a minister sent by the General Synod of the Evangelical Lutheran Church organized a congregation in Portland. The General Synod was a body whose roots reached back into the colonial period, thoroughly American in outlook and English speaking by preference. Had this church flourished, the history of Northwestern Lutheranism might have been less fractious than it was, but by 1875 it had disappeared from the scene, replaced by congregations organized along ethnic lines and often divided by sectarian disputes.

At that time, American Lutheranism was beset with dissension. In 1860 the General Synod represented nearly two-thirds of all Lutherans in America, but in that year Scandinavians in the Midwest withdrew and formed what would eventually become the Augustana Synod. The General Synod was further reduced when the synods of several southern states withdrew during the Civil War. The remnant was impoverished again when conservative Midwestern synods broke away to form the Missouri Synod. Subsequent divisions along theological and ethnic lines added to the confusion. The result was a serious reduction in the ability of the Lutheran sects to carry out missionary work among the large number of immigrants coming from and in some cases fleeing a Lutheran background.

German settlers, for example, had been arriving in the Northwest since the days of the donation claims. Those of Lutheran background, however did not form a congregation until 1884 when the Ohio Synod answered a request from several families who settled in Tacoma and sent them a pastor who organized that city's First Lutheran Church. After this, the Ohio Synod carried out missionary work among German families in communities east of the Cascades, leaving much of the Western region to the Missouri Synod. The Reverend George Finke recalled the experiences of one pastor, the Reverend Paul Groschupf, in the vast interior plains.

> ... Groschupf was a wild rider. Instead of opening gates, he with Flora [his horse] jumped over them. He rode her through deep, overflowing creeks, down steep mountains and climbed them. The deep canyons were full of rattlesnakes. In order to escape their deadly bites, the rider had to lay his feet on the horse's neck and his back on the gown and books which were tied in the saddle.

The appearance of representatives of the Wisconsin Synod in the Northwest intensified competition for the region's Germans. This was expecially so in Yakima where antipathy between a Wisconsin Synod and a Missouri Synod church became so bitter that outside arbiters had to be called in to resolve the matter.

The first Scandinavian Lutheran churches in Washington were organized by a remarkable missionary, the Reverend Anders Emil Friedrichsen, known popularly as Skindbrokpraest, "leather-breeches priest" because of his colorful and devotedly non-clerical frontier garb. Preaching in Norwegian, Swedish, Danish, German and English, Friedrichsen ignored synodal and ethnic differences. In 1871 he organized Washington's first Lutheran Church, located in Oysterville, and later founded other churches near the mouth of the Columbia, Bush Prairie (near Olympia), Centerville (later Centralia), and Tacoma. However, synodal rivalries and an explosive theological conflict over the issue of predestination flummoxed his attempt to create a broad-based Lutheran congregation. Supported by synodal associations, ethnic differences prevailed, and distinct Norwegian, Swedish, Finnish and Danish churches appeared.

Norwegian churches proliferated in the northern Puget Sound region beginning with the Stillaguamish Church at Utsaladdy on Camano Island, the Norwegian mother church. Swedish pastor Peter Carlson sought to visit every place in the Northwest where Swedes settled, and in Washington he organized at least five churches on his own, among them Gethsemane Lutheran Church in Seattle. In later years he was helped by the Reverend Jaakopi Juhonpoika Hoikka who also organized congregations among the region's Finnish immigrants, most of whom settled in communities near the mouth of the Columbia. Neither the Danish nor the Icelandic synods were large enough to support much pastoral work among their respective groups, small and scattered as they were over the immense land. However, several Danish congregations were organized in the Seattle-Tacoma area, and Icelandic congregations were established in Blaine and on Point Roberts where an Icelandic colony had settled. In Seattle the Icelanders organized Calvary Church. Many Icelanders had come from existing settlements in North Dakota, Minnesota and the Canadian prairie provinces where Lutherans suffered a series of theological disputes. These led to the development of several Icelandic Unitarian congregations, many of whose members migrated westward with their Lutheran counterparts and organized congregations of their own in Blaine and Seattle.

Perhaps it was inevitable, given the turbulent dynamism of American society, that congregations would divide along ethnic and linguistic lines. As places where people speaking the same language and sharing the same heritage could come together to worship, to wed, to be buried in an old familiar way, the ethnic churches served as havens in an unfamiliar and sometimes frightening world. In this they resembled the first churches that served the Americans when they were an ethnic minority in the Northwest. Following that pattern, they sought to help their members flourish in the new land.

In spite of the many hardships visited upon them blacks supported several 1890s humanitarian associations through their churches that sought to provide help in the community. A black branch of the W.C.T.U. brought aid to the sick and destitute and its members visited prisoners in jails. Aid societies and a variety of clubs hosted benefits and socials to fund charitable projects and to provide education and entertainment in the process.

Similar societies among Jewish congregations sought to ease the immigrants' entry into American life. The most notable example of this was the establishment of the Educational Center by Seattle's Council of Jewish Women in 1906 as a means to aid poor Jewish families primarily of Eastern European background who began entering the Northwest in large numbers as the new century dawned. The Educational Center would also serve Seattle's growing Sephardic community. Besides taking care of their own, many Jews were in a position to practice philanthrophy in the greater communities in which they lived. In Seattle, the Levy and Cooper families left large bequests to several charitable institutions, among them the new Children's Orthopedic Hospital, which relied heavily on contributions from the city's churches.

In the early years, the energies of the small Orthodox communities were devoted primarily to the construction of churches. These needed

Work-seeking Russian immigrants besiege Russian Orthodox priest Alexander Vyacheslavov.

Courtesy of the Congregation, St. Spiridon Orthodox Cathedral, Seattle, Washington

icons and altar pieces in order to be fitting places of worship, and much effort was made to obtain them. Among the Russian Orthodox, efforts were also mounted to send contributions to the motherland after the abortive 1905 revolution and to aid immigrants. With the outbreak of the Russian Revolution in 1917, Father Alexander Vyacheslavov of Seattle's St. Spiridon's church sought to aid the thousands of refugees entering Seattle. He met them on the boats as they arrived from eastern Russian and Chinese ports, found jobs for many, provided others with shelter and saw that qualified students were placed at the University of Washington. Eventually, several parish organizations took up this work and the all-important task of teaching the immigrants English.

Because many Scandinavians were sailors and fishermen, Lutheran pastors organized several missions to attend to their needs. In Seattle, Ingebrigt Tollefsen helped organize the Siloah Seaman's Mission where sailors could find room and board, receive and post mail, store valuables and hear ministers who spoke their language. The Finnish Suomi Synod also sent ministers out to communities frequented by Finnish sailors, to attend to their needs.

In many cases the proliferation of Lutheran institutions at the turn of the century represented the duplication of efforts by several synods. One Episcopalian observer noted somewhat incredulously that in Seattle's Ballard district alone there were no less than twenty-seven Lutheran churches. The same redundancy existed among Lutheran schools. The founding of the Norwegian Synod's Pacific Lutheran University was followed a few years later by the opening of the Lutheran Free Church's Bethany High School in Poulsbo, another work of Ingebrigt Tollefsen. In 1905, the Missouri Synod founded Concordia College in Portland. The United Norwegian Church founded Spokane College in 1907, and in that same year the Augustana Synod founded Coeur d'Alene College in nearby Idaho. Two years later the United Norwegian Church also founded Columbia College in Everett. The scale of building could not be sustained, however, and by 1919 only Concordia and PLU remained as independent centers of Lutheran scholarship.

Many in the ethnic synods were deeply concerned about the need to have a priesthood fluent in English to insure that their message would continue to be heard as immigrants and their children assimilated themselves into American society. In Washington, the synods were helped by the work of the Pacific Synod of the United

*Athletics, including basketball as shown in the 1909
photo, were a part of student activities at the University
of Puget Sound and other denominational schools in the
early decades of the twentieth century.*

Courtesy, Public Relations Office, University of Puget Sound, Tacoma,
Washington.

Lutheran Church—the original Lutheran church in the Northwest—
which moved its Pacific Theological Seminary from Portland to Seattle in 1914. There, next to the University of Washington, it expanded
its curriculum from two to four years. It was the only seminary in
the state (the Ohio Synod's Pacific Lutheran Seminary opened in Olympia in 1907 but had closed in 1910). Because it was an English-speaking
institution, it served as a meeting ground for representatives of the
various synods. By advancing a ministry in English, it served as a
model for the rest, particularly after the onset of World War I, when
teaching or speaking in any language but English was popularly regarded as subversive.

In spite of their heroic efforts, Lutheran pastors bemoaned the fact
that they had called into their churches only a small fraction of the
immigrants who came from Lutheran backgrounds. By 1900, for example, over 15,000 Scandinavians lived in Washington, but the various
Lutheran judicatories counted less than 5000 Scandinavian communicants in the entire Northwest. Most stayed away from church

entirely, but many had joined other churches.

The latter was the case among many of the German immigrants who had come to Washington in the 1880s from communities along the Volga River in Russia. Campaigns to Russify ethnic minorities and forced military service drove hundreds of thousands of German settlers out of Russia in the nineteenth century. About eleven percent of the Volga Germans who emigrated to the American Midwest were Catholic, but the great preponderance were Lutheran. Dislike of the doctrinal and ecclesiastical rigidity of the Lutheran Consistory in Russia however, prompted many to look elsewhere when they were free of its jurisdiction. Many were attracted to German Congregationalism which had been fostered by the American Home Missionary Society of the Congregational Church in the Midwest beginning in the 1840s. When a colony of Volga Germans emigrated from Nebraska to Washington in 1887, they brought their German Congregationalism with them and established their first church in Ritzville. With the aid of George Atkinson, the General Missionary and Superintendent of Home Missions in the area at the time, many more congregations were organized, and by 1910 their numbers approached ten percent of the total population of Volga Germans in the state.

Other Volga Germans joined Methodist, Episcopal, Reformed and Seventh-day Adventist churches as these groups carried out missions in the area. Along with the Evangelical Church and the Mormons, these religious groups also organized energetic missions among Scandinavian immigrants, but the most successful Scandinavian missions were those undertaken by the Methodists and the Baptists.

Missions to the Italian immigrant community were also organized. Italians had appeared early in the region's history and provided the Northwest with some of its most distinguished clerics. Father Louis Rossi and Jesuit Fathers Joseph Carunna, Urban Grassi and Joseph Cataldo, were only four of the more notable among that nationality to serve Washington and the Northwest. But the work of these men was spread thinly over a huge expanse of territory, and when large numbers of poor Italian Catholic immigrants began to enter Washington in the 1880s, there were few priests to serve them

At the beginning of the new century, Pope Leo XIII asked Mother Frances Cabrini, foundress of the Missionary Sisters of of the Sacred Heart to send her sisters to serve the Italian immigrants pouring into the United States. In 1903, during a tour of the country she visited Seattle and organized Mount Carmel Mission for Italian orphans. Up to that time these children had been cared for in the Methodist Deaconess Home. Even though his archdiocese was heavily in debt, Bishop Edward O'Dea assumed the burden of supporting the Cabrini sisters' mission. Both he and his associate in the newly erected diocese of Spokane, Augustine Schinner, actively recruited priests and religious to serve the needs of the Italians lest they fall into the clutches of the dread Protestants.

Two groups from non-Christian backgrounds, the Chinese and the Japanese, were targeted by the churches for evangelization. Nominally Taoist or Buddhist, the Chinese had been brought into this country to work in the railroad and burgeoning west coast farms, but in the unstable economy following the Civil War, they were violently attacked by laborers who saw their willingness to work for small wages as a threat. The Chinese organized protective associations—tongs—for mutual aid, and these sometimes sponsored individuals who officiated at funerals, but it was difficult for the religious customs of their homeland to take root amid the chaotic conditions of the West.

Efforts to evangelize the Chinese in Washington Territory began in the early 1870s when Congregational and Presbyterian ministers attracted several to their churches. In 1876 a Chinese Baptist minister, the Reverend Dong Gong, was sent on a mission to the Puget Sound region by the Church in Portland. A mission school was started in Olympia and plans for another in Seattle were made before he had to leave. In 1880 John DeVore organized a Chinese Methodist Episcopal chapel in Seattle and had a regular following of fifteen of the town's five to six hundred Chinese. As many as fifty-seven Chinese attended services, and many took advantage of night school classes that were conducted free of charge. In 1881 the school was expanded: one class of Bible study and another of English were taught weekly. Prayer meetings were held on Friday nights and by 1882, 111 Chinese had attended the school.

Several members of the Methodist chapel voiced their desire for a minister of their own nationality and offered $100 toward his support. The Reverend Andrew Jackson Hanson was given charge of the Northwest Chinese Mission with the support of the California Conference, and in 1885 the Reverend Chan Hon Fan was made his assistant.

These interesting endeavors were cut short in 1885 and 1886 by anti-Chinese riots at several Washington towns which drove most of the Chinese out of the territory. Churchmen in Seattle and Tacoma decried the vigilante action, and the Seattle Methodist Episcopal Ministers' Association denounced it as "cruel, brutal, un-American and un-Christian." Pastor W.D. McFarland of Tacoma's First Presbyterian Church scolded his congregation from the pulpit, provoking anger so great that he felt the need to wear a brace of pistols when he toured his parish. When a crowd of workers drove the Chinese from their homes in Seattle on a February Sunday morning, the Reverend Bates of Plymouth Congregational Church left the pulpit with a rifle in his hands to take his place in the Home Guard protecting the Chinese.

In spite of these churches' efforts on behalf of the Chinese, most of the Chinese left, and it was not until the 1890s that work could resume among them. One of the major problems missionaries faced in their attempts to build Chinese congregations was the law forbidding the immigration of Chinese women. Marriages were therefore few, and as a result, western-style congregations were slow to develop among the Chinese.

The law did not apply to Japanese workingmen who began to arrive on the west coast in the 1870s. Many saved wages and paid for the passage of "picture brides," women who advertised their willingness to marry in a new country with a photograph. Japanese families put down roots, purchased property when they could and became one of the largest immigrant groups in the state.

Actually, the Japanese had been here much earlier. In 1833 a group of fishermen washed ashore near Cape Flattery and were later ransomed from their Makah captors by John McLoughlin. He taught them some English, introduced them to scripture and sent them back to the orient via London where they had an audience with Queen Victoria. In Macao they worked with a missionary to translate the Bible into Japanese. They sailed to Japan full of high hopes but were denied entry since they had been given up for dead and were now deemed "foreign intruders." Apparently, some migrated back to the Olympic Peninsula and lived out their days among the Makahs, but it is believed that at least one of them, a baptized Christian, eventually returned to Japan when that nation opened its doors to the West in 1854.

The closure of Japan some 250 years before came about because of internal strife resulting from Christian missionary work which was resumed in a small way after 1854. Although nominally Buddhist or members of Shinto sects, the Japanese who came to the western United States in the 1870s may have been familiar with Christianity. The first conversion in the United States took place in San Francisco. Soon afterwards Protestant denominations trained and sent Japanese missionaries to Northwestern cities to meet immigrants as they came off the boats.

Kiyo Montoda, an early resident of Seattle's Nihon Machi or "Japan Town," recalled the powerful effect of those early missionaries.

One evening I was walking along the streets of Japan Town, my mind a blank. There was a crowd of people at one corner. From what I heard behind the crowd, it was street preaching by Christians. The sermon sounded sincere, about the value of lives, persuading people away from crime and temptation. Before he knew it, Eitaro Montoda went up to the front of the crowd. The preacher said after his sermon, "We'll talk further at the church. Please come, those who have troubles and heavy loads in life. We can give you a great promise."

Montoda went with them. Every word he heard at the Seattle Japanese Presbyterian Church struck him. The fear of sin sank into his mind... Realizing that the secret of success was to live one's life on the basis of the Bible, Motoda decided to become a Christian at once.

This was acculturation at a profoundly personal level, and it is no denial of sincerity to suggest that conversion offered practical benefits to immigrants in a Christian culture. So many Japanese men found employment through churches, especially as house servants, that they became known as "mission boys." For both men and women, church membership provided something of the closeness of the village life they had left behind. And the eagerness of the Issei, the first generation of immigrants, to acculturate themselves, to be successful, was satisfied by the churches' provision of schools, English classes and social clubs, and by the pre-schools, kindergartens and athletic clubs many churches sponsored to help keep families together.

A problem that concerned many Japanese immigrants was the plight of women who had been forced into prostitution. Some were picture brides kidnapped by pimps or otherwise sold into bondage, and others were impoverished women who had left Japan to become prostitutes in Southeast Asia and were subsequently shipped to the west coast and sold into rings. In the early 1900s, a Japanese official estimated that there were 150 to 200 Japanese prostitutes working in Seattle. To help these women, several church leaders, among them the Reverends Orio Inoue and Seimei Yoshioka, organized the Humanitarian Association. Those they rescued in Seattle they took to the Baptist Women's Home where they were given employment and the opportunity to marry legitimately. The Home also offered courses in cooking and child care as well as Bible study.

But in their drive to survive and succeed in the new land, many Japanese did not want to become entirely divorced from their heritage. Most were at least nominally Buddhist, and many desired to carry on the practices of their religion across the ocean. In the late 1890s, Buddhist missionaries from Kyoto traveled throughout the Western Hemisphere and established their first mission in the U.S. In 1902 Gendo Nakai, a monk of the Jodo Shinshu sect arrived in Seattle to serve Buddhists here. Services were held in private homes, classes in Japanese were taught so that children of immigrant parents—Nisei—would not lose the connection with their culture, and festivals like Bon Odori, a popular summer ancestoral spirits celebration, were sponsored. In 1907 a temple was established in Seattle. In the 1920s temples were established in Yakima and Auburn, and a Shinto Konko-Kokyo temple was opened in Tacoma.

In Tacoma a group of Japanese Buddhists approached representatives of the Japanese Baptist mission and offered to pay if the missionaries would teach the Buddhists English in a class separate from the one for Christians and without religious content. The mission agreed to do so but declined to accept money for teaching, charging the twenty who took the class only for the cost of the room and teaching materials.

Amid all this social and cultural tumult, the native American population continued to manifest deep religious vitality. They had not disappeared as white planners had assumed or hoped they would, but survived instead, and produced religious leaders who inspired the people to follow the ancient traditions. Native American author Vine Deloria describes how many native Americans on Washington reservations succeeded in preserving their heritage by adapting it to western customs. Forbidden from carrying out winter dances and other religious ceremonials, many simply waited until the Fourth of July when agents allowed them to celebrate the national holiday and held them then, telling the flustered agents that it was simply their way of celebrating Independence Day. The ironic humor may have been lost on the agents, but they were unable to suppress the ceremonials without appearing to be unpatriotic.

The Indian Shaker Church continued to expand its membership in native communities, but it was not the only native group active in the state. In the 1870s and 80s, Kolaskin, a Sanpoil prophet born in a mat lodge near Fort Spokane, led a religious revival among the Sanpoil, Spokane and Southern Okanogan people. In his twenties he suffered a long painful illness which led to what those around him assumed was his death. However, he revived suddenly as they were preparing him for burial. He said he had been given a message from the creator, Qwilantsutun, who commanded the people to change their lives, to refrain from drinking, stealing and adultery, to pray and sing and listen to their prophet Kolaskin, and to act kindly toward others. The prayers Kolaskin taught are said to have been like the appeals addressed to the ancient tribal diety, Sweatlodge, and the songs like love songs.

Kolaskin's message was reinforced by the steady recovery from his illness, and he attracted a wide following, especially after he successfully predicted the great Columbia Basin earthquake of November 22, 1873, that briefly halted the flow of the great river. A Presbyterian congregation among the Spokanes resisted his efforts to proselytize among them, objecting to the "sensuous" nature of his lyric songs, but without much success.

According to etnographer Verne Ray, dissension among the Sanpoil over tactics Kolaskin employed to enforce his moral code resulted in a dispute during which a man was killed. The murderer and Kolaskin were arrested and taken to Fort Spokane. After a hearing, the murderer was released, but federal authorities seeking to squelch the movement Kolaskin had inspired sent him to McNeil Island Penitentiary for three years. After his return, Kolaskin repented many of his actions, but his followers continued to honor him and follow his preachings even after his death in 1920.

Another of the prophets who rose on the banks of the Columbia in the dying years of the nineteenth century was Jake Hunt. He had been born in the 1860s in a Klickitat village near the modern town of Husum. Although his family participated in the Washat, he showed no religious inclinations until the illness of his third wife, Minnie Coon, and their child. The Shakers had established themselves in the Yakima Reservation in the 1890s, and several of that religion's practitioners were called upon to cure, but they were unsuccessful and both wife and child died. Consumed with grief at their deaths, Hunt underwent a profound religious experience after which he claimed to have received the power to heal the sick and cure drunkards, and a commission to convert people in seven lands to what became known as the Waptashi or feather religion.

This seems to have occurred around 1904. Eagle feathers and wings played a prominent role in the initiation and curing ceremonies of this religion which resembled the Washani religion in its emphasis upon traditional practices. Unique to it, however, were the initiatory rites of purgative vomiting and of spinning to induce visions. The differences between the two religions were characterized by one native informant who remarked that "The Feathers have borrowed from the Washani and put Spiritualism into it. The Washani are slow and respectful like the Catholics. The Feathers are all excitement and feeling like the Pentecostals."

Hunt's efforts to bring the religion to different groups met with great success until he attempted to cure a consumptive in the last stages of illness on the Umatilla Reservation sometime around 1906. The attempted cure became a contest between him and his followers and Christian members of the reservation who condemned the old beliefs. The Superintendent, O.C. Edwards, was alerted, and doctors were called in to witness the cure. According to one witness, the white doctors gave the man only twenty-four hours to live. Hunt claimed he could give him two more days, but by noon the next day, the man was dead. Jake Hunt was seized; his hair was cut off, and he was told to leave the reservation or go to jail. He left humiliated, fell seriously ill, and sometime between 1910 and 1914 he died, but the religion he preached still survives in isolated areas.

With the building of the railroads, Washington's population surged. In 1890 it counted some 350,000 people; by 1910 the number had passed a million. Along with this influx came a host of new religious congregations. The closing decades of the nineteenth century witnessed the growth of the Evangelical Church, the Church of God, the Church of Christ, Scientist, and the Salvation Army. Pentecostal groups like the Full Gospel Church gathered rural congregations, and the Mennonites arrived to build their colonies. In the new century their growth was matched by the Society of Friends, the Jehovah's Witnesses, the Church of the Nazarene, the Reorganized Church of Jesus Christ of Latter-day Saints, the Assemblies of God, and Spiritualist churches. Virtually each new year saw the arrival or emergence of some new group while the older bodies experienced continued growth.

Nevertheless, the great majority of people entering the state remained unchurched. According to Thomas Jessett, in 1890 only seventeen percent of the population belong to a church. In 1910 around twenty percent did, and the rate of increase remained low. Washington was one of the least churched states then and it remains so today. There were reasons for this. Washington became urban and industrial early in its existence, and well into this century men, primarily young workingmen, greatly outnumbered women. The percentage of married family men who belonged to a church may not have been that much lower than the national average, but the family-oriented, middle class character of church congregations, and their attachment to a puritanical, middle class morality did not make them attractive to many unmarried working class men.

The church provided for many needs during the early years, but they had powerful rivals. Masonic lodges, fraternal and secret societies and labor unions—even saloons—provided social support and a convivial place where people, especially workingmen, could gather. Many of the social and humanitarian institutions pioneered by the churches were eventually supported by state, county, municipal, and local organizations which could often support them more effectively through taxation. In spite of all this; in spite of low percentage of the population that was churched, the percentage grew. Moreover, churches and church leaders continued to play a major and sometimes a leading role in social and political affairs.

The transformation of the United States from a predominantly rural and agricultural society to one that was increasingly urban and industrial was attended with considerable economic dislocation and hardship. As antagonisms developed between rural and urban citizens and among the emergent lower, middle and upper classes, an increasing chorus of voices called for reforms. Known as Populists in the 1880s and 1890s, the reformers gained increasing prominence in the early 1900s as their efforts coalesced into the Progressive movement. They were inspired by the hope that science, applied to the ills of society, could led to human progress, but the moral force of their vision derived from the idealism of Judeo-Christian ethics.

Some of the earliest voices calling for reform were those of churched men and women working in urban slums and in the impoverished countryside who saw first hand the growing gap between rich and poor and the suffering that others did not recognize or chose not to acknowledge. Sometimes their protests ran counter to sentiments within their own churches, like the more comfortable view of Henry Ward Beecher, one of the most eminent American churchmen in the

1880s who proclaimed that, "...no man in this land suffers from poverty unless it be more than his fault—unless it be his sin..."

One of the more gifted advocates for those opposed to Beecher's view was Walter Rauschenbush who ministered to the poor in his Second German Baptist Church, located next door to the notorious Hell's Kitchen district in New York. His experiences there inflamed a passion for reform and inspired him to interpret the words of the Lord's Prayer, "Thy kingdom come; thy will be done, on earth..." in literal terms. His book, *Christianity and the Social Crisis* became a moral guide for those grappling with the immense problems of modern American society. Drawing upon deep wells of faith, they sought to apply the ideals of the Gospels to heal the ills of the nation. By interpreting the Christian message in social rather than purely theological terms, they authored the Social Gospel movement in American Protestantism.

In Washington, the Social Gospel found energetic expression in social work among ethnic minorities to speed their assimilation, and in work to improve the health and welfare of the community. The Seattle Bible Training School for Deaconesses, Missionaries, and Other Christian Workers opened in 1905 and trained teachers, nurses, chaplains and administrators to staff Methodist hospitals, children's homes and schools. Church work with youth and in prisons inspired reform movements that brought about the creation of juvenile courts and prison chaplaincies.

The most well-known spokesman for the Social Gospel movement in the Northwest and one of the more vocal advocates of progressive reforms, of what he called "Christian Socialism," was the Reverend Mark Allison Matthews. Leaving his native South, where he had already developed a reputation as an energetic advocate of reform, Matthews became pastor of Seattle's First Presbyterian Church in 1902.

With his dynamic leadership, First Presbyterian plunged into community work, operating a day nursery, the city's first successful kindergarten, and an unemployment bureau. It funded Reverend Inoeu's work in the Japanese community and offered English classes for Japanese immigrants. It supported development of a juvenile court and established the city's first anti-tuberculosis sanitorium. Matthews was a charismatic figure, and during his pastorate, First Presbyterian's congregation rose to 9,000, becoming the largest in the world.

He called for the development of city parks, art galleries, libraries, and the development of a medical school at the University of

Washington. He campaigned for the establishment of initiative, referendum, and recall in the political process, worked for the institution of the direct primary and supported labor-management negotiations and consumer protection.

In general, the relationship between the churches and organized labor in Washington was ambiguous. Many church members were workers and some were members of labor unions, but with the notable exception of Matthews and a few others, church leaders were not involved in the labor movement. This may have reflected the middle class character of most churches and the historic antipathy between the middle and working class in the Northwest. A few such as Thomas J. Hagerty, a Catholic priest and co-founder of the radical Industrial Workers of the World union, eventually turned against organized religion, a move that resulted in Hagerty's dismissal from the priesthood. There were labor evangelists, however. One, the Methodist Reverend Oscar H. McGill, assisted lumber workers in their efforts to organize cooperative sawmills.

The most influential labor leader in the state in the early decades of the twentieth century, secretary of the Seattle Central Labor Council, James "Jimmy" Duncan, also happened to be a leader in his church, Seattle's Westminister Presbyterian, and later, University Christian Church. Duncan came to Seattle in 1904 and rose quickly throught the ranks of the American Federation of Labor to his position on the council. In the meantime, he took an active role in his church, teaching Sunday school and helping lead several church organizations. His tough, no-nonsense, pragmatic approach to labor issues won him enormous respect, and his brand of management, dubbed "Duncanism," made the Central Labor Council one of the most effective labor organizations in the country. By centralizing control of Seattle unions, he gave the Council great power and provided the unions with a cohesiveness that enabled them to successfully stage the first city-wide general strike in the nation's history—an act that horrified Mark Matthews.

Evangelical Protestants like Matthews, McGill and Duncan were not the only local religious leaders who believed that their faith required their active participation in efforts to reform society. The desire for reform and for social justice motivated many Catholics and Jews as well, and out of these two religious groups came individuals who made notable contributions to the public good.

Although many of their efforts, in the settlement house movement for example, were directed toward Catholic immigrant groups, the results of Catholic efforts such as the Mount Carmel Mission, benefitted more than just the Catholic community. A more mainstream effort, the Northwest's—and the nation's—first effective minimum wage law was passed by the Oregon legislature largely because of the work of Father Edwin O'Hara, a noted advocate of social reform, and his co-worker, Caroline Gleason, a professional social worker, who later became a Holy Names sister.

In Washington, the Jewish leader best known for his efforts on behalf of reform and social justice was Rabbi Samuel Koch of Seattle's Temple de Hirsch. Born in Denver in 1874 to a family of immigrant German Jews, Koch attended Hebrew Union College in Cincinnati, Ohio, a Reform Jewish seminary, and was ordained by its faculty. Accepting the position of rabbi at Temple Beth-El in Pensacola, Florida, he developed a reputation as an advocate of education and child welfare programs. In 1905 he was invited to Temple de Hirsch in Seattle and accepted the offer of its pulpit.

With his energetic leadership, Rabbi Koch's new congregation enjoyed a long period of growth. In short order, it built a new synagogue, undertook an ambitious religious education program, published a newsletter, obtained a cemetery, and in the process, doubled its size. Koch built strong ties with the local Jewish community by marrying a daughter of a prominent family, Cora Dinkelspeil, but he also reached out to the non-Jewish community.

Building upon his reputation as an effective advocate of reform, Koch served on the board of virtually every social service organization in Seattle and was instrumental in organizing the Central Council of Service Agencies which managed their work more effectively. He worked for the creation of Children's Hospital, today's Children's Orthopedic Hospital, and supported the creation of an independent Seattle newspaper, the *Sun*. In order to increase understanding between Christians and Jews, he fostered ties with other churches and was a frequent guest speaker from their pulpits. One of the more fruitful relationships to arise from this effort was his close personal friendship with the Reverend Sydney Strong, pastor of Queen Anne Congregational Church, another progressive religious leader and father of radical activist Anna Louise Strong.

With Anna Louise Strong, Rabbi Koch helped organize the important Child Welfare Exhibit that opened in Seattle in May, 1914, and ran for nine days. This was dedicated to informing the public about

the needs of children in their community, to provide practical information about the ways to improve children's lives and to show the
connection between municipal problems and child welfare. The exhibit included dramatic photographic displays, charts, live demonstrations and even provided free dental exams. It was a dramatic success; attendance exceeded 40,000, and it was universally lauded in
the press. Moreover, when the time came for it to be dismantled, parts
of it were requested for use in other similar exhibits in Everett, Wenatchee, and Victoria, British Columbia.

The energy generated by religious idealism during this time also
expressed itself architecturally. The simple meeting hall of the pioneer
era was replaced by a complex of offices, classrooms, auditoriums,
libraries and gynmasiums in order to enable congregations to fulfill
their ambitious social goals. To emphasize the churches' claim to moral
leadership within the community, religious edifices aspired to a gothic,
baroque or neoclassical grandeur. Sometimes, as in the case of the
Catholic's St. James Cathedral in Seattle and Episcopalian's Cathedral
of St. John the Evangelist in Spokane, and St. Mark's Cathedral in
Seattle, these structures strained the financial resources of their respective congregations, as the vision came periously close to outstripping
the capacity to realize it. In the case of St. Mark's Cathredral, vision
did outstrip reality. When interest payments on the mortgage could
no longer be made, foreclosure proceedings were undertaken, and
the Cathedral was closed from 1941 to 1946.

The benefits of religious idealism in the community were also
tempered by an often narrow and self-righteous zeal. Involved as
church leaders were in economic and social reform, the greater
energies of most were directed toward moral issues. Mark Matthew's
support of progressive reforms was only part of his larger plan to make
Seattle a holy community and an important staging area from which
missionaries could embark for Asia to complete the Christian conquest of the world and hurry its moral transformation. Jimmy Duncan's pragmatism did not extend to his inclination to impose a rigid
Calvinist morality upon his town. Historians Robert and Robin
Friedheim credit Duncan with the claim that, "...as far as booze and
vice goes I will make a Sunday school out of Seattle. I will make them
all obey the law, whether he lives on Capitol Hill or in the Rainier
Valley, it will be all the same to me, and they will all toe the mark."
If beyond such figures as McGill, O'Hara, Matthews, Koch and Strong

Growth and change: First (circa 1879) Methodist meeting house in Spokane.

Courtesy Earl Howell Photo Collection, Pacific Northwest Methodist Annual Conference Archives, United Methodist Church, University of Puget Sound, Tacoma, Washington.

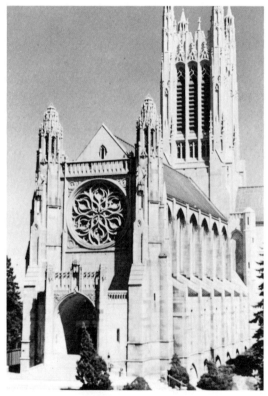

Episcopal Cathedral of St. John the Evangelist: Contrast the simple lines of the early Methodist meeting house with the Gothic detail of the Episcopalian Cathedral of St. John the Evangelist which held its first service in 1929.

Courtesy of St. John's Cathedral Book Store, Spokane, Washington.

Catholic St. James Cathedral showing the dome that was to fall during a 1916 snow storm.

Courtesy Special Collections Division, University of Washington Libraries, Negative #8833, Seattle, Washington.

Window commemorating Spokan Garry in Cathedral of St. John the Evangelist, Spokane, Washington. Belated recognition came to Spokan Garry in 1932 when this stained glass window was placed. Garry is shown being baptised, teaching catechism, and conferring with Gov. Stevens.

Courtesy of St. John's Cathedral Bookstore, Spokane, Washington.

One has to dig to find clerics actively involved in support of progressive reforms, one has no trouble finding those who worked tirelessly to ban prostitution, drinking, gambling, horse racing, Sabbath breaking and dancing. While their concern for the victims of the more nefarious of these activities was laudable, their provincial, middle class piety, their negativity and their impulse to authoritarianism provoked the ire of many thoughtful people, including many in the churches themselves.

With the century's turning, the attack on demon rum absorbed the greater part of the churches energies. Instead of merely restricting the sale of liquor, the reformers sought to prohibit completely its manufacture and sale. An attempt to include an article in the new state constitution that would have accomplished this was defeated by a public vote of 31,000 to 20,000, however, and after that, supporters of prohibition aimed their attacks against the institution most closely associated with the liquor trade, the saloon. In 1898 the Anti-Saloon League of Washington (ASL) was organized. A child of the Anti-Saloon League of America organized in Ohio three years before, it drew its leadership and support from the churches and their allies in the community.

In league with other groups such as the WCTU, the ASL directed its energies toward the enactment of local option laws which gave communities the right to prohibit saloons from operating within their boundaries. This was regarded as only a first step toward complete, statewide prohibition. Such groups also worked for womens' suffrage and for the adoption of a constitutional amendment that would grant state voters the right to pass legislation directly through the use of the initiative. The reformers played the political game well. When the bill enabling local option was killed in the state House of Representatives in 1907, the ASL published the names of those who voted against it and organized successful campaigns against their re-election. In 1908 both the Democratic and Republican parties supported the measure, and the next year it was voted into law.

With that, campaigns between prohibitionists, "drys," and their opponents, the "wets," erupted in communities throughout the state. The dry vote received an enormous boost when women once again received the vote. By 1912, when the right of initiative was amended to the state constitution, the ASL estimated that out of some 220 local option elections, 140 had resulted in dry victories leading to the closures of saloons in communities representing forty-two percent of the state's population.

The first exercise of the people's right to direct legislation was the campaign for Initiative No. 3 that called for an end to the manufacture and sale of liquor on January 1, 1916, a move intended to destroy the state's liquor industry. The drys waged the campaign with the ardor of a crusade. A good part of the money came from Presbyterians who contributed $150,000 for prohibition in the Northwest and California. The Methodists, nationally the denomination most active in the fight, sent 700 ministers to help in the effort. Zealous support for prohibition was manifest in virtually every denomination, from Adventist to Unitarian. In fact, a notable record for the promotion of abstinence from drink was one of the factors favoring the selection of Augustine Schinner as the first Catholic bishop of Spokane, a town that advertised a saloon with the country's longest bar. Old antagonisms were put aside temporarily as Protestant and Catholic clergy and laity worked together to pass No. 3.

The drys felt confident of victory in rural parts of the state, but less so in its urban areas, especially in Seattle. They were supported there, however, by the most eloquent and fanatical champion of prohibition, Mark Matthews, whose persuasive skill was hardly less im-

Mark Matthews slim frame as seen by a cartoonist.

Courtesy, Special Collections Division, University of Washington Libraries, Negative # 3357.

pressive than his gangly frame. In one of his sermons printed in the local newspapers, he described the liquor trade as, "the most fiendish, corrupt and hell-soaked institution that ever crawled out of the slime of the eternal pit." A knack for vivid phrases led a writer for *Collier's* magazine to suggest that, "it is doubtful if in the American pulpit there is a man more skillful in the arts of public denunciation than Mark Matthews. Few men can paint black blacker than he."

The election to decide the fate of No. 3 was held on November 2, 1914. Beginning in October, Matthews launched a series of impassioned attacks on the liquor industry and all who supported it, including the Democratic and Republican parties which he derided as "rum soaked and saloon cursed, and without conscience on the quesiton of the abolition of this great enemy." His attacks continued daily until October 31, when he ceased with a blast entitled "Satan at the Polls."

Satan, in this case, was represented by an interesting mix of elements: the liquor industry obviously, but also the major Seattle papers which opposed No. 3 as an infringement of personal freedom. Joining them was the Washington Federation of Labor which had voted to support those of its member locals like the brewery workers, waiters, and wagon drivers who would be harmed by the passage of the initiative. It was a difficult position for the Federation to take since many of its members, most notably Jimmy Duncan, had actively supported No. 3. The opposition was not strong enough, however, to overcome the popular resentment excited against saloons and liquor dealers, and No. 3 was passed by a vote of 189,840 to 171,208. The turnout was immense; no subsequent initiative has received a higher percentage of votes cast. Predictably, the dry vote was heaviest in rural areas, but even in Seattle, thirty-nine percent of the voters supported No. 3

The efforts of the prohibitionists did not end there. Other campaigns were mounted to turn back attempts to overturn No. 3, and in 1917, the legislature was persuaded to pass the "bone dry" law that forbade the importation of liquor into the state. Finally, in 1919, Washington added itself to the list of states ratifying the 18th Amendment to the U.S. Constitution. The cause of prohibition, victorious in this state and twenty-seven others, became the law of the land. The great crusade had been won.

Samuel Hill: Roads and Globes

According to legend it was Sam Hill's ancestor, Oliver Crom-·
well's Finance Minister, who gave the world the epigram
"What the Sam Hill." That same ancestor left England, and
a cranky employer, for the more salubrious and peaceful climate of
North Carolina. Cromwell's wars were no longer old Sam's, and to
make his point he joined the Quaker church.

Washington State's Samuel Hill, born in 1857 on his farther's North
Carolina farm, left the South at the beginning of the Civil War. A
southern Quaker family with pro-Union views may not have been
popular in North Carolina.

Sam's mother, Eliza L. Mendenhall, was a descendant of Thomas
Pearson, who accompanied William Penn to the American colonies
in 1688. The Mendenhall family established a Quaker meeting house
near Jamestown, Virginia. When the Hill and Mendenhall families
joined through marriage, it was a true-blue Quaker contract.

According to Sam Hill's recollection of events, his family, after leaving the South, first stopped in Indiana, home of a friend who ran part
of the fleeing slaves "underground railroad." Later, young Sam was
raised in Minneapolis. His father and brother were doctors. Sam
entered the world of business, specifically as an agent of the St. Paul
& Pacific Railway.

Other than Hill's Quaker upbringing, the one event that most
changed his life occurred in a modest little railway office. The new
owner, James J. Hill (no relation) of the Great Northern, poked his
head in during an inspection trip. Finding everything in good shape,
and a handsome, intelligent employee in charge with ready answers
to all his questions, the boss James J. Hill was impressed. Telling the
great railroad magnate that if the opportunity arose he wanted to
become a lawyer, young Hill was soon contacted by President Hill
and offered a scholarship to Harvard.

Cynical observers noted that despite Sam Hill's talents and education he also married the boss's daughter, Mary. The James J. Hill family
was, through his wife's side of the family, Roman Catholic. James,
however, was surrounded by books as a young man and his early
education was gained in part from two Quaker teachers, an Irishman
and an Englishman. It might not be stretching things to deduce from
that impressionable Quaker experience that James' interest in young

Samuel Hill's Columbia Gorge Stonehenge monument to pacifism and memorial to World War I war dead.

Bob Spring photo, courtesy of Exploration Cruise Line, Seattle, Washington.

Samuel Hill, builder of railroads, peace monuments and world traveller.

Courtesy Special Collections Division, University of Washington Libraries, Negative #3014.

Sam might have been influenced by the Quaker "connection." In those days Sam, despite the fact he eventually dropped using "thee" and "thy" in correspondence, made no bones about his religious background. Although his marriage to Mary Hill would eventually sour, and his connections to the James J. Hill railroad empire dry up, his fortune was made and a legend had begun to take shape.

Sam Hill seemed to be in everything: successful attorney; founder and promoter of the Washington State Good Roads Association; world traveler and hobnobber with royalty and Russian revolutionaries; initiator and banker for the Canadian Border Peace Arch at Blaine, Washington, ("May these gates never be closed"); financial sponsor of the Chief Joseph monument on the Colville Reservation and Stonehenge Monument on the north bank of the Columbia River. As a kind of symbol of his interests, and especially his penchant for travel, Hill distributed world globes as gifts. Many a business associate or even casual acquaintance boasted a Sam Hill globe in his den.

Born a Quaker, Hill never wandered far from the basic instincts and teaching of his family religion. Detractors pointed out that his tough business dealings and strong personality—edging toward ruthless behavior, were "not Quaker-like." His church attendance was sporadic and he expressed anti-German views during the First World War. This apparent hedge on Quaker pacifism also put him at odds with some members of his faith. Nevertheless, threaded among the busy, worldly fabric of Hill's life was a consistent, quiet, often behind-the-scenes support of Quaker projects and issues.

Guilford College, a Quaker school in North Carolina, received $5,000 in 1901 from the hands of Sam Hill. He also contributed generously to Haverford College, another Quaker institution. Later he mused about establishing a Quaker college in Seattle. With Hervey Lindley and Elbridge Stuart he financed the first Quaker meeting house, called the Friends Memorial Church, at 23rd Avenue and Spruce Street in Seattle. Hill's grandest project with religious underpinnings was the Maryhill Estate near Stevenson, Washington.

Sam Hill's Minneapolis law clerk had, in 1903, acted as a land agent for the Great Northern Railway in Klickitat County. Shortly after that Hill himself became interested in a water power plant at Lyle on the Columbia River. In 1906 Hill asked a young Quaker pastor in North Carolina to "come out to Washington and help us build another Whittier." Whittier, California, had begun as a 2,000-acre tract for Quaker barley farmers. That North Carolina minister, J. Edgar Williams, did indeed accept Hill's invitation and took over the Friends Memorial Church in Seattle. The 4,000-acre Columbia River spread was bought by Hill at about this time. It was to be a planned community for Quakers ($300 an acre for pioneers). Not an acre was sold, not a brave Quaker recruited, although a number of prospects visited the barren, scenic site. Hill built a tiny Quaker meeting house above his Stonehenge replica, which was later torn down by Great Depression farmers for lumber.

Sam Hill's personal life was complex. He drifted apart from his wife and children, had liaisons with several other women, sired three children out of wedlock, and then found himself beset with lawsuits. After his death in 1931 his fortune shriveled. Lawsuits continued against his estate. The old Quaker builder and planner, however, had become a robust symbol of the Pacific Northwest. Downhill from his failed Quaker colony at Maryhill, which now houses an extraordinary museum with an unparalleled view of the Columbia Gorge, is Sam Hill's crypt. An inscription on the monument reads: "Amid nature's unrest, he sought rest."

Agnes Healy Anderson &
The Horse-Drawn Brougham

Oldtimers still talk about the great mansion on Seattle's aristocratic First Hill. Located at the corner of Columbia and Minor, the gabled structure with marbled bathroom walls and floors was built by Alfred H. Anderson, Shelton lumberman, former Mason County legislator, and husband to Wisconsin-bred Agnes Healy Anderson.

Philanthropist Agnes Anderson and her horse drawn coach.

Courtesy Special Collections Division, University of Washington Libraries, Negative #8829.

Negative #8830

Agnes and Alfred were pillars of the Shelton, and later Seattle, communities. He possessed, besides a keen sense of commerce, a 7'8" custom-made bathtub, and a gargantuan appetite. Until 1935 Mrs. Anderson proudly rode her coachman-driven brougham drawn by horses named Lord and Lady. She also controlled one of the largest estates in Washington State following the 1914 death of her husband.

When Agnes Anderson died in 1940, the funeral was held in her imposing Seattle home. Christian Scientist readers led the service—a surprise to some attendees. Mrs. Anderson's Christian Science roots, in fact, went back to her early married days in Seattle.

Perhaps her closest friend after coming to the Pacific Northwest was Mae Riley. Mae was a state tennis champion and devout Christian Scientist. (The Riley family had known Mary Baker Eddy in their home town of Boston.) Mae and Agnes were inseparable, the former acting as personal secretary and travelling companion to the grande dame in the horse-drawn brougham. Until Mae's 1915 death, she and Agnes were frequently seen drawing up to Seattle's First Church of Christ Scientist behind the prancing team of Lord and Lady.

Mrs. Anderson, like Mary Baker Eddy, believed that "the science of Christianity makes pure the fountain, in order to purify the stream. It begins in mind to heal the body..." In the late 1890s and early 1900s, the period of Mrs. Eddy's early writings and influence, Agnes Healy Anderson was reading everything published by Eddy, and listening to her devoted friend Mae Riley. "The less medicine the better, until you arrive at no medicine," made perfect sense to a woman who had been physically "delicate" as a girl.

Alternatively, one can imagine this grand lady's puzzlement with Mark Twain's writings about Mrs. Eddy whom he labeled at one time "queen of frauds and hypocrites" and on another occassion described as "the benefactor of the age." It was a turbulent and trying time for a cultured, wealthy woman to single-mindedly choose a new, controversial religion. During her lifetime Agnes Anderson reportedly gave $500,000 to Principia, a small Christian Science secondary school and college near St. Louis. That school, by the way, had other Pacific Northwest supporters, including the Baillargeon family.

Agnes had asked close friends to help her keep a personal vow: never to consult a physician. Her Christian Scientist beliefs were firm. However, she changed practitioners from time to time, due to their varying abilities or personalities.

With an estate of over $12 million, Agnes Anderson was a focal point for philanthropy. Her largesse resulted in a high-profile project such as paying off Cornish School's mortgage. Nellie Cornish described Agnes as "tall and stately, endowed with great natural dignity, and yet naive and modest to a degree." Agnes also underwrote the Alfred

H. Anderson School of Forestry at the University of Washington. She was invited to serve as a director—the first woman—of the National Bank of Commerce (later Rainier Bank), Seattle, where, it was noted, she was the second largest shareholder. Her 1940 will confirmed other longtime interests: the Shelton Public Library, Children's Orthopedic Hospital, the YWCA, King County Humane Society, and Whitman College. She left her laundress, Ida Johnson of Suquamish, $1,000. Seventy large diamonds and 272 other small precious stones were also listed in the estate inventory. Principia College, a symbol of her Christian Science experience, was again a beneficiary of Mrs. Anderson's generosity.

Agnes and Alfred Anderson, along with her parents, the Benjamin Healys, are buried side by side in Lake View, Seattle's Pioneer Cemetery atop Capitol Hill.

Sister Ray's Hairpiece

After the 1776 American Revolution, free blacks seceded from white churches and established African societies. Many of those groups set up African Methodist Episcopal Churches. Blacks saw these churches as a refuge, a place where they were shielded from white hatred and discrimination. Emancipation after the 1861-65 American Civil War caused black dislocation. Churches again served as a stable element to refugees from the South.

Emma J. Ray and her husband L.P. were part of a curious, hopeful black migration from border and southern states in the late 19th century. Missouri was native land to the Rays; Washington State would become their outpost. Emma Ray, born a slave, wrote that she "was born twice, bought twice, sold twice, and set free twice."

Early experiences with her husband's drinking bouts and their empty bank account, convinced Ray that she must find salvation from both Missouri and a rocky marriage. After moving to Seattle in 1889 she attended meetings of the new (1890) African Methodist Episcopal Church. At one service a young preacher raised the roof, beating a tatoo on the pulpit with his knuckles. Emma Ray thought a hammer was striking her heart. She fled to the altar and asked to be saved. One of the church sisters bent down and whispered "this is the very best step you have ever taken in your life." Her next task was to get Mr. Ray off the bottle and through the church doors. That job was accomplished within a year. L.P. Ray would later describe his baptism on the 3rd of July, 1906, in the clear waters of Lake Washington.

Upgraded to "Sister" following her sanctification and re-dedication to the church, Ray took charge of Seattle's first black Woman's Christian Temperance Union meeting. This adventure was followed by an association with Mrs. O.S. Ryther, famous missionary to Seattle slums. The work was permeated with disappointment, violence and tragedy. Dope and drink were frequent causes of human misery. Sister Ray spent hours at the city jail, trying to help dissolute female prisoners.

During the Klondike gold strike Seattle's waterfront boomed. Sister Ray's husband found work at McDougal and Southwick, a major purveyor of dry goods for the Alaska crowd. When prospectors geared up for cold northern days they frequently left their old clothes behind. The Rays gave those goods to the poor, and managed to simultaneously distribute religious tracts. Sister Ray sadly noted that some of the gold-seekers "left their Bibles behind, and...many left their salvation also."

In May 1900, Sister Ray decided that her conversion and church work comprised a story worth telling to her Missouri relatives. After all, when she left home several years before, her life was "in sin and darkness." L.P. had a job to complete, so Sister Ray left her 5th Avenue home in Seattle and watched the warehouses and old county hospital disappear through windows of a slow-moving train. About then she noted with some embarrassment that since age fifteen she had worn a fulsome hairpiece. Now perhaps it was time to remove the hairpiece and bare her head, as she had bared her sinful soul.

The Missouri visit started off with Sister Ray proclaiming "praise the Lord" to her surprised sister. After visiting family haunts, she contacted the Kansas City W.C.T.U. chapter. That was the catalyst to get Sister Ray going again. When her husband arrived they established a dilapidated Christian mission in Hick's Hollow. It didn't take long to fill every bed and chair of this poor two-story bungalow. Street gospel meetings, jail visits, offerings to the sick, and her first experience at honest, heart-filled "preaching" (in a tent meeting) filled her days and nights. After two busy years, Sister Ray and L.P. joined a family of friendly Quakers on the return train trip to Seattle.

Finding rooms in an old downtown alley house between Third and Second Avenues, Sister Ray hit the streets, religious tracts in hand, on behalf of a Skid Road mission called The Stranger's Rest. Her most vivid memory of that mission was not souls in torment, nor the near empty collection plates, but instead, swarms of mosquitoes. Sister Ray was perversely happy with that buzzing presence because they helped keep drowsing customers awake to hear her sermons.

L.P., who had now assumed the sobriquet "Brother," put $30 down on two lots near Seattle's jewel-like Green Lake. Finding stone, window frames and doors lying about, with the help of friends Brother Ray constructed two solid homes on Sunnyside Avenue. Sister Ray's father and step-mother came from Missouri to occupy one of those structures. "When the Lord got ready for us to have a home, how quickly it was done," Sister Ray wrote.

With the Rays' help, "holiness meetings" were held in the African Methodist Episcopal (A.M.E.) church on 14th Avenue. Reverend Donohoo called on this dedicated couple to help him "revive" Seattle's oldest black church. No sooner had deaconesses been ordained and A.M.E. put on a solid footing, the Rays turned their attention to the Olive Branch Mission on Pine Street. This activity led to their joining the Free Methodist Church of Reverend C.E. McReynolds, also on Pine. Sister Ray has recounted numerous examples of tramps, sailors, prison inmates and "fallen" women who came into her life. The results, of course, were the same: with her help they found God.

The great experiment (Prohibition) was cause for joyous celebration by the Rays. Sister Ray had long prayed that she "might live to see the saloons closed and old John Barleycorn voted out." Shortly before passage of state prohibition (1914) an anti-booze rally and a two-mile-long parade were held in downtown Seattle. Sister Ray joined the banners, flags and celebrants on that march. At Second Avenue and Yesler Way she noted that a large sign was flashing "Rainier Beer." When the mug houses closed, she watched with satisfaction the extinguishing of that devil sign-board.

Back on the road, years of revival meetings were held by Sister Ray and Brother Ray. Their stops included the towns and crossroads of: Byrn Mawr, Cascade Tunnel, Grandview, Burlington, Blaine, Chewelah and many more.

Among Washington State's predominately white population, Sister Ray's skin color was apparently not a hindrance to her evangelistic duties. She once explained that God had made all sorts of animals, birds and flowers, each of a different color. "I want to be," she said, "just myself."

James. H. Clawson:
Patriarch, President and Parent

Jack Clawson, Bishop and Patriarch, Church of Jesus Christ of Latter-day Saints.

Courtesy of Leora Clawson, widow of L.D.S. Bishop James H. Clawson.

Industrial Manchester in England had heard of the great Mormon trek to Utah. So had Copenhagen, Denmark. Jack Clawson's fore-bearers came from those two regions. Both branches of the family drove wagons west during the chaos of the American Civil War.

Born in 1899, Clawson's childhood in Providence, Utah, was a rural, hard-hands existence. His grandmother made mittens, underwear and socks from home-spun wool. Timber from Logan Canyon, a few farm animals, and flourishing garden helped sustain the growing family.

Although his American ancestors came to Utah as committed members of the Mormon Church, and at a time when polygamy was tolerated, Clawson had no record or memory of other than monogamous marriages in his family.

The Providence area, including Cache Valley, was a self-contained economy. Eggs and chickens were exchanged for groceries; soap was made from pork and lye; a potato cellar rested below every home; grain was ground at a cooperative mill, half of it being returned as flour to the grower; wagons, sleighs and draft horses provided transport; and, fortunately, small streams were everywhere, irrigating the rich soil. Brigham Young had designed the townsites and the Church members carried out his plans.

With family and neighbor encouragement, Clawson graduated from Brigham Young College in 1920, then entered Harvard Business School. Not a robust lad, he looked at teaching, and then business, as possible careers. Joining Stone and Webster, a large utilities company, Clawson eventually moved over to one of its subsidiaries, Puget Sound Power and Light. The road to the top began — from junior auditor to chairman of the board.

Jack Clawson's business career included world-wide travel as a utilities consultant. At home (Washington State), his friendship with M.L. Bean provided business opportunities with a growing chain of stores called Pay and Save. In his spiritual life, Clawson's commitment to the Church of Jesus Christ of Latter-day Saints (Mormon) was deep.

In an informal, friendly memoir Clawson wrote, he recalled that he never had "an absence...from Sunday School." He modestly claimed that his activities only filled leadership vacuums when taking on such tasks as scoutmaster, presidency of the Deacons Quorum and secretary of the Priest Quorum. While on the road, for business or vacation, Jack Clawson would seek out the nearest LDS meeting. His religious commitment and sound business sense were recognized by Church officials. Those qualities led to his being chosen in 1938 as bishop of the Seattle First Ward (Queen Anne). He was the first in the state to hold that position. Clawson's talents ultimately found employment as Patriarch in the Mormon Church — a signal honor to him and to the state of Washington.

Though Jack Clawson died in 1984 at age eighty-five, his two families: 1) the extended Church; and 2) his immediate family of wife Leora, three sons, grandchildren and great grandchildren; continue to prosper. At Clawson's funeral it was remembered that he had officiated at many similar services while bishop of the Church. Upon returning from one funeral where no relative or friend appeared, Jack Clawson said: "Surely every person has the right and need to be loved." On another mission he brought a shovel, boots and raingear in preparation to dig a grave. Upon arrival at the cemetery he discovered that his duty was to dedicate, not dig the grave. Whatever the call, Clawson was available.

Twenty-two grandchildren sang at Jack Clawson's funeral. To the melody of "Teach Me To Walk In The Light", one stanza was as follows:

"All 22 of us love you so much.
All of our lives we've relied on your touch.
All of your wisdom and all of your care;
Grandma, Grandpa, you've always been there".

The Smooth Cheeks of
Stephanos E. Phoutrides

In 1870, following years of Pacific Northwest rivalry between Russian, American, British, and Spanish interests—to name only the main contenders—the first American Orthodox Church was established. Because of strong ties to Russia, that new world initiative was called the Diocese of the Aleutian Islands and Alaska. In two years it moved to the raucous seaport and Orthodox center of San Francisco.

Pacific Northwest Orthodox candidates meanwhile, were primarily Greek fishermen and loggers. Other Eastern European and Russion emigres soon followed. Seattle responded to this activity by establishing St. Spriridon Orthodox Church on Capitol Hill. In time—certainly by the 1920s—the Greek and Russian congregations had their own churches. Greek parishioners took matters a step further, they split into two congregations: one clung to the old world language and liturgy, while the other acquired a priest who was fluent in both Greek and English.

Puget Sound Greek immigrant families had of course brought their language and traditions to the new soil. Many Greek men married non-Greek women. Those families tended to wander away from the Orthodox Church unless services and most church activities were held in English. In the mid-1920s several members of Seattle's Greek Orthodox Church of St. Demetrios decided that a relaxation of traditional ways—including the relentless use of Greek in Church services—was necessary. Conservative members disagreed. The reformers, however, were a majority. At this point the congregation launched a nation-wide search for a pastor. He was found at Holy Trinity Parish in Waterbury, Connecticut. His name was Stephanos Evangelos Phoutrides.

Father Phoutrides startled many parishioners by arriving in the Pacific Northwest clean-shaven. Clerical beards were virtually a badge of office in the Orthodox faith. Razor or no razor, Father Phoutrides undertook his task in 1923 with confidence and aplomb.

Born in Greece, Phoutrides graduated from Embetios Gymnasium in Cairo, Egypt. For two years he studied at Holy Cross Theological

St. Demetrios Greek Orthodox Church, established
1921, in Seattle at Yale Ave. N. and Thomas, now
converted to secular use.

Courtesy of Special Collections Division, University of Washington
Libraries, Negative #8832, Seattle, Washington.

Seminary in Jerusalem. In 1911 he came to America, studied English
at a preparatory school, and then entered Yale University in 1913.
Upon graduation in 1917 he practiced his new English skills and
learned about America by teaching and writing for a local newspaper.
He decided that his true calling was the church, however, and in 1921
he entered St. Athanasius Theological Seminary, Long Island, New
York.

Seattle's burgeoning Greek Orthodox community provided rich soil
for the activist priest. Moving at a pace that some traditionalists found
breathtaking, Phoutrides introduced English in all phases of church
activity. Several of his innovations were "firsts" in American Orthodoxy. For example: Sunday school classes held in English and Greek;
a lay mixed choir; a youth organization called the Junior Orthodox
League which studied the liturgy, history and sacraments in both
English and Greek.

In 1932 Phoutrides was called to Oakland, California, where he stayed only two years: the St. Demetrios membership had voted overwhelmingly to invite him back to Seattle. His second Seattle career proved a trial, however. A significant number of members thought that the activist priest had gone too far. Now a majority, the traditionalists at St. Demetrios voted to fire Phoutrides and re-affirm the use of Greek in church affairs. The church hierarchy, also traditionalist, supported the old ways. After acrimonious debate and several unpleasant incidents, St. Demetrios Orthodox Church was temporarily closed on August 15, 1939.

Attempts to establish another membership, with the Phoutrides English-language innovations as the modus operandi, were undertaken. A new church name was chosen, Assumption of the Virgin Mary, and the reformers sought approval from the Archiodiocese.

Father Phoutrides was of course their first choice as spiritual leader. To soften the blow, so to speak, the Assumption group promised to achieve harmony with their colleagues at the revived St. Demetrios. The Archdiocese said "no," it would only approve one church, the resuscitated St. Demetrios.

Reconciliation and negotiation had failed. A bold step was then taken. The Phoutrides congregation bolted, sought religious sanctuary with the Russian Orthodox Greek Catholic Church of America, and borrowed St. Barnabas, an old Episcopal Church on Seattle's Capitol Hill. (St. Barnabas had sheltered Orthodox believers once before, during the time St. Spiridon had been condemned as unsafe.) The Phoutrides innovations continued, along with a colorful mix of traditional icons, candles, censer and chalice.

In later years members of the Greek Church of the Assumption claimed they harbored no regrets about the schism. A parish poet would describe Stephanos Phoutrides in these words: "...When attacked (which happened often), his gentleness, his power, his courage helped young and old...he cleared the way."

Hans Andrew Stub:
St. Olaf's Own

Seattle's raucous nature was on full display when a young, wavy-haired, handsome Norwegian-American clergyman arrived in Seattle. That was the summer of 1903, and Hans Stub had completed a long train ride from his native Minnesota. Klondike fever was still in the air and Seattle waterfront noises dominated the panorama of life. Nearby, the Lava Beds, later to become famous in Murray Morgan's book as the original Skid Road, bustled with a life of its own.

In 1900 there were seven Lutheran Churches in Seattle. By 1910 eleven additional Lutheran churches were built. Some local Lutheran churchmen had called for even more, and that appeal was no doubt heard by Hans Stub in St. Paul. Lutheran activity, however, was only a fraction of the religious bustle in turn-of-the-century Seattle.

In 1901, just two years before Stub's arrival, another lean purveyor of the gospel had come to Puget Sound. His name was Mark Matthews, and he was destined to become one of the most famous Presbyterian preachers in America. In just a few years he was already dominating the Seattle scene by attacking city officials who allowed Skid Road enterprises like saloons and brothels, to flourish. To the fledgling Reverend Stub, all this commotion must have made him pause. Seattle appeared to be a purgatory, perhaps a mid-point between an earthly heaven and hell.

In 1953, Rev. Stub and his wife Victoria celebrate fifty years of marriage and Seattle ministry.

Courtesy Seattle Post-Intelligencer Collection, Museum of History and Industry, Seattle, Washington.

184

Reverend Stub, despite his youth, was at ease with the life of a pastor. With an active wife, Victoria, at his side, he could accomplish many tasks. His maternal and paternal grandfathers had been clergymen and his father was president of the Norwegian Lutheran Synod of America. Grounded in the keen sense of competition and rivalry between Lutheran Synods, Stub found that his primarily Norwegian-speaking parishioners didn't object to the occasional use of English in church services. Pacific Northwest Lutherans tended to be more flexible than their mid-western brothers and sisters; however, the Lutheran evangelical thrust at first did not reach for American Indians or Asians. After many decades in his pulpit, Reverend Stub would change all that.

On August 1, 1903, Hans Stub stepped into the pulpit of Immanuel Lutheran Church at Minor and Olive Streets, in downtown Seattle. His first challenge was to expand the pathetic rolls of eleven parishioners (only three of whom were voting members). Like his volatile Presbyterian neighbor Mark Matthews, Stub was an organizer. He also took a special interest in young people. Repeating his Norwegian language sermons in English each Sunday, his flock grew quickly. In fact, growth of Immanuel Lutheran became a problem, not necessarily a blessing. Standing-room only Sunday services led the leadership to move the church to a new location. About ten blocks away, in the Cascade neighborhood, below the west side of Capitol Hill, property was found at Pontius and Thomas Streets. By 1912, with over 300 members, Immanuel Lutheran was the largest Norwegian church on the West Coast.

Earnest and direct, Stub gained reputation as a stem-winding speaker. He avoided the "uptown" secular battles of Matthews, but wasn't shy about laying lessons of his time on listeners during Sunday sermons. His community activism extended primarily to assistance for the underprivileged. Indigent travellers heard that Reverend Stub had a soft spot in his heart. No one was turned away. That concern would, in Stub's late years, lead to the installation of beds and meal service for thousands who were down on their luck.

Further physical growth of Immanuel Lutheran included a gymnasium (Stub's dedication to youth activities remained keen all his life), parsonage, offices, choir loft, Sunday School classrooms and kitchen facilities. With all this going on, Stub found time to serve for twenty years on the Seattle Public Library Board and gain wide reputation as a popular "marrying" preacher who officiated at over thirty-seven hundred marriage services.

In 1936 Reverend Stub received an honorary Doctor of Divinity degree from Whitworth College. In 1947, while celebrating his forty-fifth year as a pastor, he was knighted by the king of Norway—the Order of St. Olaf—for a lifetime of promoting good will between the U.S. and Norway.

Another milestone came in June of 1953: his fiftieth anniversary. Three signal events were feted: 1. his ordination; 2. his call to Immanuel Lutheran; and 3. his marriage to wife Victoria. Wearing a familiar cut-away black coat, winged collar, black bow tie and gray-striped trousers, white-haired and tall, Reverend Hans Stub returned the salute to his well-wishers.

Another change took place in 1950 that was beyond Stub's power to prevent. His Cascade neighborhood, close to downtown and a block or two from the proposed new I-5 freeway, was changing rapidly. Commercial rather than residential uses dominated. Although people came from all over Seattle to hear Stub's sermons, the surroundings were in decline. In the 1930s and 40s he held four Easter Sunday services. In the 1950s the church would barely fill once on that special Christain day.

After a fifty-five-year pastorate, longest in the city's history, Hans Stub, a vigorous seventy-seven years old, resigned. City notables of all parties and faiths turned out to hail this extraordinary man who claimed he was guided in life by two words: "Be kind." Hans and Victoria Stubs had raised and lost two children, Gerhard died in 1937, and Sylvia, 1940. Those losses were private, however, and Hans Stub had turned his affection and energies to the life of a proud, busy, ever-changing inner city church, Immanuel Lutheran.

A Touch of Karma:
Tatsuya Ichikawa

Jodo Shinshu Buddhism was founded in the Pacific Northwest on November 15, 1901. At 624 Main Street, Seattle, seven Issei Japanese immigrants met to organize Buddhist services. Those young men had heard tales of Alaska gold and the great seaport of Seattle. Upon arrival from Japan they instead found raw prejudice, loneliness, meager pay and dingy rooming houses. The spiritual and cultural

Reverend Tatsuya Ichikawa survived the Great Depression, Japanese-American War Relocation camps to earn his Buddhist Temple the honored status of Betsuin.

Courtesy of Etsuko Osaki, daughter of Rinban Tatsuya Ichikawa.

needs of these earnest pilgrims needed a boost. The ceremony on Main Street was a first step toward reclaiming their heritage and creating a new community.

Shortly after the State's first Japanese-owned department store and bank opened, Buddhist Reverend Gendo Nakai arrived in May, 1902, to serve the growing Issei population of Puget Sound. He roamed the

Seattle Buddhist Church 1965 Procession.
Courtesy Seattle Post-Intelligencer *Collection, Museum of History and Industry, Seattle, Washington.*

Japanese communities of South Park, Green Lake, Vashon Island, Tacoma, Bellevue and other hamlets. Finally, despite restrictive laws preventing Asians from owning real estate, a Buddhist temple was established at 1020 Main Street in 1907—under the control of three trustees, two of whom were Caucasian.

In 1925 Reverend Tatsuya Ichikawa visited Seattle as part of a Japanese delegation commemorating the twenty-fifth anniversary of the founding of the Buddhist Churches of America. Ichikawa would return eleven years later to serve the young Seattle Buddhist church during its most crucial and harrowing years.

The Great Depression caused Seattle's Japanese community to stagger. The old bank and many businesses failed. Overseas, a growing restiveness among Japan's military leaders was contributing to anti-Asian violence and discrimination in America. Tatsuya Ichikawa returned to Seattle in the midst of this foment.

Reverend Ichikawa was born in Nagano-ken, Japan on January 21, 1903. After taking his degree at Ryukoku University in 1927, he was ordained and immediately took up missionary duties in Fresno, California. Following a two-year visit to Japan, Ichikawa accepted the position as minister of the Seattle Buddhist church in 1936. Described as a gentle, humble man, he was about to undergo an ordeal of leadership in a time when his adopted country would wage war against the nation of his birth.

A new temple was built in 1941 under Reverend Ichikawa's direction. As the cost of construction rose, and tensions mounted in the Far East, the job at hand seemed impossible. On October 4, 1941, the new temple was dedicated with a celebratory five-block-long procession. Two months later, December 7th, the Japanese military government bombed Pearl Harbor. Within months president Franklin Roosevelt signed Executive Order 9066—later to become one of the most controversial wartime measures in U.S. history—which sent all West Coast Japanese, including those who were American citizens, to "relocation" camps. It was Ichikawa's turn in May, 1942. He would spend the next four years behind barbed wire in enemy alien internment camps in the states of Montana, Louisiana, New Mexico and Texas. He and his family were eventually reunited in a family internment camp in Crystal City, Texas.

Settling the temple's debt was one of Reverend Ichikawa's postwar duties. He was aided in his work by an English-speaking Nisei minister, Reverend Shoko Masunaga. The "Americanized" Nisei were fast supplanting the "old country" Issei. Scouts, Camp Fire Girls, an active Sunday School, athletic programs, clubs and celebrations such as Bon Odori helped push war memories out of view. In spite of the war and the indignities of incarceration, the Nisei made a name for themselves in local schools as scholars, athletes and leaders. Ichikawa and his wife Yasashi proudly watched their seven children participate in this cultural revival. On March 11, 1954, the busy temple was elevated to the honored status of Betsuin. As the head minister, Reverend Ichikawa was now addressed as Rinban, a formidable title in the Buddhist church. The Seattle temple, in fact, became the third Betsuin in America.

Rinban Ichikawa's health began to fail as rapid changes in the Pacific Northwest and in the Japanese Buddhist church accelerated. By the end of 1959, almost twenty-five years from the time he moved permanently to Seattle, Ichikawa resigned due to failing eyesight. A testimonial banquet was held in January, 1960, to salute the Rinban. That occasion was also a celebration of new beginnings for Americans of Asian ancestry. In 1968 Rinban Ichikawa died in Seattle at age sixty-five. The road from the small 1901 gathering at 624 Main Street, Seattle, to the retirement of Tatsuya Ichikawa, was littered with pain, war, racial prejudice and eventually the evolution and survival of a proud people.

Mark A. Matthews:
"Soap, Soup, Salve and Salvation"
(A Matthews' Sermon Title)

C alhoun, Georgia, to Seattle, Washington, is a large jump. Mark Allison Matthews did it in one stride and on his own terms. Matthews' father was not sympathetic to his son's religious zeal. Nevertheless young Matthews, born two years after the Civil War ended, knew what he wanted. With eleven siblings, and the privation of Reconstruction all around, the future Presbyterian firebrand worked as a printer's helper, dry goods salesman and prohibition volunteer.

Although he never graduated from high school his religious education was at full throttle. He preached his first sermon to a home-town congregation at age seventeen. By twenty he was an ordained minister of the Southern Presbyterian Church. Matthews studied for the bar, passed, and practiced law briefly in Tennessee. That achievement, and a three year pastorate in Dalton, Georgia, was all he needed to build what would become the world's largest Presbyterian congregation in early Seattle.

Mark Matthews accepted the call of Seattle's First Presbyterian Church, but only after being assured that his salary was $6,000 a year and that every elder and officer of the church would resign so he could run matters his own way. With startling prescience the *Seattle Mail and Herald* on February 1, 1902, welcomed Reverend Matthews with the prognosis that "He will henceforth wield a wide influence in the social and moral affairs of the city."

During that 1902 inaugural year Matthews bounded from pulpit to City Hall to neighborhood, changing and challenging as he went. Lean, standing 6'5", a long neck emerging from a stiff white collar, his mane of black hair swooping in several directions, Matthews literally stopped traffic. One of his first sermons was to a church full of saloon-keepers (present by special invitation) about the evils of spiritous liquors. By mid-year he visited Alaska and advocated its statehood—over fifty years before the fact.

In August he had drawn up a church manual: 1. Repair and beautify the church; 2. Paint a church at Interbay (then a suburb of Seattle); 3. Build a church at Georgetown (another suburban community); 4.

The Reverend Mark Allison Matthews, one of Seattle's notable church leaders shown at a Christmas service.

Courtesy of Special Collections Division, University of Washington Libraries, Negative #8827, Seattle, Washington.

Build the manse (his own home); 5. Erect an "old people's home;" 6. Charter and build an "emergency hospital;" 7. Erect an auditorium and open an "academy of music;" 8. Install a new pipe organ; 9. Establish a "general mission;" 10. Organize a junior endeavor and kindergarten; 11. Inaugurate an afternoon Sunday School; 12. Find 1,000 new members by January 1, 1903 (four months hence).

Matthews' early sermons were peppered with terms such as "blood-stained dollar," "murderous practices," and "kill sin." As a crusader he was without peer. Shifting from sermonizing about public bribery, the lack of moral backbone in Seattle churches (an "invertebrate church" he exclaimed) and striking blows at sin's "hydra head," he directly entered the fray as civic reformer. From 1910 to about 1918 Mark Matthews clashed with police officials, city politicians—including the redoubtable Seattle Mayor Hiram Gill—gamblers, purveyors of whiskey and the keepers of Seattle's infamous houses of ill fame. He won a few and lost a few. Undoubtedly his greatest victory on behalf of "morality" was in the recall of Mayor Gill. The voters returned Gill to office four years later.

Matthews was accorded a signal honor in 1912-1913: Moderator of the General Assembly of the U.S.A. Presbyterian Church. In May of 1913 he presided over the Assembly in Calhoun, Georgia, his home town. Fresh from crusades against Seattle sin, it must have been the zenith of his professional life.

Called a "Prophet of God," "the Preacher" and "the Tall Pine of the Sierras" by his admirers, very different appellations were applied to him by his foes. "Sensationalist," "rabble-rouser," "effeminate" and a reputation as an erratic vehicle driver were among the criticisms.

It's clear that Matthews' executive and sales skills were impressive. During his thirty-nine-year Seattle pastorate he oversaw the efficient growth of the nation's largest Presbyterian church. Within seven years after his arrival he built a new acoustically perfect church with an auditorium seating 3,000. He was reputed to have one of the most resonant, mellifluous voices in Christendom. Besides sponsoring the founding and construction of "satellite" Presbyterian churches throughout greater Seattle and Alaska, he is credited with undertaking the first local efforts to combat tuberculosis. He also opened Seattle's first kindergarten. He founded the first day nursery, organized a juvenile court, established a Red Cross chapter and engaged in prisoner and jail reform.

On February 5, 1940, white-maned Mark Matthews died of a stroke at Seattle General Hospital. His wife Grace and two married children were present at his death. Seattle Police Badge No. 455, his own, was retired. A former overseer of Whitman College, trustee of Whitworth College, and Scottish Rite Mason, Mark A. Matthews passed into history. His stormy, passionate life continues to live in the edifices, organizations and leaders he helped create.

Seattle has only one public statue to a religious leader. In historic Denny Park, under the clear, stern gaze of Reverend Dr. Mark Allison Matthews, are the inscribed words: "Preacher of the Word of God and Friend to Man."

Searching for a Path

The 1919 triumph of Prohibition ultimately proved to be an illusion. Prohibition was a law enforcement nightmare, and by 1933 most of the states that had voted for the Eighteenth Amendment voted for the Twenty-first repealing it. Rather than leading the nation to a higher moral plane, the churches' efforts resulted in a humiliating debacle. Meanwhile, the mood of popular idealism that crested in 1919 broke in a tumult of reaction that swept the nation.

More than just a crusade against drink, historians regard the prohibition movement as a revolt of rural America against the increasing power of the city, of the old Protestant Anglo-Saxon stock against a polyglot tide of immigrants. There was more than just drink on the mind of one reformer who declared that, "Our nation can only be saved by turning the pure stream of country sentiment and township morals to flush out the cesspools of cities and so save civilization from suicide." Taking another step, many were quick to identify racial, religious and non-English speaking minorities as the sources of pollution.

It is interesting to note that well into this century, groups such as Italians, Greeks and Slavs were still indentified as races rather than nationalities. A macabre example of this is a gravestone in the Fall City cemetery marking the burial site of three nameless victims of an accident, identifying them only as "Two Eye-talians and One White Man." Prejudice against poor European immigrant laborers was inspired by many of the same fears that had prompted white workers to brand Chinese workers as "Coolie Slaves," fears that bosses would use them as pawns in their battle against labor unions and to keep wages down. Because many immigrant workingmen from southern and eastern Europe were Catholics or Jews, xenophobia was inflamed by religious prejudice as well. Bowing to pressure from the American Protective Association, an anti-Catholic organization prominent in working class communities, the Mayor of Spokane had made it city policy in 1896 not to hire Catholics in order to keep Italian laborers out.

During World War I German-speaking groups were made targets of war hysteria, and the experience spurred many congregations to begin holding services in English. After the war, anti-foreign sentiment continued to build, and in the 1920s, laws severely restricting immigration into the United States were passed. At the same time, the Ku Klux Klan entered the Northwest and succeeded in making bigotry an election issue.

Revived in 1915, the Invisible Empire of the Ku Klux Klan grew rapidly after the war, feeding on a climate of fear, particularly in the economically depressed Midwest. Its hatred was focused primarily upon Catholics, Jews, foreigners and blacks, the latter group eventually becoming its primary target. The Klan spread rapidly, and by the 1920s claimed over 4,000,000 members nationally.

In 1921 it entered Oregon from California, adding its strength to a movement seeking the closure of parochial schools. The Klan came to power in several Oregon communities, including Portland, and succeeded in electing a Klan sympathizer governor. On July 6, 1922, the Compulsory School Law bill requiring children between eight and sixteen to attend only state schools was submitted to the electorate under the motto, "One Flag, One School, One Language." The Masons, who earlier had supported compulsory attendance, and most religious groups opposed it, but in spite of their protests, the bill was voted into law by a substantial margin. Flush with this victory, the Klan directed its efforts north of the Columbia.

Washington seemed an appealing target. Few state constitutions are as avowedly secular regarding school support as Washington's, which provides no means to support private education with public funds. Created at a time when faith in public education as a guarantor of liberty was at its height, the constitution committed the state entirely to public education. Possibly, this may have been in reaction to the pre-eminence of private educational institutions at the time of the constitutional convention.

On December 4, 1922, in Spokane, the King Kleagle of the Klan, L.J. Powell, claimed publically that a bill identical to the Oregon Compulsory School Law would win support in Washington, "and when we have won in Washington we will move into Idaho, and so on until we have won the entire nation." The Klan entered the state in force, electing municipal officers in several communities and printing a newspaper, *The Watcher On The Tower,* in Seattle. Cloaked in a weird religiosity, the *Watcher's* editorials declared that all plots against the government were hatched in Rome, that Seattle's government was riddled with Catholics and that Greeks and Mexicans should be deported. Klan activity increased in 1924 when the Imperial Wizard, Hiram Evans, came to Seattle and was given cordial receptions by several civic organizations.

On January 8, 1924, five men from Tacoma led by John A. Jeffries, the Grand Dragon of the State of Washington, filed initiative petitions at Olympia as representatives of the Washington State Good Govern-

Handbill distributed by Catholic school children during the 1924 Initiative 49 campaign which defeated a K.K.K.-sponsored attempt to outlaw parochial schools in Washington State.

Courtesy of Catholic Archdiocese of Seattle Archives, Seattle, Washington.

ment League. Afterwards, Klan members traveled to a clearing north of Seattle and celebrated their efforts by burning a huge cross.

Seeking to avoid the confusion that had attended their efforts in Oregon, Catholics in Washington and their allies, among them Episcopalians, Lutherans and Seventh-day Adventists whose own school systems were at risk, mounted a subdued campaign against the petition drive. In spite of their efforts, however, 55,638 signatures were gathered. This was more than enough, and on July 3 Initiative 49 requiring compulsory attendance at state schools was filed in Olympia.

In the meantime, the Sisters of the Holy Names in Oregon and the Episcopal Hill Military Academy of Portland sued in United States District Court to have the Oregon Law declared unconstitutional. In support, *amicus curiae* briefs were filed on behalf of the Domestic and Foreign Missionary Society of the Protestant Episcopal Church, the American Jewish Committee and the North Pacific Union of Seventh-day Adventists. The case was argued on January 15, 1924, and the three justices of the court declared in favor of the plaintiffs on March 31. Immediately, supporters of the Oregon law appealed the decision to the U.S. Supreme Court.

In Washington, foes of Initiative 49 astutely downplayed the Catholics' role in their opposition and emphasized the fact that passage of the initiative would require millions of dollars in added taxes to educate the thousands of students it would force into the public schools. Newspapers, business and political leaders, the Seattle Central Labor Council, and the leaders of most churches vigorously opposed the measure. Parochial school students and their parents leafletted and doorbelled prospective voters. On November 5 the polls opened, and the Initiative was defeated by nearly 60,000 votes.

There was a collective sigh of relief in church schools when the results were announced. The jubilation of the victors was heightened further when the Supreme Court handed down its unanimous decision on June 1, 1926, denying the appeal. Justice James C. Reynolds, author of the Court's opinion, declared:

"The fundamental theory of liberty upon which all governments in this Union repose excludes any general power of the state to standardize its children by forcing them to accept instruction from public teachers only. The child is not the mere creature of the state; those who nurture him and direct his destiny have the right coupled with the high duty, to recognize and prepare him for additional obligations."

It would not be the last time churches would resist the growing power of the state to direct the lives of its citizens.

Catholics, the primary targets of the Klan's campaign, could congratulate themselves on their success and bask in the wide support their plight inspired. Nevertheless, the fact remained that more than 131,000 citizens had voted for the Initiative, and the struggle reinforced in Catholics the ghetto mentality that had made them suspect in the first place. They were by no means the only ones to suffer the effects of bigotry. Increasingly, Jews found themselves banned from organizations they had helped organize, and blacks fought an uphill battle against efforts to isolate them socially and economically.

Despite the resolute stand many churches had taken against religious intolerance, the fact that it had become an election year issue did not flatter them. Likewise, the zealous efforts of many religious leaders on behalf of disarmament and international welfare issues left them open to the charge of substituting sentimentality for critical thinking, particularly as militarist regimes assumed power around the world and problems at home multiplied. "All I can remember the churches emphasizing during the twenties," wrote Episcopal priest Thomas E. Jessett, historiographer for the Episcopal Diocese of Olympia, was our moral obligation to "feed the starving Armenians" and to support petitions to "end war." The zeal for disarmament may have come in part from the guilty consciences of some religious leaders who had earlier likened America's involvement in World War I to a crusade against barbarism. In 1934 the Methodist General Conference declared war a sin and stated that, "No Christian should engage in war for any purpose or give it his sanction or approval." Such ringing pronouncements rang a little thinly a year later when the Italian dictator, Benito Mussolini, invaded Ethiopia, an act precipitating a decade of war.

Jessett's criticism of the churches was not entirely fair, however. Their stand against war helped pass legislation that legitimized conscientious objection. Locally, the churches were active in other areas too, and the Twenties witnessed the attempts of many religious bodies to come to grips with the problems of labor and the economy.

This could be observed in the deliberations of the various conferences of the Methodist Episcopal Church in Washington. In 1915 the Puget Sound Conference gave polite support to the idea of a half-day holiday for working men, an eight-hour day for working women and the enactment of child labor laws. In 1922 Tacoma Methodists organized Goodwill Industries, a novel economic welfare program that provided the poor with jobs rather than handouts. Its success and Conference-wide support encouraged expansion to Seattle in 1923, and later to Grays Harbor and Spokane. Eventually it was turned over to an interdenominational board of directors. By 1928, the Conference was calling for a revised workman's industrial insurance bill and hospital contract system and pensions for the poor in lieu of the common practice of sending them to county work farms. In that same year the Columbia River Conference sided with workers declaring, "We affirm the social creed of our church, a living wage for every laborer and the best wage that any industry can afford for its employees." This declaration, part of a longer statement of support, was read from pulpits on the eve of Labor Day.

By 1928 the Puget Sound Conference was also calling for an impartial investigation of the trial of several members of the I.W.W. who had been convicted and sentenced for their part in a bloody 1919 Armistice Day riot in Centralia. This was a vindication of those pastors who earlier had taken the bold stand of offering their pulpits to union men after the infamous "Everett Massacre" of 1916 when vigilantes fired into a crowd of workers, who had come up from Seattle to support a local strike, as they stood ready to disembark from the steamer *Verona*. The pastors' actions infuriated many in the business community who succeeded in getting them removed from their churches.

The Methodists were not alone in their growing concern for labor issues. Rabbi Samuel Koch was a member of the Central Conference of American Rabbis' (CCAR) Commission on Social Justice when it prepared a powerful report in 1928 that addressed the nation's social and economic problems and called for reforms that echoed many of those put forward by the Methodists' conferences. Koch had the report and the entire Social Justice Platform of the CCAR printed in the Temple de Hirsch newsletter, *Temple Tidings*. He also twice functioned as an arbiter in labor disputes and was a member of the committee of Washington State ministers that investigated the Centralia affair and recommended the release of I.W.W. prisoners. In works such as these the churches here and nationwide provided much of the groundwork for the economic and social reforms of the New Deal.

Among the churches themselves, there were moves toward greater cooperation that helped pave the way for the ecumenical movement of the 1960s. Examples of this were attempts by sects within denominations to overcome the divisions that separated them. In 1906, for example, most of the Cumberland Presbyterian Church rejoined the Presbyterian Church U.S.A., healing the rift that had divided them for nearly 100 years. In 1920 they were joined by the Welsh Calvinistic Methodist Church. Among Lutherans too, the tide of division that had splintered their denomination had begun to reverse itself. Synods had split and merged in the flux of dispute, but by the 1900s, the move was decidedly toward merger. In 1917 three large Norwegian synods united to form the Evangelical Lutheran Church. A year later other groups combined to form the United Lutheran Church, and by 1930, three German-origin synods succeeded in merging to form the American Lutheran Church.

Moves toward union also absorbed the attention of Methodist sects, who together made up the largest religious group in the state. In the middle 1920s, the Methodist Episcopal Church and the Methodist

Episcopal Church, South, divided since the Civil War, voted on a plan of union with the Methodist Protestant Church. Unfortunately, the southern Methodists balked over the issue of blacks in the congregation, and agreement was stymied. In 1930, however, the plan was revived, and in May, 1939, the three sects merged to form the Methodist Church.

As these moves took place within denominations, cooperation facilitated relations between them. In 1916, for example, the Congregational Church withdrew from the Cascade Mountain town of Index in favor of the Presbyterian Church which bought the church property and held services there. In Olympia, Presbyterians, Congregationalists and the United Churches cooperated to develop a federated church in which all the denominations contributed toward expenses. In Ridgefield, near Vancouver, Presbyterians and Methodist Episcopal church members formed a federated church that was served by a Methodist Episcopal pastor. During the construction of Grand Coulee Dam in the early 1930s, a community church serving at least a dozen denominations was organized at Mason City, which later became the town of Coulee Dam.

Twentieth century pioneering as the church follows construction workers to the Grand Coulee Dam. The Mason City Community Church Junior Choir (1940)

Courtesy the personal papers of Reverend D.E. Peterson.

One of the more notable cooperative efforts among denominations was the United Protestant Church organized in Richland in 1944 through the efforts of the Seattle Council of Churches and the Washington and Northern Idaho Council of Churches. To serve the community of more than 30,000 that had grown up around the atomic energy facility at Hanford, the government built two churches, one for Catholics and one for Protestants. Under the plan devised by the councils, Protestants of all denominations could belong to the Richland church without giving up their denominational affiliation. Funds were prorated among the cooperating denominations, and ministers served turns as pastors.

Efforts such as these to develop community, union or federated churches were not always successful, but in a region where people cared less about theological differences than the basic Christian message their denominations shared, they made economic sense, especially in straitened times.

Beyond the interests of economy, many denominations cooperated to pursue common goals. This had been true nationally and regionally since the days of the ABCFM missions, in the campaigns for abolition and temperance and in support of organizations like the Y.M.C.A. and Y.W.C.A., but in the new century, local institutions arose to address local needs. In 1902, lay people east and west of the mountains seeking to promote Sunday School work organized the Western Washington Sunday School Association and the Inland Empire Sunday School Association. Another interdenominational group and possibly the oldest continuous ecumenical body in the state was the Seattle Japanese Christian Church Federation, the "Seattle Nikkei Kirisuto Kyohkai Dohmei," organized in 1912, that brought together Japanese Baptist, Methodist, Presbyterian, Congregational and Episcopal churches in cooperative work.

The most influential of these cooperative associations was the Seattle Federation of Churches, the ancestor of today's Church Council of Greater Seattle. In 1918 Dr. Roy Guild, representing the Commission of Interchurch Federation, the ancestor of the National Council of Churches, worked with the Reverend James E. Crowther of First Methodist Church of Seattle to organize the Seattle Federation. Interdenominational federations of churches were being organized in Los Angeles, San Francisco and Portland at the time, and on July 19, 1919, the first meeting of the Seattle Federation was called. Although only one person attended, the idea caught on, and soon over sixty-two congregations met to approve the Federation's new constitution. These represented Baptist, Christian, Congregational, Evangelical, Episcopal, Federated, Free Methodist, Lutheran, Methodist Episcopal, Methodist Protestant, Presbyterian, United Brethren and United Presbyterian churches.

In spite of serious financial problems, the Federation continued to grow. It was closely associated with the Washington—North Idaho Council of Christian Education (the body born from the merger of the Western Washington and Inland Empire Sunday School Associations) sharing staff members in the same building, and in 1930 the secretary of both organizations, the Reverend Gertrude Apel, became the Federation's Executive Secretary. Under her skillful leadership the Federation's members overcame onerous differences and learned to work together effectively. Reorganized as the Seattle Council of Churches, their reputation inspired other groups to join them. In 1934 the Council of Christian Education merged, and they were followed by the Seattle Federation of Women in 1936. When the Interdenominational Ministerial Association joined in 1937, the Council became the largest and most influential religious organization in the Northwest.

As denominations increased their cooperative efforts, however, church members who held liberal theological and social views moved further apart from those whose views were more conservative. This had been the case since the time of Beecher and Rauschenbusch, but it was exasercbated at the turn of the century by the controversy over the application of modern methods of historical criticism to scripture. Accepting the analyses of critics, liberals allowed that much of scripture was myth and allegory, whereas conservatives stoutly maintained their belief in its literal truth and its basis in Divine inspiration. Many conservatives had also come to reject what they regarded as the excesses of the Social Gospel Movement: the substitution of sociology for theology, of secularism for spirituality. They sought, instead, a return to what they regarded as the fundamentals of Christianity.

Because of the region's youth, its isolation and its sparse population, organized religion in the Northwest remained a relatively unsophisticated affair with practical concerns. Its few seminaries existed to train ministers rather than serve as centers of theological inquiry. An emphasis upon familial values and personal piety gave Northwestern religion a distinctly conservative tone that colored its involvement in secular affairs. Locally, the pre-eminent conservative critic of liberal "modernists" was Mark Matthews. A figure of national consequence in 1915, he threw himself into an unsuccessful effort to purge modernist theologians from the prestigious Union Theological Seminary of New York. Yet, while theological disputes between liberals and conservatives might have excited clerics, the laity remained largely uninvolved. What involved them more were disputes over public morality. Thomas Jessett recalled one such dispute that took place in eastern Washington.

In the spring of 1927 the young people of the Church of the Good Samaritan in Colfax, where I was the lay-minister, came to me with a problem. The school board, badgered by the Methodist, Baptist, Assembly of God and Christian ministers, had banned all high school dances, except the Senior Prom. They were now pressing to have this abolished. I told the young people, who were among the school leaders, to tell the superintendent that if this were done, the Episcopal Church would sponsor the Senior Prom. The school board retreated, but got even with me by refusing the request of the Senior Class that I be invited to deliver the baccalaurate [sic] sermon.

Much was stirring the churches during the 1920s and 1930s, a time marked by upheaval around the world, and although events might take place far away, some had direct impact on churches here. Revolution in Russia, for example, brought strife to local Russian Orthodox churches. Shortly after the Bolsheviks came to power in Russia, they began a systematic persecution of organized religion. As part of their plan to dominate the Russian Orthodox Church, the new Soviet government supported the creation of the so-called "Living Church," a group led by Orthodox clergy who supported the regime. Abroad, representatives of the Living Church laid claim to Russian Orthodox Church property. After a six-week court suit in Seattle in 1931, Living Church representative Father Vladimir Alexandrov gained possession of the St. Spiridon church and rectory, but the congregation fled, taking with them icons and altar pieces which they hid in nearby St. Barnabas' Episcopal Church. Aided by the Episcopal Church, the Orthodox continued to hold services at St. Barnabas' as a member church of the Orthodox Metropolia, the ancestor of today's Orthodox Church in America, which sought to retain ties with the Patriarch of Moscow.

Not all of the congregation remained at St. Barnabas', however. Following the call of the Russian Church in Exile, which regarded the elections of Moscow Patriarchs after 1925 as invalid, about half of the congregation moved to an empty storefront on nearby Capitol

Hill. There they organized a new parish, St. Nicholas, named in honor of the late Tsar whom they revered as a martyr. Both parishes raced to build their own churches. On December 19, 1937, the exquisite St. Nicholas memorial temple was blessed, and six months later, the elegant, nine-domed St. Spiridon's church building was consecrated, both having been designed by the same architect, M.I. Pavlov.

A division of another kind occurred within many local churches after 1924 when Congress halted Japanese immigration into the country. It was but one of a long list of legal restraints and actions that had been taken against Japanese immigrants along the West Coast, and like the rest, it served to heighten feelings against them and widen the gulf separating them from the rest of society. Consequently, the ties binding Japanese congregations to their respective denominations weakened as relations between the United States and Japan worsened.

One outside of the Japanese community who saw the dangers of this happening and worked to bridge the growing rift was Floyd Schmoe, a forestry Professor at the University of Washington and Clerk at the Society of Friends Meeting in Seattle. He took a three month leave of absence from his post at the university to study the problem in Hawaii and published his findings and reflections in an article, "Pregnant with Disaster," that appeared in the February, 1940 issue of *Fellowship*. In it, he challenged the churches and the larger community to reach out to Japanese Americans as neighbors and friends in order to prevent a calamity.

What can be done about it? The problem is immensely difficult but we must not consider it hopeless. We can give it thought and study... Understanding is certain to increase goodwill. Goodwill is essential to any solution. It is already late to begin but there is no earlier starting point.

Sadly, events overtook the effort.

In spite of the difficulties they had faced, Japanese churches had grown. Buddhist churches developed in innovative ways as their congregations adapted to Western culture, giving their religion a distinctly Western tone. Clerics dressed in western-style robes, held services on Sunday and delivered sermons. Marriage ceremonies were shortened and simplified to more resemble Christian weddings, and in Sunday Schools, children were taught Buddhist hymns in surprising new forms (Buddha loves me, this I know...). In 1936 Tatsuya Ichikawa arrived in Seattle and began to develop youth programs. Until his coming, services had been held in private homes, but he encouraged his congregation to build a temple where they could be celebrated in a more suitable setting. In spite of straitened times, construction went ahead, and the first Buddhist temple in the Northwest was completed in 1940.

Another ethnic group to suffer restrictions like those imposed upon the Japanese were Filipinos. Having acquired the Philippine Islands during the Spanish-American War, the United States gave its new colonial subjects immigration privileges, and by the 1930s, several thousand had settled on the West Coast. Most were men, nominally Catholic or Muslim, and unions rather than churches served as centers of immigrant life. Nevertheless, Filipino missions were carried out by Catholic Maryknoll fathers, who also had a Japanese mission in Seattle, and by several Protestant denominations. As it prepared the way for eventual Philippine independence, Congress bowed to demands for limits on Filipino immigration and passed the Repatriation Act of 1936, which provided one-way tickets to those who wished to return to their home islands.

The contribution of Asia to Washington's religious heritage increased with the appearance of two new faiths, Baha'i and Vedanta, in the first half of the century. In 1905, Tacoma attorney and one-time Adventist preacher, Nathan Ward Fitz-Gerald, returned from a pilgrimage to Acre in Palestine where he had met Adbu'l-Baha, the leader of the Baha'is and son of Baha'u'llah, the prophet-founder of the Baha'i religion. Baha'u'llah taught that there is one God who brings religion to mankind through a series of prophets and that he was the latest of these whose revelations fulfilled Judeo-Christian and Islamic messianic prophesies. Fitz-Gerald gave lectures to large audiences in Seattle and asked the Tacoma Ministerial Association for the opportunity to address it on the topic of the Baha'i faith. The Association gave him only fifteen minutes, but he excited interest among several who attended his lectures. That same year in Tacoma he published one of the first books on the Baha'i faith in the United States, *The New Revelation: Its Marvelous Message,* which announced that the spirit of Christ had returned in the person of Baha'u'llah and the Kingdom of God was at hand.

Some of the first Baha'i meetings in Seattle were held in the home of Wallace Bussel, son of a prominent land speculator, and for several years, Bussell was the treasurer of the Seattle Baha'i Assembly which organized in 1907. Artist Mark Tobey served on the Seattle Assembly, offered his studio for Baha'i public meetings and often spoke at Baha'i functions. Beginning in the 1920s, a black Baha'i, Bob Roberts, promoted interracial meetings in Seattle working with the Mount Zion Baptist Church which sponsored Baha'i lectures.

Spokane Baha'is organized shortly after 1907, and the Baha'i message was carried to other parts of the state and beyond by traveling teachers. Two who attended Fitz-Gerald's lectures, Clara Davis of Walla Walla and John Hyde-Dunn of Seattle, married and introduced the Baha'i faith to Australia. Seattle Baha'i Kenzo Torikai returned to his native Japan in 1916 to spread the Baha'i message and was the first Japanese Baha'i to publish a book on the Faith in Japan.

Vedanta, a philosophical and religious system deriving its inspiration from the Vedas, the sacred Sanskrit books of ancient India, was introduced to the United States through the efforts of Swami Vivekenanda. A disciple of the Indian philosopher Shri Ramakrishna, Vivekenanda attended the World Parliament of Religions in Chicago in 1893, and back in India, organized the Ramakrishna Order to help spread the message of Vedanta to the world. It captured the imagination of many in this country, including Chester Nelson of Everett who invited another monk, Swami Vividishananda, to come to the Northwest from Denver where he had started a Vedanta center. In 1938 Vividishananda came to Seattle and helped organize the Vedanta Society which, in 1942, settled in a home on Capitol Hill.

Like the Baha'is, the members of the Vedanta Society were almost wholly white middle class professionals. In the late 1930s, Washington's East Indian population was very small, although it had once been larger. In the early years of the century, several hundred came to the state primarily as laborers. Like the Chinese, their presence excited fears in white workers who organized exclusion societies and drove them out. The most notorious incident was the riot of September, 1907 in Bellingham when 400 East Indian laborers were driven by a mob from their shanties beside a lumber mill. They and several hundred others driven from other communities fled across the border into British Columbia where a similar fate awaited them. Predominantly Sikh and Muslim men, it is not known whether they formed any religious associations, and more than sixty years were to pass before others like them were able to do so.

The appearance of the Spiritual Assemblies of the Baha'is and the Vedanta Society reflected the growing cosmopolitanism of the Northwest as well as a marked religious volatility among its citizens. Increasing numbers of people, disturbed by the tumult of the time and unsatisfied by analyses of it provided by secular institutions or traditional Western religions looked elsewhere for answers. Eastern religions satisfied some, while others were attracted to local cults such as the Seventh Elect Church in Spiritual Israel founded in 1920 by Daniel Salwt. Its followers believed Salwt to be the reincarnation of Jesus Christ, who, they also believed, had appeared in history in the guise of several famous figures including Alexander the Great, Martin Luther and George Washington. In 1929 the eighty-four year-old Salwt died, but his followers refused to give his body up, hoping to see him rise again. When he did not, several sued the church to retrieve the money they had contributed to it. A sensational trial followed, and newspapers focused their attention upon the figure of Eva Falk Firpo, described as the "long-haired priestess" of the cult and Salwt's lover. The Church won the case in 1932, but the issue was brought to court again in 1934 and again in 1980. In spite of the rancor, a small group of followers remained loyal to Salwt's memory.

The coverage of this and other sensationalized events served to divert minds from the economic hardships of the 1930s, which were no kinder to the churches than to the rest of the state and nation. During the Great Depression, congregations shrank, cleric's salaries were slashed, programs were cut back or eliminated, and some churches were closed and abandoned. Church-run hospitals and schools struggled to survive, and in their drafty convents, many sisters went hungry so that those they served could eat.

The problems were so intense and pervasive that private institutions could do little more than offer handouts. Dr. Dale Soden, Mark Matthew's biographer, writes that the otherwise fiery and resourceful minister seemed stunned by the scale and longevity of the suffering. By 1933 the crisis was so severe that the Social Committee of the Columbia River Conference of the Methodist Episcopal Church called for the common ownership of natural resources and the means of production. These had been the radical goals of the I.W.W. whose espousal two decades before had horrified church leaders. In 1936 the new Catholic Archbishop of Seattle, Gerald Shaughnessy, organized his archdiocese's department of Catholic Charities. In August of that year, the National Conference of Catholic Charities held its twenty-second Annual Meeting in Seattle where thousands heard Washington Governor Clarence Martin and Seattle Mayor Fred Dore reiterate the need for action. Most denominations were hard pressed to help their own, but a few such as the Salvation Army and its offshoot, the Volunteers of America, made it their goal to help whomever they could.

Following the example of these last two groups who provided work and relief to the poor through the sale of second-hand goods, the Catholic St. Vincent De Paul Society established salvage bureaus in several Washington cities. The largest and most famous of these was the one in Seattle, organized by the remarkable Peter Emt in 1926, which provided aid to tens of thousands of needy people during the Depression.

The times radicalized many. Dismissed from Seattle's Pilgrim Congregation for his outspoken criticism of war and social indifference, the Reverend Fred W. Shorter organized the Church of the People in the University District. Shorter had been instrumental in having the Federal Council of Churches investigate the Centralia trials, and from his pulpit, he actively confronted the problems of the day and sought solutions. He sponsored weekly forums where troublesome issues could be debated, and speakers at his church included luminaries such as Norman Thomas, Anna Louise Strong and British labor leader Harold Laski. His weekly church paper, *The New Religious Frontier,* focused attention on local, national and international examples of racial discrimination, abuse of the poor and suppression of free speech. It drew a national audience and prompted one Midwestern minister to

The anti-war murals, partly responsible for Fred Shorter's being voted out of the Pilgrim Congregational Church and forming his Church of the People.

Courtesy of Chester Kingsbury's personal papers.

The New Religious Frontier

Issued by The Church of the People, 4033 University Way, Seattle, Wash.
FRED W. SHORTER, WALTER R. HUNDLEY, *Ministers.* Subscription Two Dollars a Year.

Vol. 19 No. 1   September 22, 1955

"HOME BUILDERS face Crisis in Northwest" was an item buried on the gardening page of the Sunday TIMES, an issue devoted to the "Parade of Homes". Amid some 50 pages of advertising of super-duper new developments on easy credit terms were these startling statements. There is a money shortage. There were quotes from the outstanding builders that "they will never build another home and are liquidating their assets and commercial interests." One builder cited eight prospective purchasers for a home, each of whom could arrange a small down payment, but ALL of whom were turned down by financial institutions as "poor risks". The Mountlake Terrace developer said he is tired of trying to operate a "private enterprise" that is as completely controlled as the building industry.

All this indicates that "Suburbia", developed by private enterprise and sold on credit will not answer the problem of housing that under-

MORRIS RUBIN, editor of The Progressive, in discussing the change in the international climate, says he believes "we are moving through the most significant, and perhaps the most decisive, development in our lifetime." It presents, we might add, a special challenge to pacifists. This period of relaxation of tension must be used to bring home the fact that more than conferences and banquets and visitation are necessary if the tensions are not to arise again and perhaps in a more virulent form. As Alfred Hassler, editor of Fellowship, says, the basic economic and political causes of war must be dealt with.

PUBLIC POWER will be a hot election issue especially here in the Pacific Northwest. Since some of us might get into arguments about the pros and cons of public power we might do well to keep this in mind: TVA is now debt-free. This year it paid off and retired its remaining

Fred Shorter's Church of the People newsletter The New Religions Frontier.

Courtesy of Chester Kingsbury's personal papers.

write, "Every week I read your sheet of uplift and protest and feel an admiration for the man and institution that stay right out there on the firing line all of the time." It was indicative of Shorter's progressivism that in 1940, when there were 553 birth control clinics operating in the United States, the only one in Washington was that run by the Church of the People. Commenting on criticism of their church's support of birth control, Shorter's wife, Billie, observed wryly, "The only ones agin' dancing are those who can't."

Not all church leaders had the Shorters' plentitude of spirit. Many considered the 1933 repeal of Prohibition to be a terrible defeat, although most accepted the fact that Prohibition was unenforceable. Locally, they grimly continued to support "blue" laws that banned the sale of liquor on Sundays and kept businesses closed. If, as many believed, America was "the nation with the soul of a church," then it was possible to imagine the defeat of a cause so just as the work of sinister, anti-American forces. In the thickets of delusion, there was a search for scapegoats.

Thomas Jessett recalled an episode when the Episcopal Bishop of Spokane, Edward Cross, invited a European professor to address the

Spokane Summer School.

> *This professor insisted that Europe's and the world's problems were all due to the Jews, who were the instigators and propagators of Communism. This and the bishop's admiration for Mussolini made me skeptical of him, in spite of his great abilities.*

The professor was not the only one to entertain such ideas. The rise of National Socialism in Germany and the restoration of the German economy, albeit at the expense of civil liberties, excited many Lutherans and Catholics of German background, although their enthusiasm cooled when German armies invaded Poland in 1939 and Norway in 1940. On the radio, Catholic demagogue Father Charles Coughlin blamed Jewish financiers for leading America toward war. With faith in reasoned debate, Jews protested these slanders, so cruel to those who knew what was happening inside Adolph Hitler's Germany.

When Hitler assumed dictatorial powers in 1933, he began the brutal and systematic persecution of Jews, inaugurating a program aimed at their eventual destruction. Many fled, and congregations in the United States undertook efforts to receive them. In Seattle the Council of Jewish Women sent members to meet ships carrying refugees enroute from Vladivostok. After the war broke out in Europe, President Roosevelt closed ports in the eastern United States to refugees, and Seattle became the major port of entry on the West Coast.

As the plight of European Jewry became more ominous, several church leaders were moved to protest. During World War I, Mark Matthews accused Jews of supporting government subversion, but Hitler's actions horrified him. "The idea of confiscating the properties of Jews," he declared in a sermon, "then herding them like cattle across the borders of a country, is indescribably corrupt and hellish." One hopes he would have been equally vehement denouncing what the American government was about to do to Japanese-Americans, but he died in February, 1940.

The shock and anger generated by the Japanese surprise attack on Pearl Harbor on December 7, 1941, and the onset of war placed Japanese-Americans in a dangerous situation. Along with others, church leaders counseled calm, and many pointed out the need to treat Japanese-Americans with justice and humanity. In a sermon delivered shortly after Pearl Harbor, Rabbi Koch urged his congregation to act with good will.

Japan has gone beserk... But one admonition seems necessary. There are many aliens on the coast—especially Japanese. The great majority of them are highly commended for their Americanism... They are anxious to remain good Americans... We should remind ourselves that the American way is tolerant, sympathetic, cooperative. Let's be on our guard to treat all Americans as Americans.

In an official Pastoral Letter, printed in *The Catholic Northwest Progress* on December 12 and read at all Masses in his archdiocese on December 14, Archbishop Shaughnessy reminded Catholics of their Christian duty.

Our Catholic heritage especially inculcates us in these momentous hours that we embrace our fellow American citizens of Japanese extraction in a special bond of charity, for they who are no less loyal than others, and no less claimants of true American citizenship and of all rights thereunder, need our sympathy and our love in Christ, innocent victims, as in many cases they will be, of antipathies and unreasoning prejudices.

Even before war broke out, the government had collected information enumerating and locating Japanese residents on the West Coast from the Bureau of the Census. Hours after the attack on Pearl Harbor, the F.B.I. arrested hundreds of Japanese community leaders including all Buddhist and Shinto clergy. In February 1942, Congress passed Executive Order 9066 designating much of the West Coast a restricted area from which Japanese-Americans were to be removed.

The order did not go unprotested. Fred Shorter vehemently opposed it in the pages of *The New Religious Frontier.* A resolution supporting the removal of Japanese-Americans presented at a meeting of the Olympia Rotary Club met with vigorous opposition from Thomas Jessett who prevented it from being adopted. When General DeWitt, the military officer in charge of the removals, visited Seattle to observe their progress, he was confronted by the Reverend Newton E. Motts of the Seattle First Methodist Church who protested the action. Taken aback, DeWitt averred that he represented the authority of the President of the United States. Undaunted, Mott replied, "Sir, I represent a higher authority."

Such protests had little effect, however, and ultimately some 112,000 Japanese-Americans—13,400 from Washington—were removed to relocation and internment camps. Shorter, Jessett and Motts were not the only religious leaders to protest this massive and, as it proved, unnecessary violation of civil rights, yet others remained silent or approved. "Some of the strongest pulpit preachers of the west coast," wrote the Reverend Lester Suzuki, a Methodist minister who carried out his pastoral duties while incarcerated, "were not vocal in their utterances against the injustice of the evacuation." In the camps, Buddhist ministers were not permitted the privileges enjoyed by Christian clergy. And because they were members of the state religion in Japan, Shinto priests were barred from holding services at all. Nevertheless, churches remained active in the camps and were one of the few links the imprisoned had with the outside world. The impression one receives reading the reminiscences of evacuees is that of the few Caucasians that helped them in the camps and during their release, most came from the denominations that had ties with Japanese congregations.

One of the crueler ironies of the evacuation was that Japanese-Americans were kept in the camps more than two years after the government determined that the West Coast was no longer in danger of attack. Many church leaders called repeatedly for their release, and some were finally allowed out in 1945. Even victory did not lessen the hostility many felt toward them, however, and church leaders joined with others to protest anti-Japanese meetings and rallies that were organized to prevent their return. Many denominations sought to help their Japanese-American members reestablish themselves, and the Society of Friends and United Brethren helped as many as they could whether or not they were affiliated with any group.

The Japanese-Americans had not been treated as the Jews were by the Nazis, but there was a disturbing parallel in the fact that in both cases the state had decided the fate of an entire population. Japanese-Americans could observe with dark humor that they shared with native Americans the dubious distinction of having been administered by the Department of the Interior. The extraordinary growth of government in the 1930s and 1940s, and its capacity to intrude into the lives of citizens was something new in American life, and it was a problem the churches would have to confront in the post-war period.

At the end of World War II, the nation entered a period of accelerating and often bewildering change. Quickly, the euphoria of victory gave way to a building sense of anxiety as the United States and the Soviet Union, wartime allies, became increasingly deadly enemies. As they armed themselves with the weapons of Armageddon, the world divided into hostile camps. Paradoxically, as it was troubled by visions of the Apocalypse, the nation experienced an unprecedented economic boom and enjoyed unrivaled affluence. In Washington, economic growth was matched by growth in population and church membership. The 1950 census enumerated 1,378,963 people in the state, of whom approximately thirty-four percent belonged to a church—considerably above the twenty percent of 1910. In 1960 the census counted 2,853,214 and church membership approached forty percent of total.

The greatest growth took place in the suburbs where new congregations undertook energetic building programs. Church buildings sprouted like mushrooms on the outskirts of town or in housing projects, often in new, contemporary designs. As the baby boom generation reached school age, there was a boom in school construction as well. Virtually every denomination offered classes in Bible study and religious training, and Catholics, Lutherans and Seventh-day Adventists continued in their efforts to develop a complete program of education for their children, from kindergarten to college. Although not numerically large, the Adventists had succeeded in building a system that served the majority of their children. Much of the work was begun in this century. By the 1960s, their Walla Walla College in the town of College Place received students from a secondary school there and from others in Battleground, Auburn, and Spangle. These in turn drew students from a host of Adventist primary schools. Adventists also moved boldly into health care, opening Walla Walla General Hospital in Walla Walla and numerous clinics throughout the state.

The churches' impulse toward conservative morality continued to manifest itself, in vigorous efforts to censor books and films. They lost the battle to retain Sunday closure laws, but were effective in killing a statewide referendum to legalize gambling. They took a stand for clean government, morality in public life and strong families, issues few would care to debate.

On the more contentious political and social issues of the day, there was less consensus. Regarding American relations with the Soviet Union, the Social Service Committee of the Methodist's Columbia River Conference fretted in 1946, "We do not profess to know the answer. We are opposed to appeasement, we are equally opposed to steps which will involve us in war with her." More positively, they declared, "we are convinced that within these limits peaceful solutions can be evolved." In the "Red Scare" that followed, many church leaders chose to follow rather than lead. A few such as Fred Shorter and several Unitarian pastors provided forums for debate, but some of the loudest anti-Communist voices arose from the churches, nationally from preachers like the Reverend Carl McIntire, head of the ultra-conservative American Council of Christian Churches, and the Reverend Billy James Hargis, or, from those involved in ephemeral movements such as the Reverend James W. Fifield Jr.'s Spiritual Mobilization and Dr. Fred C. Schwarz's Christian Anti-Communist Crusade.

Churches were involved more positively with the issue of civil rights. Locally, several denominations had taken public stands against racial discrimination, and during the war, they were involved in efforts to eliminate restrictions on blacks entering the labor force and to provide housing for immigrant black workers. They met with only limited success, however, and it would be long after the war when more effective actions could be taken against such discriminatory practices as restrictive housing ordinances, and only after blacks led the way. After segregation became a national issue, the Seattle Council of Churches was influential in local efforts to eliminate discrimination in public facilities and led efforts to end discrimination in its member churches.

Another positive development commanding public attention was the continuing effort of the churches to heal the rifts dividing them and achieve greater unity. Among Lutherans, for example, the Lutheran World Federation, organized in Uppsala, Sweden in 1946, enabled synods and sects to cooperate more fully with one another. In this country the desire for unity led in 1960 to the merger of the American Lutheran Church (German background), the Evangelical Lutheran Church (Norwegian) and the United Evangelical Lutheran Church (Danish), creating the American Lutheran Church, which was joined in 1963 by the Lutheran Free Church (Norwegian). In 1962 the Augustana Synod (Swedish), the United Lutheran Church in America, the Suomi Synod (Finnish) and the Danish Evangelical Lutheran Church in America merged to form the Lutheran Church in America. The most recent merger in 1987 has brought the American Lutheran Church, the Lutheran Church in America and the Association of Evangelical Lutheran Churches—an offshoot of the conservative Missouri Synod—together to create the Evangelical Lutheran Church in America.

These mergers were especially significant in the Northwest, but even more interest was attached to ecumenical conversations between Protestants, Catholics and Jews. The most significant example of this development was the production of the popular and award-winning television show, "Challenge."

This was the inspiration of Rabbi Raphael E. Levine, Rabbi Koch's successor at Temple De Hirsch. In 1952, Levine had an idea for a television show featuring local Protestant, Catholic and Jewish clergy discussing timely issues from a religious perspective. It would be, he hoped, a way to combat religious intolerance and promote inter-faith understanding, but the new Catholic Archbishop of Seattle, Thomas J. Connolly, declined his church's participation, arguing, according to Levine, that such a program would promote religious indifferentism.

The nomination of John Kennedy in 1960 as the democratic candidate for the Presidency excited anxiety in many who feared the election of a Catholic to the highest office in the land. In the Northwest, a group calling itself Protestants And Others United For America spoke out loudly against it. In his Seattle office, Levine received a number of calls from those fearful of the same thing. Concerned, he resurrected his earlier idea. With backing from KOMO TV of Seattle, he invited the Reverend Martin Goslin of Plymouth Congregational

The KOMO Television Challenge Panel. Standing, Reverend Martin Goslin, to his left Rabbi Raphael Levine and to his right Father William Treacy.

Courtesy of Garry Darragh, KOMO-TV Tape Librarian, Seattle, Washington.

Church to participate, and once again approached Archbishop Connolly. This time, Connolly agreed to the proposal and selected Father William Treacy to be the Catholic member of the panel.

The ground rules the panelists agreed upon reflected the tensions of the time: there were to be no arguments about theology, no baiting of one another, and the issues discussed would be those of common concern to all three and their respective denominations. At first the three were defensive—none wished to lose points—but they quickly found that they could be open and candid with one another.

"Can We Have a Catholic President?" aired in September, 1960, and the show rapidly gained a wide audience. The program aired on Palm Sunday, 1961, "Who Crucified Jesus?," confronted the issue of anti-Semitism and won an award from the National Association of Christians and Jews. To see representatives of faiths that shared a long and bitter history of antagonism discussing the issues dividing them in a lively, rational and amiable manner was extraordinary. The show lasted fourteen years. Interestingly, because the Protestant panelist was changed regularly in order to represent several denominations, Levine and Treacy became the show's dominant personalities. The rapport and affection that developed between them was celebrated, and when Treacy asked Levine to carve an altar for his new parish, St. Patrick's, its installation was a national media event, and became a symbol of reconciliation.

Much had made all of this possible, not the least of which was the new openness of the Catholic Church which emerged with the accession of Pope John XXIII in 1959, and bloomed dramatically in the Second Vatican council. Torpid under his predecessor, the Church came to life in Pope John's papacy, and its opening toward other faiths elicited from them an equally generous and enthusiastic response.

This was historically important, and in Washington as elsewhere in the world, Catholics came to work with their Protestant and Jewish colleagues rather than at some distance beside them. In another positive development, the general sympathy in this country for the victims of the Holocaust and popular enthusiasm for the new nation of Israel helped to improve relations with Jews. Because of these things, Rabbi Levine's inspiration was able to elevate the three faiths into a position of moral influence in the community that they could not have achieved alone. With a heightened image and enhanced credibility, the churches were able to play an important part in the racial and social turmoil of the 1960s.

Throughout the state, black churches had striven to combat discrimination and promote civil rights, but given the massive indifference of the white community, their accomplishments had been minimal. For a time, black militants derided the black churches' apparent ineffectiveness, but the influence of national figures like Dr. Martin Luther King and the presence of dynamic local church leadership induced many critics to regard the churches as allies rather than obstacles.

Black churches were also important as places where whites could approach the black community on some degree of common ground. The ties uniting blacks and whites in Methodist and Baptist churches provided an important avenue of communication and helped in developing a concensus among churchmembers about what should be done to improve race relations. In the 1940s and 1950s, volunteer inter-racial groups such as Christian Friends For Racial Equality performed a similar service. In the 1960s the Seattle Church Council became more involved along with Catholic and Jewish groups. Programs like CURE, "Churches United For Racial Equality," helped to get an open housing ordinance passed in Seattle, and the Church Council played a crucial role in the effort to desegregate the city's schools. The importance of black churches was underscored during the 1977 Seattle mayoral campaign when candidate Charles Royer made a visit to the Mount Zion Baptist Church. During the service, the Reverend Samuel McKinney announced to his congregation, "the next mayor of Seattle is worshiping here this morning." It was good politics on Royer's part, since it recognized the influence of black churches and their unique role in the community.

An institutional innovation that made the Seattle Church Council more effective in this challenging period was the Denominational Executive Advisory Committee, formed in 1963, in which church leaders gathered together at regular intervals to discuss problems and assess progress in dealing with them. The leadership the committee provided helped guide the churches through the turmoil that attended American involvement in the Vietnam War.

Strong feelings for and against American involvement in the war polarized churches as they did the rest of American society, and clerics risked splitting their congregations if they spoke out for or against it. Pacifist denominations such as the Society of Friends, United Brethren, Mennonites and Jehovah's Witnesses opposed the war on principle. Methodists and Baptists supported the principle of conscientious objection, but many within these and other denominations had also spoken out strongly against the spread of Communism. The war posed a cruel dilemma: some of the clergy defended it; others counselled youth on draft-resistence boards. The religious convictions of Baptist Alice Franklin Bryant led her to run twice against Senator Henry Jackson on the issue of the war, and she could often be found at the head of protest marches.

The polarization brought about by the war helped speed the division of churches into liberal and conservative camps. In the Northwest, the division reflected something of the region's conservative bias. Regarding the Protestant clergy, Methodist Reverend William Cate writes:

Most young ministers taking churches in the Northwest in the last 30 years, in the established churches, have been trained in the seminaries of the East, Midwest or at the seminaries in California staffed by Eastern trained scholars. The Fundamentalists have been largely trained in local Bible schools or nationally known fundamentalist colleges.

The division was also a sign of spiritual disquiet in many Northwesterners, and of the rootless character of modern Northwestern life. Long associated with rural people, conservative churches have become increasingly attractive in the suburbs and cities where the socially isolated appreciate the conservative churches unequivocal message and appeal to the emotions. Like ethnic churches, the conservative churches often provide believers with a sense of community and sharing they no longer find in more liberal churches.

The division between liberals and conservatives reshuffled many denominations as conservative members joined conservative churches or developed ties with growing radio and television ministries. This reshuffling affected Catholics and Jews as well as Protestants and coincided with a falling-off of membership in traditional mainline churches. As a result, while the percentage of the state's residents belonging to a church shrank during the 1970s, it also appeared to become more conservative. This shift in character, however, was muted by the fact that, in spite of their growth, conservative congregations were unable to develop a strong, unified voice, while liberal churches continued their efforts to work cooperativley.

The religious flux of the period was further complicated by the fact that many people sought association with new, often esoteric groups such as the Church of Scientology, the Aquarian Foundation, the International Society for Krishna Consciousness and Sokka Gakkai Buddhism. Others sought to form their own churches, for example, the Church of Armageddon, headquartered in Seattle.

These were almost exclusively urban phenomena, attracting disenchanted members of the middle class, but the Northwest also saw growth in denominations such as the Seventh-day Adventists, who emphasized health and vegetarianism, in Christian Science and among the Mormons because of their strong emphasis upon family life and community. The construction of the Mormon Temple in Bellevue in the 1970s, the first temple in the Northwest, signaled the arrival of this denomination to a position of prominence within the state.

Another reflection of increasing disenchantment with public and secular institutions was the growth of enrollments at private religious schools even as the number of children in the total population declined. Many new schools were organized and supported by conservative groups of believers who did not like what they identified as the humanistic content of the public school curriculum. Within the Catholic school system at this time, a decline in the numbers of teachers available from religious orders required the schools to hire more expensive lay teachers with the result that tuitions increased dramatically.

The Northwest also continued to attract groups who, like the early settlers, were attracted by the fertile soil and a liberal attitude toward religion. This was true of Russian pietist sects such as the Dukhobors in British Columbia and the "Old Believers" who settled in Oregon's Willamette Valley after World War II, and it is true of the Hutterites, the followers of a religious movement founded in the sixteenth century by the Swiss Anabaptist, Jakob Hutter. In 1961 the Hutterites, who much resemble the Amish and traditional Mennonites in their conservative ways, established their first agricultural colony in Washington at Reardon, fifteen miles east of Spokane. Later, three other colonies were established, one near Odessa in Lincoln County and two others in Grant County.

Meanwhile, new ethnic groups were adding their cultural weight to the state's religious heritage. Of the more recently arrived groups, the ones with the longest history in the region are those of Hispanic origin. Their first representative in Washington was Alferez Manuel Quimper who raised the cross at Neah Bay in 1790. They were present in all periods of the Northwest's history, but they did not arrive in force until the 1930s when Chicanos—American citizens of Hispanic background—began to move into the agricultural regions of Washington. Predominantly Catholic, they nevertheless attracted the attention of several Protestant denominations which carried out missions among them and organized several congregations. Many remained in the Catholic fold, however, and that church's heirarchy scrambled to find priests and religious to serve them in Spanish as well as English. Taking up the issues of poverty and exploitation on behalf of migrant workers, many of whom were Hispanic, church leaders and workers were also led to focus on the problematic relations between the United States and Latin American countries which in many cases had driven Hispanic immigrants from their homelands.

Another group to appear here were Koreans. As a result of the Korean War and this country's growing relationship with the Republic of South Korea, many Koreans began to emigrate here in the 1960s. Catholics and several Protestant denominations had organized missions in Korea, and several were carried out here among immigrants, resulting in the development of several Korean congregations. From Korea itself came the ministry of the Reverend Sun Myung Moon, a Presbyterian minister who in 1954 founded the Unification Church, a new Christian denomination that promoted disciplined communal living. The church's Holy Spirit Association for the Unification of World Christianity won many converts in Korea, Japan and the United States, but criticism of the church's methods of recruitment and the arrest and imprisonment of Dr. Moon in this country on tax evasion charges slowed its rapid growth.

Although small in number, another Asian group to make a religious impact locally were Tibetan refugees fleeing the Communist Chinese takeover and subjection of Tibet. One of those who came to Seattle was H. H. Jigdal Dagchen Sakya Rinpoche, a high official in the Tibetan government and head lama of the Sakya sect of Tibetan Buddhism, who was invited to the University of Washington in 1960 to help develop its East Asian Studies Department (begun earlier by Episcopal priest and scholar, the Reverend Herbert Henry Gowen). In 1974 he and the Venerable Dezhung Rinpoche founded the Sakya Tegchen Choling, the Center for the Study of Vajrayana Buddhism and Tibetan Culture in Seattle. A nearby church was purchased and converted into a Sakya monastery in 1984. A branch of this monastery was also organized in Olympia. The Center and the monastery have become important sites in the United States for the study, transmission and dissemination of Vajrayana Buddhism which, like Zen Buddhism, appeals to many because of its emphasis upon meditation.

Other groups to make a recent religious contribution to the Northwest are its Middle-Eastern immigrants, most of whom come from Islamic backgrounds. Many came as students to attend schools and universities, others as professionals to work in the region's industries. One who arrived in Seattle in the late 1950s to work for the Boeing Company was Jamil Abdul Razzak. In 1974, he helped open the first Muslim gathering place in the south Seattle community of Burien, and later he played an important part in the building of the North Seattle Mosque. Completed in 1981, it was the first Muslim mosque west of the Mississippi River to be built in a Middle-Eastern design.

Construction of this edifice was made difficult by tensions that arose when Shi'ite Muslim militants held fifty Americans hostage in Iran. Islam gained high visibility in this country as a result, albeit in an undesirable fashion, and Muslims like Abdul Razzak felt the weight of hostility much as Buddhist and Shinto congregations had during the war. The mosque in Seattle was built with money donated by Saudi Arabian Sheik Abdel-Keder Idriss, but while it is unique in style, it is only one of several Muslim places of worship that have grown up in the greater Seattle area, in Tacoma, Pullman and the Tri-Cities.

The mosque with its tall brick minaret near Seattle's Northgate shopping mall is one more visual example of how religion serves to create a sense of community. Not all Middle-Eastern immigrants are Muslim, of course. Many Baha'i immigrants from Iran have been integrated into local Baha'i communities, while Maronite Christians from Lebanon and Coptic Christians from Egypt and Ethiopia have joined congregations or developed their own. They join other recent newcomers like Vietnamese, Cambodians, Laotians, Samoans, Russian Jews and Latvians who have organized their own congregations or joined others, which, as they always have, provide refuge in a strange land while they open doors to a new life.

Finally, we must return to that first community, to the native peoples of the state who continue to treasure their ancient religious traditions and adapt them to ever-changing conditions. Even today, many people continue to believe that the native people would do themselves a favor if they simply assimilated themselves out of sight and became like everyone else. When the construction of huge dams on the Columbia River inundated burial grounds and sacred sites, the native people protested, but their protests generally went unheeded or were regarded as unprogressive. These attitudes on the part of the white majority began to change in the 1960s, however, as movements celebrating native pride developed at a time of widespread concern over environmental problems.

One such problem, a declining fishery resource, exacerbated the conflict that had grown up between native groups and state agencies and sport fishermen. In their efforts to examine the problem and seek ways to resolve it, the American Friends Service Committee put together a report which gave considerable attention to native views. Nothing so significant or comprehensive had appeared on the topic, and in 1967 it was published by the National Congress of American Indians. Three years later a revised version appeared as *Uncommon Controversy: Fishing Rights of Muckleshoot, Puyallup and Nisqually Indians,* a book that did much to increase public awareness of this long-festering problem.

When so much in American life seemed spiritually bankrupt, many native people and not a few whites took a renewed interest in native spirituality and its deep regard for the natural world. In Seattle this rekindled interest led to the development of the Daybreak Star Arts and Culture Center. In Toppenish it led to the development of the Yakima Nation Cultural Center, and in Spokane to the remarkable Museum of Native American Cultures, one of the finest native American museums in the West, and largely the work of a single man, Jesuit Father Wilfred Schoenberg. Like black churches, these centers help celebrate the native heritage and provide common ground where non-natives can approach the native community and come to a more sensitive understanding of it.

East of the mountains native religious leaders continued to call their people to honor the ancient customs in the old ways, and west of the mountains, interest in spirit dancing revived. This was most notable among the Nooksacks and neighboring groups, where dances initiating members into societies attracted considerable attention. There was a renewal of interest, too, in first salmon ceremonies, inspired in large part by the leaders of the Tulalip Tribe, Stan Jones and two other tribal members, Morris Dan and Harriette Shelton Dover. Since 1976, the return of Yo Bauch, the big king salmon, has once again become an important communal event for many tribes.

Throughout the state, the Indian Shaker Church continues to serve its members, and other native people, Catholics and Protestants, continue to worship in the way taught by the missionaries. In many of these congregations there is increased use of native rituals, art and language as native pride continues to reassert itself. The life of Washington's native peoples is still hard, the hardest of all its minority groups, and native religious bodies are challenged to mediate the problems facing the community. In prisons the purificatory rites of the sweatlodge have been introduced for the benefit of native American inmates. In another development, dance leaders such as Bruce Miller of the Skokomish Reservation and Johnny Moses, a young shaman sent by his native community on Vancouver Island on a mission to the Puget Sound region, lead dance groups to help native youth at risk in white society reestablish a link with their heritage.

Today, religion in Washington is as vital as it ever was. With 4,132,353 people according to the 1980 census, and with "baby boomers" returning to churches in some number, the percentage of the state's population affiliated with a denomination will likely increase. All of the world's major religions are represented in the state along with a host of minor ones. Nevertheless, the fact remains that at least two-thirds of the population belongs to no religious group.

Wesley Gardens Retirement Home, south of Seattle in Des Moines. This home was one of many established nationwide after World War II.

Courtesy Earl Howell Photo Collection, Pacific Northwest Methodist Annual Conference Archives, United Methodist Church, University of Puget Sound, Tacoma, Washington.

This has been an historic constant in the region, and churches have responded to it by eliminating much of the exclusiveness they brought in with them and reaching out to one another for support. Important divisions still exist, especially between liberal and conservative churches, between those who embrace ecumenism and those who reject it. Many denominations are racked with dispute over issues such as women's rights, abortion, and gay and lesbian ministries. Indeed, divisions within denominations are probably now more intense than those that used to divide them.

To the unchurched, this contention is one of the things that makes organized religion such a bewildering phenomenon. Many are quick to point out the churches' failings and rightfully so. The notorious high-jinks of some televangelists, the hate-mongering, brazen hypocrisy, cynicism, and the smug complacency of some church figures are the churches' shame. Many observers are genuinely disturbed, too, by "New Age" cults, by sybaritic communes, and by many faith healers and "channelers" who seem anxious to separate the needful from their money. Yet, there is no denying that literally thousands are attracted to these individuals without coercion.

On the other hand, the churches also present an edifying spectacle as representatives of many faiths gather together before nuclear arms depots to demonstrate their desire for peace and the elimination of these costly and hellish weapons. Some may argue points, but few can quibble with the generosity of spirit and high idealism of those involved. Local religious leaders and groups have chosen to call the public's attention to issues confronting the community and the world to which Washington is now so inextricably involved. Seattle's Catholic Archbishop, Raymond Hunthausen, witholds part of his taxes to protest the arms race, and the University Baptist Church chooses, along with others, to play an active role in the Sanctuary movement aiding refugees from Central America. Others call attention to the abuse of human rights in the Soviet Union, in South Africa and Latin America. A host of church-sponsored groups and agencies seek to aid the homeless and the abused, street people, battered wives and children, the disabled, the hungry and the dying.

In the meantime, churches and religious groups continue to administer and upgrade their institutional systems: their schools, hospitals, rest homes, clinics, reading rooms, missions, and counselling and support centers that promote the health and welfare of the whole community. Even as they support these, they continue to develop new institutions to address new needs. In 1970, for example, the Church Council of Greater Seattle developed "Neighbors in Need," a program that established food banks and distribution centers throughout Seattle to feed a growing number of hungry people. It was expanded to serve the greater Seattle area and has become a model for other programs throughout the nation. Recently, University Unitarians have opened the Mark De Wolfe House in Seattle to care for residents afflicted with AIDS.

Many of the state's religious leaders continue to seek better relations between denominations and to extend them to others. In his 1988 "Manifesto To The Seattle Religious Community," Unitarian pastor Peter Raible calls for the creation of a new council body that will include all religious traditions on an equal footing, a truly ecumenical group.

Few chances come in every age to transcend what presently exists and to stake a claim on the future. Usually the dead hand of the past kills these opportunities aborning, but occasionally there are those with boldness, creativeness and daring, who reach beyond what is presently known and risk for human understanding. Such prophetic religious leaders ever declare a basic human faith—a faith that we can have life and have life more abundant.

Anticipating this, a group of church leaders sought to begin work healing the rift between Native Americans and the rest of the state, a rift which the churches played a major role in creating. On Thanksgiving Day, 1987, the bishops and leaders of nine Christian denominations met with representatives of several native groups on what had been an old native burial ground in downtown Seattle to present an apology to the native peoples of the Northwest "on behalf of our churches for their longstanding participation in the destruction of traditional Native American spiritual practices." It was a first step only, but also a move of inspired reconciliation that for the first time voiced a sympathy for native spiritual traditions so tragically lacking in the first missionaries.

Since its presentation, the apology—reproduced at the back of this book—has attracted considerable attention. Most of the local media picked up on the story and featured it in news broadcasts. It was read aloud by native leaders to over 3,000 Northwestern native people gathered for ceremonial purposes, and a copy was submitted by the Affiliated Tribes of Northwest Indians in a resolution to the National

Congress of American Indians. A copy of it was given by Dr. William Cate, President-Director of The Church Council of Greater Seattle, to Dr. Emilio Castro, a representative of the World Council of Churches, and a copy of it is now on display at World Council offices in Geneva, Switzerland. The apology was also translated for leaders of thirty tribal groups in Brazil who are presently engaged in a struggle to protect their native lands.

By identifying themselves so closely with American cultural and national aspirations, the churches in the Northwest participated in an historic tragedy that continues to dog the region. The churches had been critical of American institutions such as slavery and the saloon, and the abolition of slavery was rightly counted a triumph, but here the romance of nation building proved irresistible. It took time for them to distance themselves from the national culture and take a more balanced view of it, but many have begun to do so. They have looked to their original inspiration to find the energy that makes it possible for them to transcend ideas of nation and race and offer insights into personality and culture that are uniquely theirs.

Religion and its institutions have been powerful shaping forces in this region's history, and they always will be. Religion taps the deepest emotions in human beings and releases energies its institutions seek to control and direct. It enlivens even as it constrains. What role the churches will have as Washington enters its second century is a matter of speculation, but that they will have a role—and a major one—is assured. Representing a diverse and voluble minority in a population that is often critical of them, they are fated to be vigorous.

Willard Jue's Two-World Legacy

erhaps it began in Seung Gok, China, Province of Guangdong. Goon Dip was born in 1862, emigrated to Portland, Oregon, and then moved to Tacoma, Washington. In the 1880s Tacoma had the largest West Coast Chinese community outside of San Francisco. Beginning as a laborer, the intelligent Goon Dip manifested management traits that were noticed by his white bosses. Before long, he was an independent businessman—a labor contractor. From there he moved into dry goods and hotel ownership and management.

Goon Dip married, sired children and watched his grandchildren prosper despite exclusion laws, anti-Chinese riots, and the gnawing presence of race prejudice throughout his life. During that active life Goon Dip gave little evidence of a religious conscience. However, an American-born grandson named Willard Jue would become a devout Christian and leave his imprint upon the Chinese and international communities of Seattle.

Williard Jue was born in Portland, Oregon, 1905. As the eldest son it was his duty to study Chinese language and literature. These subjects included poetry, history, Confucian lore, and traditions of the Jue clan. (A ten-volume genealogy of the Jue family, presented to him by his tutor, became one of his proudest possessions.) These intellectual opportunities reflected the relative affluence of his family. In Portland public schools Jue not only learned English, but came to appreciate the heterogeneous nature of America. His classmates were, besides Caucasians, many Japanese-Americans ("Nisei"—the second generation).

Following summers of hard work in fish canneries, Jue graduated from the University of Washington in 1929 with a degree in pharmacy. Race prejudice, no other reason, prevented him from working in his profession. Instead, he took on sales clerk, janitorial and other menial tasks. His grandfather, the irrepressible, honored, Goon Dip, counseled Jue to "look for (another) way." For awhile that "way" was as typesetter for the local Seattle Chinese language newspaper, *Seattle Star.* Later he tried his hand at operating his own small grocery store.

Throughout this period Willard Jue diligently practiced his Christianity. His compassion for others helped mask the indignities he suffered as a college graduate unable to get work. His grandfather died, an important link with his past. Married to Ammie Law, with a young daughter and son to support, Jue had to assume special community responsibilities. Among these were scout master duties for Troop 54, and renewed dedication to the Chinese Baptist Church in Seattle's International District (formerly referred to as "Chinatown").

Shortly after the 1886 anti-Chinese riots, the Baptist Northern Convention formed Seattle's Chinese Baptist Church. By 1920 local Chinese had taken over, in part because they didn't feel comfortable in Caucasian churches. The new church was re-established at King Street and Tenth Avenue. Jue served as usher, Sunday School teacher, and deacon. Driven by his devout Christianity, he became a self-appointed counselor and helpmate to Chinese at the Immigration Service's Detainment and Processing Center near Seattle's famous Pike Place Market. However, Jue also served Seattle's wider religious community, giving time to First Baptist and University Baptist congregations.

In the 1960s a revival of interest in Asian studies occurred. Willard Jue, a history buff and later founder of the Chinese Historical Society of the Pacific Northwest, found himself speaking to college classes about the Chinese experience in America.

One year after the 1976 death of his wife Ammie, Jue visited Hong Kong and Taiwan. It was the first of several pilgrimages to the "Old Country." In 1979 he finally managed to see Guangdong Province, ancestral home of Goon Dip—103 years after his grandfather came to Portland, Oregon.

A few years before Willard Jue died, he remarried, dabbled in Chinese herbal medicine, helped establish Seattle's Wing Luke Asian Museum, and received humanitarian awards from several organizations, including the Japanese American Citizens League. Quiet, unwavering service to the Chinese Baptist Church—now settled in commodious surroundings on Seattle's Beacon Hill—may be Willard Jue's greatest legacy. He was proud to be both Chinese and American, and never wavered in his Christian duty to all humankind.

Mark Tobey's Balancing Act

In January 1928 the Seattle papers had great fun describing the hanging of a Mark Tobey painting—upside down. Seattle claimed Tobey, but the artist himself claimed the world—at least Europe—as his spiritual home.

Born in 1890, Mark George Tobey was the youngest of four children from a Wisconsin small town family. His upper Mississippi, horse-drawn carriage youth gave way to a teenager's life in the burly streets of Chicago. The remainder of his life, in fact, would be spent as an

Mark Tobey, world renowned painter and follower of Baha'i.

Courtesy Special Collections Division, University of Washington Libraries, Negative #2421.

urban-based artist with the joy and heart of a country boy. The light, movement, and interruptions of New York, Seattle, Paris and Basel would influence the range and intensity of his work. The miracles of nature, however, never lost their fascination to Tobey.

Throughout his artistic growth—reaching a peak in his early fifties—Tobey was influenced by contemporary artists. Paul Klee, Picasso, Georgia O'Keeffe, and Oriental painters were important to his artistic growth. Also, the meditations of Zen impressed Tobey. But perhaps the most powerful allure came from his conversion to the Baha'i faith.

Most Tobey biographers trace the date of his conversion to 1918, the year he met Juliet Thompson. Thompson was a portrait painter and Baha'i enthusiast. She invited Tobey to immerse himself in Baha'i teachings at camp Green Acre in Eliot, Maine. The exposure worked. Tobey would eventually be claimed by the Baha'i as sort of artist-in-eternal-residence. Tobey, on the other hand, while acknowledging his strong belief in the principles of his faith, claimed that Baha'i "found him."

With roots in early 19th century Persia (Iran) and a history of violent persecution, including beheadings, hangings, and believers blown from the mouths of cannon, Baha'i evolved into a demonstrably peaceful, forgiving faith. Teheran-born Abbas Effendi, who took the title Abdul-Baha (i.e. servant of Baha), is the modern day prophet of Baha'i. When asked "What is a Baha'i?" Abdul-Baha replied: "(It means) to love all the world; to love humanity and try to serve it; to work for universal peace and universal brotherhood."

Tobey was the product of a country emerging from the Great War, 1916-1918. Woodrow Wilson, the idealist, was pressing hard for U.S. Senate approval of the League of Nations. Baha'i taught that the unity of mankind is inevitable; that world citizenship and world civilization signaled humanity's coming of age. This idealistic, mystical approach included the respect of all religions and their prophets. In other words, different routes to the same godly end. Tobey was comfortable with that view of his troubled world. His new-found curiosity and studies began to be reflected in his art. "Progressive revelation," or as Abdul-Baha described it: "The century of motion, divine stimulus and accomplishment" was at hand. Tobey felt prepared to transfer this motion to his sculpture, sketch pad and canvas.

Besides being artistically gifted (his first show was at New York's M. Knoedler and Co. at age twenty-seven) Mark Tobey had the curiosity of a modern Renaissance man fueled by inordinate physical energy. The goateed artist became an amateur pianist and composer, wrote prose and poetry, and enjoyed an insatiable appetite for film, science, concerts, travel and the theater. As abstraction crept into Tobey's work he infused it with the principles of music. Not only, it was said, did his brush dance on the canvas, he occasionally physically broke into a jig or pas de bourée while painting.

In 1922 Tobey and George Brown took a cross-country rail trip to Seattle. They had only enough money for two coach tickets and a bag of oranges. Nellie Cornish, founder of Seattle's Cornish School, remembered Tobey in his early years as "very timid, I would say frightened." After he started an "outside" art class for children, Nellie invited him to teach in the school. He was paid $2.00 a class, of which $1.20 was taken by Cornish. Tobey supplemented his income by painting wooden parrots which he sold for twenty-five cents each. One wonders what one of those parrots would bring today?

The Seattle experience saw Tobey discover cubism, learn about Chinese brushwork and study Japanese color prints. With the strong influence of Mrs. Eugene Fuller and her son, Dr. Richard Fuller, who were close to Miss Nellie Cornish, Seattle's reputation as an Occidental center of Oriental art grew. Tobey took advantage of these connections. His Baha'i principles also found nurturing ground in the Pacific Northwest's rustic beauty and heterogeneous people. Along with Kenneth Callahan, Morris Graves, and Guy Anderson, Tobey helped found what would be called the Northwest School of art. It was in Seattle that Tobey sketched and painted memorable scenes of the Pike Place Market. The first examples of his "white writing" style of painting, perhaps inspired by his association with artist Teng Kuei at the University of Washington, were done on the shores of Puget Sound.

By the mid-fifties, with his artistic reputation secure, Mark Tobey left Seattle. He visited the Orient, New York, Paris and in 1960 settled in Basel, Switzerland, his last home. In 1961, three hundred of his paintings were displayed at the Louvre in Paris. Tobey died in Basel on April 24, 1976, leaving behind a body of work that frequently reflected Baha'i themes. Tobey told an interviewer that Baha'i teaches "science and religion (as) two great powers which must be balanced if man is to become mature. I feel my work has been influenced by these beliefs."

Conservative Roots Of The Inland Empire: Abraham Huppin

Spokane's conservative synagogue, Temple Beth Shalom, began as a troubled partnership between traditional and Reform Jews. Abe Huppin represented one faction, the historic — and Orthodox — Keneseth Israel Synagogue, in protracted negotiations toward establishing a new temple. His role was significant because he headed the committee charged with resolving basic differences: e.g. religious rituals; interpretation of the Halacha (Jewish Law); and virtually all aspects of Jewish conduct, education and living.

Abe Huppin's father Samuel came to the United States from Turisk, Russia — near Chernobyl — in 1921. It was not uncommon then for the breadwinner to precede his family and get established in the New World. The senior Huppin found housing, genial neighbors and a second-hand store in Spokane. Several years later, having saved money and achieved a modest stake in Washington's burgeoning Inland Empire, he sent for his wife Batsheva and young Abe.

When Abe Huppin steamed into New York Harbor aboard the S.S. *Estonia* in June 1921, he had seen nothing of the world and did not speak a word of English. What occurred first was a tragedy. His father died a few months after he and his mother arrived in Spokane. The

Abraham Huppin of Spokane's Keneseth Israel Synagogue and Temple Beth Shalom.

Courtest of Gene Huppin, son of Abraham Huppin.

young Huppin had to step behind the counter of the second-hand store. While studying English in a night course, he waited on bemused and occasionally impatient customers who at first had to rely on sign language to haggle for Huppin's used goods. To further complicate this early family struggle, Abe's mother was pregnant with her deceased husband's second son, Samuel, Jr.

Keneseth Israel Synagogue was the cultural, religious and social hub for much of Spokane's early Jewish population. To young Abe Huppin it provided the family and society he had lost or left behind in Russia. His skills as negotiator for the later amalgamation of Keneseth Israel and Temple Emanual were honed through a series of experiences related to his beloved synagogue. For example, Huppin served as recording secretary and president of Keneseth Israel. He also helped organize the Spokane Hebrew Free Loan Society (interest-free loans to members "of good character": its motto was "to help one to help himself"). For over forty years Huppin was a member of the Chevra Kadisha, the holy society for the ritual cleansing and dressing of a body for burial. In that connection, he simultaneously looked after Spokane's Mt. Nebo Cemetery.

William Toll, in his essay, "Judaism As A Civil Religion In The American West" (1987), described the Jews who came west as "predominantly young men who had quite self-consciously cut themselves loose from the routines of their fathers." That statement did not apply to Samuel, Sr. or his first son. Abe Huppin saw in religious affiliation and activity a bond with the past. His life-long love affair with Keneseth Israel, and later Temple Beth Shalom, signaled support for civic stability, a condition missing from his youthful experience in Russia. Although western U.S. Jews created institutions to support their ideological differences with gentiles, they also cooperated with neighbors of all races and religions. Through broad mercantile and civic efforts their contributions were extensive. Abe Huppin played both roles: dedicated pillar of the Jewish community and participant and leader in Spokane's civic issues.

During the 1940s Huppin was active in B'nai B'rith, an esteemed American Jewish service organization founded in 1842. He was president of a Spokane lodge and traveled throughout the West to help install lodges and attend conventions.

Mt. Nebo, the Spokane Jewish Cemetery which Abe Huppin served for forty years, is the final resting place for Abe and his wife Marian.

Marian died in October 1985; Abe followed her to Mt. Nebo in July 1986.

Perhaps only Abe himself guessed what rich and vital years lay ahead when he saw his handsome, well-groomed visage staring from the pages of Spokane's October 25, 1929, edition of the *Jewish Voice.* He was then secretary of Keneseth Israel Synagogue. He had learned English, was raising a family, and had begun the subtle process of maturation leading to the presidency of Keneseth Israel and, later, the respected ritual committee chair to negotiate the synagogue's re-birth as Temple Beth Shalom.

Gertrude Apel
and the Morals Committee

Evangelical beginnings in Minnesota proved to be prophetic omens. Young, diminutive Gertrude Apel took her frontier Methodism seriously. Sunday school, and studies at the Chicago Evangelistic Institute and McCormick Theological Seminary were but signposts along a path to her dream: having a church of her own.

After bumping along Montana's Hi-Line in a Model T Ford for two years, serving a Methodist pastorate in the Glacier Park district of Montana, Reverend Apel was assigned a circuit rider's life in eastern Washington State. From 1920 to 1929 she delivered sermons and comforted the congregations of five rural churches from Twisp to Mazama.

Although efforts had been made to unify English Protestant churches in the 1840s, the U.S. did not form an ecumenical organization until 1895 (N.Y.C.). Gertrude Apel's circuit riding and tolerance for diverse characters and disparate religious views had nurtured a patient, forgiving spirit. One day that rare talent would find an appropriate outlet. The opportunity came to Apel in 1929 in the guise of Pacific Northwest ecumenism.

Ecumenism has been described as promoting Christian unity or cooperation. In the Pacific Northwest, with its frontier history of individualism, European mores and values, and a kind of nontheological diversity among churches, the local ecumenical movement embraced the following: 1. oneness in Christ; 2. providing assistance to achieve a cooperative ministry; and 3. aiding local congregations. In other words, the less specificity the better. Later, as Gertrude Apel and her successors would experience, the hard issues and wide-ranging debates emerged.

Taking up an associate pastor's duties at the Trinity Methodist Church in Seattle's Ballard neighborhood, Apel was intrigued by a new organization: the Federation Of Churches. Within ten years the Federation merged with its rural counterpart, the Inland Empire Sunday School Council and another organization, to seriously urge Protestant religious cooperation. Under the banner of an organization called the Washington North Idaho Council of Churches and Christian Education, Gertrude Apel entered the new world of ecumenism as executive director of the Council. Debts and spotty parish support almost

Gertrude Apel's years of work recognized by the Council of Churches (1954).

Courtesy of the Seattle Post-Intelligencer Collection, Museum of History and Industry, Seattle, Washington.

doomed the new group. Apel's energy and her concentration upon religious education and teacher training, however, brought enough people together to breathe new life into the Council.

While Apel had been driving through Montana snow storms and Palouse back roads, tiny Pacific Northwest ecumenical stirrings had occurred. Reform movements aimed at peace, prohibition, abolition, religious education, home missions and early women's groups occasionally brought Christian faiths together. The alliances sometimes only lasted for the duration of a campaign or when given strong leadership. The new Council, however, would endure and grow under Apel's patient direction.

Ecumenical reorganization and revitalization occurred during the 1930s while Apel plunged ahead with her Council duties. Jessie Kinnear Kenton in her 1985 masters thesis *(Changing Values In Ecumenical Strategy In The Greater Seattle Area, 1919-1984)*, describes a basic problem undermining ecumenical effort: ambivalence in the choice of issues to be addressed.

Gertrude Apel, for example, had to draw on reserve grit, self-control and probably some gentle guile to deal with the Council's Morals Committee. Strongly held views about the content of books and films, gambling, temperance and sexual conduct were sometimes passionately expressed by members of the Morals Committee. Other committees such as Peace, International Goodwill, and Industrial Relations tended to mitigate the more militant, personalized deliberations of the Morals faction. The job got done, however, as Apel reminisced: "Men tried to be polite to me and so long as I was around it was hard for them not to be polite to one another".

Gertrude Apel oversaw an era of great controversy. In 1932 the Council opposed national rearmament and favored recognition of Russia. The *Seattle Post-Intelligencer,* a Hearst paper, characterized the Council's pacifism as giving "aid and comfort to the communist movement and party". When America entered the Second World War, the Council spoke up on behalf of Japanese-American internees. Later, it protested the government's failure to grant amnesty to conscientious objectors. Fluoridation of Seattle water was endorsed; Sunday dancing at the Eagles Auditorium was opposed. Apel's escape from these fracases is further testimony to her qualities of leadership and to her personal dictum not to press an issue until a congenial atmosphere existed.

Honored by Matrix Table, and the general board of the National Council of Churches, Gertrude Apel had achieved several firsts: the first woman to be ordained by the Methodist Church; the first woman to receive an honorary degree from the College of Puget Sound (Doctor of Divinity); and the first woman to serve as president of the National Association of Council Secretaries. In 1959, after twenty-nine years as the region's chief catalyst for ecumenism, Apel retired. Her Council then split and is known today as the Greater Seattle Council of Churches and the Washington Association of Churches.

The little girl from Worthington, Minnesota, had accomplished a great deal. Her last years were spent in a replay of her childhood dream: to have a church of her own. She died on March 15, 1966, while holding the pastorate of Marine View Methodist Church in Federal Way, Washington.

Fred Shorter's Personal Revolution

Australian-born Frederic William Shorter would not be stopped. His credentials (Yale Divinity School) and platform (Seattle's Pilgrim Congregational Church) were impeccable. In 1925, a year of national excesses and experimentation, he might have mingled unobtrusively with the crowd and been forgotten. However, Shorter proclaimed himself a socialist, militant pacifist and founder of something off-beat—heretical to many—called Church of the People. No one, as a result of those involvements, forgot him.

Fred Shorter's first controversial act was to help win the 1929 release of a member of the I.W.W. Eugene Barnett had been in prison on false charges linked to the 1919 Centralia "riot." Following a 1934 melee over satirical church murals depicting American social problems in stark, violent form, Pilgrim's membership voted to fire Reverend Shorter. Sixty of his followers marched out with him and helped found the Seattle Church of the People. An open forum was established to hear talks on everything and anything, the more topical and radical the better. The state American Civil Liberties Union used Shorter's University District hall to hold organizational meetings. Likewise a cooperative dairy, The People's Memorial Association (inexpensive cremations), early versions of Planned Parenthood, and interracial social gatherings. Shorter seemed to be everywhere, pushing and prodding his personal revolution.

During the early Senator Joe McCarthy turbulence, Shorter's church reached its zenith. Then everything slowed down. National fear and hysteria, changing social values, and Shorter's unabated criticism of war and everyone who even spoke mildly of "defense" needs, caused membership to shrink.

Shorter died in 1963, but his revolution, typified by a 1980s pacifist resurgence over nuclear armaments and U.S. involvement in Central America and the Persian Gulf, gave evidence of new life—or perhaps it was the distant pulse of Fred Shorter's personal revolution?

Reverend Fred Shorter, minister of Seattle's Church of the People.

Courtesy of Chester Kingsbury's personal papers.

Billie Shorter at work in the Church of the People Student Center.

Courtesy of Chester Kingsbury's personal papers.

Stephen Bayne's Mixed Grill

The Right Reverend Stephen Fielding Bayne, Jr., STD, DD, LLD, Episcopal Bishop of Olympia.

Courtesy Special Collections Division, University of Washington Libraries, Negative #8828.

On June 9, 1947, the Rt. Rev. Stephen Fielding Bayne, Jr. STD, DD, LLD, arrived in Seattle to assume his duties as Episcopal Bishop of Olympia. His election at a robust 39 years of age was considered a surprise to his peers. Although New Yorker Bayne had spent some World War II time in Bremerton as a navy chaplain, his Amherst College, General Theological Seminary, and Columbia University (where he had been chaplain) background seemed out of left field.

During an exploratory visit to Seattle in 1946, he teased the press with the riposte that he was "considering acceptance of the post," and would first "measure" himself against the job. It wasn't long after he noted 77 percent of Washington State residents were "affiliated with no organized religious body," that the political weal and organizing genius of handsome Stephen Bayne took charge. During his twelve years as Bishop of Olympia the Episcopal Church in western Washington established fifty new parishes and other units and doubled its membership. The paripatetic Bishop was all over the place, presiding, anointing, hectoring, sipping cocktails, and at times raising his voice on controversial secular issues.

Bayne's Eastern education, required an intellectual outlet. The administrative tasks of his office only filled the workday. Writing, therefore, became a preoccupation, and his subjects ranged from a KJR radio broadcast on "Seasick Souls" to a 1959 NBC sermon called "Middle Age Spread." He contributed forewords to church cookbooks, ruminations on Ceylon and Pakistan, and a serious study on the impact of biology and medicine on religion *(Space Age Christianity)*. His work, *The Optional God,* is, according to his son Duncan, still sold in bookstores.

A tinge of show biz was not outside the Bishop's league. In celebration of the 100th Anniversary of the diocese's existence, Bayne held a May 25, 1953, rally in the cavernous Seattle Civic Auditorium to which 7,000 faithful came and signed their names in a register. That Centennial Jubilee celebrated the 1853 arrival in Vancouver, Washington Territory, of Rev. John McCarthy, the region's first Episcopal missionary. Such Seattle events were noted by the Anglican hierarchy in England as well as Bayne's stateside superiors.

During the late 1950s U.S. Senator John McClellan's committee investigating racketeering was the hottest show on television. Young Robert F. Kennedy, chief counsel, kept up a relentless nasal grilling of star witnesses. Seattle's own Dave Beck, President of the sprawling Teamster's Union, appeared before McClellan's committee and firmly defied its mandate and belittled the peregrinations of young Kennedy. At this same time, Bayne addressed the forty-seventh annual Diocesan Convention being held in St. Mark's Cathedral, Seattle. After thanking the attendees for their contributions, he gave a little lecture on the "immorality of inflation" and how that circumstance negatively impacts the poor. From there he took a swipe at the U.S. "tangled tax laws." Without missing a beat, the Bishop then assailed the "almost comic peccadilloes" of Dave Beck, who had allegedly misrepresented his income with the Internal Revenue Service.

Bayne, who had not met Dave Back, must have been feeling irrepressible that day, as he expounded on the "plain evidence" showing Beck's "moral irresponsibility." Letters came in supporting and criticizing the Bishop. Some were crank, others were reasoned statements from ordinary citizens. *Time* Magazine described the brouhaha in a boxed story on May 27, 1957. Dave Beck took a moment to "remind the Bishop" that he had helped "save" St. Mark's Cathedral as co-chairman of a fund drive to pay off the cathedral's mortgage, and he'd been feted at a dinner sponsored by Episcopal bigwigs. After everyone had had their say on this matter, the Bishop was "unavailable" for further comment.

An enthusiastic joiner, Stephen Bayne supported groups such as the World Affairs Council of Seattle, the Japan Society, the National Urban League, Friends of Canterbury Cathedral and the Shrine Circus Fund. He chaired the Seattle Housing Authority for six years and distributed FISH pins to lay church leaders who signed a pledge dedicating their energies to church matters. Bayne placed ads in local newspapers asking readers to take a look at the Episcopal Church. He noted that "over 500 good responses" resulted from that campaign after "weeding out the eccentrics."

Archival correspondence from Bayne bristles with pithy, humorous comment. He wrote and thanked one correspondent for his "prompt and courteous reply to my outraged squall." To another he joked about his own mixed metaphor when describing an event as "a kind of mixed grill . . . you had a finger in too many pies." Even his priests joined in the fun. The Rev. Elmer Christie wrote and thanked Bayne for helping a communicant find public housing, signing his letter "Love and Kisses, Elmer."

One might conclude that Stephen Bayne's many-faceted interests and high-speed schedule caused burnout. Honored in 1957 as the first Executive Officer of the Anglican Communion in London, England, and later as Vice President of the Episcopal Church in the U.S., Bayne fell ill and died in Puerto Rico, January 1974, age sixty-six. (Ironically, he had once written: "January...is a miserable, harassed, snivelling, crass, over-bearing, worldly wretch of a month.")

The young eastern priest had become a popular man of the west. Stephen Bayne's personal and spiritual influence was truly international, while his heart remained in the Diocese of Olympia where the sparks and ideas of a brilliant career began.

Raphael H. Levine:
Name Changes and Epithets

Rabbi Raphael Levine's journey from the ghetto of Vilna, Lithuania, then under Russian control, to Duluth, Minnesota, is a uniquely American immigrant story.

Rabbi Raphael Levine, founding member of the Challenge Television panel.

Courtesy Special Collections Division, University of Washington Libraries, Negative #8851.

Born in 1901, the little Jewish boy would later recall his early memories of Christians as purveyors of anti-semitic epithets and abuse who simultaneously sold his father their eggs. In the 1960s, Rabbi Levine teamed with Irish-bred Catholic priest William Treacy and several Protestant ministers on the Seattle KOMO-TV program "Challenge." That media performance (originally proposed by Levine) would surprise critics and sponsors by lasting fourteen years, eventually spawning a Pacific Northwest ecumenical center and inter-faith camp near Mt. Vernon, Washington. A four-year-old who had struggled with the Hebrew alphabet in Vilna, Rabbi Levine would ultimately display an erudition and patience that transcended the boundaries of his state and the tenets of his ancient faith.

Poor but steeped in Jewish traditions, the Levine family of Vilna alternated between love for religion and the past, and hatred of their unpredictable non-Jewish neighbors. Challah, the twisted loaves of white bread; busy Sabbath preparations, including the beaker of wine used for Kiddush; the holy day's prayers; and a stream of guests with unceasing talk, remained Rabbi Levine's happiest childhood memories. These reveries were broken by the arrest of his brother in 1905. A labor union activist, brother Louis spent nine anxious months in jail. Soon after that scare, the Levine family sold everything and left for America.

The name Raphael, Hebrew for God the Healer, was not appropriate for America, or so Levine's Duluth, Minnesota relatives decided. So Harry Levine graduated from high school, Ralph Levine attended law school, and Raphael Levine entered Hebrew Union College in Cincinnati. Rabbi Levine retained the middle initial "H" as a memento of those days.

Upon graduation in 1932, the new rabbi, with an equally new wife and baby in tow, became the only Reform leader in Liverpool, England. Here, Levine would begin his ecumenical work by joining the local ministers' association for intellectual company and free-swinging religious conversation. Out of that experience emerged the "World Order Group," a kind of listening post against Nazism which was on the rise in 1930s Germany.

When Levine's new synagogue in London took a wartime direct hit from German bombing, the congregation continued services across the street in the Lords Cricket Club. Meanwhile his wife Madeline, daughter Lori, and mentally retarded son David returned to the safety of "fortress" America.

On June 4, 1942, following a call from the congregation of Temple De Hirsch in Seattle, Rabbi Levine became a citizen of, and whirlwind presence in, the Queen City. His duties and ambition, by his own words, "led to a…separation (from Madeline) in 1953 after nearly twenty-five years of marriage." He later married Reeva Miller and embarked upon an extraordinary path of teaching, writing, counseling and civic activism, much of it ecumenical, that would characterize what he called "my spiritual odyssey."

Although Levine stepped aside in 1969 as rabbi of Temple De Hirsch Sinai, he remained a civic and religious figure. By 1980 he had garnered the following responsibilities and honors, among others: college teacher; Seattle's First Citizen (1976), elected by the Seattle-King County Board of Realtors; board member of Rotary, the United Way of King County, the Washington Society for Crippled Children, Council for the Aging and the Seattle Human Rights Commission. In demand as a speaker before all manner of secular and religious organizations, the slightly bent, usually smiling, gray-haired rabbi kept a full calendar.

About a year before his November 1985 death from a car accident, Rabbi Levine appeared before a Lutheran congregation. He told his startled audience that Pope John XXIII was a great figure. After all, Levine argued, he "abolished all the taboos about Catholics fraternizing with Protestants...and" he added with a smile, "Jews." Levine's Reform ecumenism was deplored by strict religionists, while it perplexed others. What does one say about a truly dedicated religious figure like the venerable rabbi emeritus who believed that God was not Jewish, Catholic, Protestant, Hindu or Buddhist? Instead, he asked his listeners to believe in God as the creator who governs everyone with love.

Sought after as a counselor, Rabbi Levine had a few precious words for anyone who asked his help. One example suffices. One of Temple De Hirsch's prominent families had a troubled son who had found solace and friends in a somewhat off-beat Christian church. In a fretful state, the young man asked the old counselor what he should do? Levine advised him to stay with his friends and seek answers to his problems in the Christian setting. Raphael "God the Healer" Levine, Reform Jew and neighbor to all, gave the only advice he could.

Chants and Meditation:
Swami Vividishanada

S wami Vividishanada was a native of Bengal, India, but found his spiritual mission on the shores of Puget Sound. When Vividishanada came to the U.S. as a young monk in 1929, it was by invitation of American admirers of the Vedanta Society—a combination church and ancient Hindu philosophy based on the Ramakrishina Mission. In 1938 he helped found the Seattle-based Vedanta Society and then remained as its spiritual leader. Taking no salary, but receiving food, clothing, housing and medical expenses from his followers, Vividishananda provided a focal point for private instruction—not proselytization, and as an example to his followers of a pure, simple, unselfish life.

Swami Vividishanda organized the Seattle Vedanta Society in 1938.

Courtesy of Devra Freedman, Vedanta Society of Western Washington.

While a young man, Vividishananda took a Master's degree in Philosophy in Calcutta. He then edited an English language newspaper in India, and wrote three books. Later, in Seattle, he had to cautiously cross the forbidden threshold of politics. His Seattle attorney, upon applying to the city building department in December 1941, for a permit to convert an old residence in a residential district to church use, lauded the Swami and his small group. He noted that the apolitical, quiet organization had been peacefully established in America since the Chicago World's Fair (1893) and that it "includes some of our nicest people." Despite the fact that no address for the proposed church was given, Corporation Counsel granted the Swami's request in three days.

Members of the Vedanta Society believe that all beings and things are divine. They also respect every religion as representing a different path to the same goal. Swami Vividishananda, according to his followers, exemplified humility, dignity and a gentle nature. Under his direction the Society remained small (less than 200 members) and quietly practiced meditation and rituals—including ancient Indian chants—at their Paul Thiry-designed Capitol Hill Temple of Worship. In the 1970s Vividishananda, far from his native Bengal, and surrounded by a tiny band of American believers, succumbed to a series of strokes. He died in September, 1980.

Perhaps the gentle Swami was fortunate to have missed the June 1984 pipe-bombing of his temple. No explanation was given for that act. The new leadership expressed surprise at such violence because, they noted, "we accept all religions as true, and we don't get involved in anything with political overtones..."

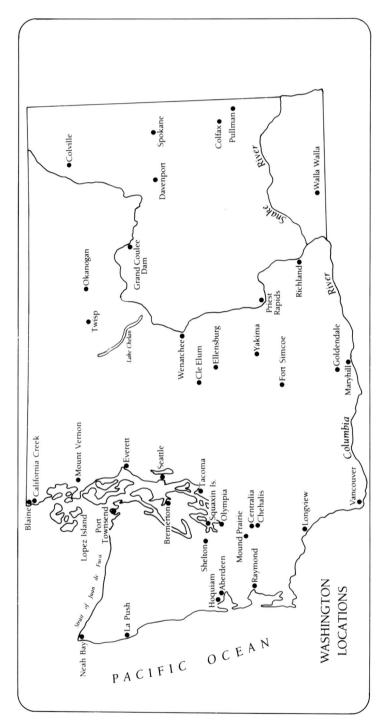

Major towns and cities of Washington state, 1980, map prepared by Larry Cort, Rainier Mapping, Tacoma, Washington.

Appendix

A PUBLIC DECLARATION

**TO THE TRIBAL COUNCILS AND TRADITIONAL SPIRITUAL LEADERS
OF THE INDIAN AND ESKIMO PEOPLES OF THE PACIFIC NORTHWEST**
In care of Jewell Praying Wolf James, Lummi

Seattle, Washington
November 21, 1987

Dear Brothers and Sisters,

This is a formal apology on behalf of our churches for their long-standing participation in the destruction of traditional Native American spiritual practices. We call upon our people for recognition of and respect for your traditional ways of life and for protection of your sacred places and ceremonial objects. We have frequently been unconscious and insensitive and have not come to your aid when you have been victimized by unjust Federal policies and practices. In many other circumstances we reflected the rampant racism and prejudice of the dominant culture with which we too willingly identified. During the 200th Anniversary year of the United States Constitution we, as leaders of our churches in the Pacific Northwest, extend our apology. We ask for your forgiveness and blessing.

As the Creator continues to renew the earth, the plants, the animals and all living things, we call upon the people of our denominations and fellowships to a commitment of mutual support in your efforts to reclaim and protect the legacy of your own traditional spiritual teachings. To that end we pledge our support and assistance in upholding the American Religious Freedom Act (P.L. 95-134, 1978) and within that legal precedent affirm the following:

1) The rights of the Native Peoples to practice and participate in traditional ceremonies and rituals with the same protection offered all religions under the Constitution.

2) Access to and protection of sacred sites and public lands for ceremonial purposes.

3) The use of religious symbols (feathers, tobacco, sweet grass, bones, etc.) for use in traditional ceremonies and rituals.

The spiritual power of the land and the ancient wisdom of your indigenous religions can be, we believe, great gifts to the Christian churches. We offer our commitment to support you in the righting of previous wrongs: To protect your peoples' efforts to enhance Native spiritual teachings; to encourage the members of our churches to stand in solidarity with you on these important religious issues; to provide advocacy and mediation, when appropriate, for ongoing negotiations with State agencies and Federal officials regarding these matters.

May the promises of this day go on public record with all the congregations of our communions and be communicated to the Native American Peoples of the Pacific Northwest. May the God of Abraham and Sarah, and the Spirit who lives in both the cedar and Salmon People be honored and celebrated.

Sincerely,

The Rev. Thomas L. Blevins, Bishop
Pacific Northwest Synod —
Lutheran Church in America

The Rev. Dr. Robert Bradford,
Executive Minister
American Baptist Churches of the Northwest

The Rev. Robert Brock
N.W. Regional Christian Church

The Right Rev. Robert H. Cochrane,
Bishop, Episcopal Diocese of Olympia

The Rev. W. James Halfaker
Conference Minister
Washington North Idaho Conference
United Church of Christ

The Most Rev. Raymond G. Hunthausen
Archbishop of Seattle
Roman Catholic Archdiocese of Seattle

The Rev. Elizabeth B. Knott, Synod Executive
Presbyterian Church
Synod Alaska-Northwest

The Rev. Lowell E. Knutson, Bishop
North Pacific District
American Lutheran Church

The Most Rev. Thomas Murphy
Coadjutor Archbishop
Roman Catholic Archdiocese of Seattle

The Rev. Melvin G. Talbert, Bishop
United Methodist Church —
Pacific Northwest Conference

Bibliography

Bibliographies, Reference Works

Corning, Howard McKinley, ed. *Dictionary of Oregon History.* Portland: Binfords & Mort, 1956.

Historical Records Survey; Division of Community Service Programs; Work Projects Administration. *Guide to Church Vital Statistics Records in Washington, Preliminary Editon.* Seattle: The Washington Historical Records Survey, 1942.

Maloney, Frank, ed. *Directory of Churches, Ministers, & Agencies 1986.* Seattle: Church Council of Greater Seattle, 1986.

Preston, Ralph N. *Early Washington Atlas.* Portland: Binfords & Mort, 1981.

Scott, Dr. James W. and Roland L. DeLorme, eds. *Historical Atlas of Washington.* Norman, OK: University of Oklahoma Press, 1988.

Smith, Charles W. *Pacific Northwest Americana.* Portland: Binfords & Mort, 1950.

Steward, Jennifer. *Washington State Materials For The Centennial: An Annotated Bibliography.* Olympia, WA. Superintendent of Public Instruction, 1988.

Pacific Northwest Regional and Local History

Bagley, Clarence B. Vol. 1 of *History of King County.* 3 vols. Chicago: S.J. Clark Publishing Company, 1929.

Bonney, W.P. Vol. 1 of *History of Pierce County, Washington.* Chicago: Pioneer Historical Publishing Co., 1927.

Chittick, V.L.O., ed. *Northwest Harvest: A Regional Stocktaking.* New York: MacMillian, 1948.

Clark, Norman, *Washington: A Bicentennial History.* New York: W.W. Norton & Company, 1977.

Dodds, Gordon B. *The American Northwest: A History of Oregon and Washington.* Arlington Heights, Ill.: Forum Press, 1986.

_____. *Oregon: A Bicentennial History.* New York: W.W. Norton & Company, 1977.

Dryden, Cecil. *Dryden's History of Washington.* Portland: Binfords & Mort, 1968.

Hawthorne, Julian, ed. Vols. 1 and 2 of *History of Washington: The Evergreen State from Early Dawn to Daylight.* New York: American Historical Publishing Co., 1893.

Holbrook, Stewart H. *The Columbia.* New York: Rinehart & Co., Inc., 1956.

Johansen, Dorothy O., and Charles M. Gates. *Empire Of The Columbia.* New York: Harper & Row Publishers, 1967.

Lavender, David. *Land of Giants: The Drive to the Pacific Northwest 1750-1950.* Lincoln: University of Nebraska Press, 1979.

Meinig, D.W. *The Great Columbia Plain: A Historical Geography, 1805-1910.* Seattle: University of Washington Press, 1968.

Pomeroy, Earl. *The Pacific Slope.* New York: Alfred A. Knopf, 1965.

Shiach, William Sidney, ed. *An Illustrated History of Skagit and Snohomish Counties.* n.p.: Interstate Publishing Co., 1906.

Primary Sources

Bailey, Margaret Jewett. *The Grains; or Passages in the Life of Ruth Rover, with Occasional Pictures of Oregon, Natural and Moral.* Eds. Evelyn Leader and Robert Frank. Corvallis: Oregon State University Press, 1986.

Blaine, The Reverend David E. and Catherine Blaine. *Letters and Papers of Reverend David E. Blaine and his Catherine: Seattle 1853-1856, Oregon 1856-1862.* Seattle: Historical Society of the Pacific Northwest Conference of the Methodist Church, 1963.

Clark, Ella E. *Indian Legends of the Pacific Northwest.* Berkeley: University of California Press, 1953.

Eddy, Mary Baker. *Christian Healing and the People's Idea of God, Sermons Delivered at Boston.* Boston: Allison V. Steward, 1915.

Eells, Myron. *The Indians of Puget Sound.* Ed. George Pierre Castile. Seattle: University of Washington Press, 1985.

Jessett, Thomas E., ed. *Reports and Letters of Herbert Beaver, 1836-1838, Chaplain to the Hudson's Bay Co., and Missionary to the Indians at Ft. Vancouver.* Portland: Champoeg Press, 1959.

Lee, Daniel and John Frost. *Ten Years in Oregon.* New York, Privately Printed, 1844.

Mattoon, The Reverend C.H., Vol. 1 of *Baptist Annals of Oregon 1844 to 1900.* McMinnville, OR.: Press of the Telephone Register Publishing Co., 1905.

Merk, Frederick, ed. *Fur Trade and Empire: George Simpson's Journal; remarks connected with the fur trade in the course of a voyage from York Factory to Fort George and back to York Factory 1824-1825.* Cambridge: Harvard University Press, 1931.

Pambrun, Andrew Dominique. *Sixty Years on the Frontier in the Pacific Northwest.* Fairfield, WA; Ye Galleon Press, 1978.

Parker, Rev. Samuel. *Journal of an Exploring Tour Beyond the Rocky Mountains Under the Direction of the A.B.C.F.M. Performed in the Years 1835, '36 and '37.* Minneapolis: Ross & Haines, 1967.

Powell, Wilbur, ed. *Narratives of the Trans-Mississippi Frontier: Hall Kelley on Oregon.* New York: Da Capo Press, 1972.

Ross, Alexander, *Adventures of the First Settlers on the Oregon or Columbia River, 1810-1813.* Lincoln: University of Nebraska Press, 1986.

Rossi, Father Louis. *Six Years on the West Coast of America.* Ed. and Trans. W. Victor Wortley. Fairfield, WA; Ye Galleon Press, 1983.

Seiber, Richard A., ed. *Memoirs of Puget Sound, Early Seattle 1853-1856, the Letters of David and Catherine Blaine.* Fairfield, WA: Ye Galleon Press, 1978.

Swan, James G. *Almost Out of the World.* Tacoma, WA: Washington State Historical Society, 1971.

_____ . *The Northwest Coast: Or Three Years Residence in Washington Territory.* Ed. Norman H. Clark. Seattle: University of Washington Press, 1972.

Whitman, Narcissa Prentice. *My Journal, 1836.* Ed. Lawrence Dodd. Fairfield WA: Ye Galleon Press, 1984.

_____ . *The Letters of Narcissa Whitman.* Fairfield, WA: Ye Galleon Press, 1986.

Secondary Sources

Ahlstron, Sydney A. *A Religious History of the American People.* New Haven: Yale University Press, 1972.

American Friends Service Committee. *Uncommon Controversy: Fishing Rights of the Muckleshoot, Puyallup, and Nisqually Indians.* Seattle: University of Washington Press, 1972.

Amoss, Pamela. *Coast Salish Spirit Dancing: The Survival of an Ancestral Religion.* Seattle: University of Washington Press, 1978.

Andrews, Mildred. *Seattle Women: A Legacy of Community Development.* Seattle: YMCA of Seattle-King County, 1984.

Atwood, The Reverend A. *Glimpses of Pioneer Life on Puget Sound.* Seattle: Denny Coryell Co., 1903.

Baker, J.C. *Baptist History of the North Pacific Coast.* Philadelphia: American Baptist Publication Society, 1912.

Barnett, H.G. *Indian Shakers: A Messianic Cult of the Pacific Northwest.* Carbondale: Southern Illinois University Press, 1957.

Bayne, Stephen F., Jr. *Now Is the Accepted Time.* Cincinnati: Forward Movement Publications, 1982.

Berkhofer, Robert F., Jr. *Salvation and the Savage: An Analysis of Protestant Missions and American Indian Response 1787-1862.* n.p: University of Kentucky Press, 1965.

Blankenship, Mrs. George. *Early History of Thurston County, Washington, together with Biographies and Reminiscences of those Identified with Pioneer Days.* Olympia, Washington: n.p., 1914.

Blankenship, Russell. *And There Were Men.* New York: Alfred A. Knopf, 1942.

Bloom, David and Lisa Jankanish. *State of the City: A Report to the Churches and the Community.* Seattle: Church Council of Greater Seattle, 1985.

Bloomberg Ray, ed. *Our First Baptist Heritage 1869-1984.* Seattle: Frayn Printing, 1985.

Bowden, Henry Warner. *American Indians and Christian Missions.* Chicago: Chicago University Press, 1981.

Boyd, Rev. Robert. *History of the Synod of Washington of the Presbyterian Church in the United States of America.* Seattle: The Synod, 1909.

Brosnan, Cornelius. *Jason Lee: Prophet of New Oregon.* New York: Macmillan, 1932.

Buerge, David M. *Children of the Sacred Heart, A History of Forest Ridge.* Seattle: Northwest Press, 1982.

Clark, Norman H. *The Dry Years.* Seattle: University of Washington Press, 1987.

_____ . *Mill Town.* Seattle: University of Washington Press, 1982.

Cole, Jean Murray. *Exile in the Wilderness: The Biography of Chief Factor Archibald McDonald 1790-1853.* Seattle: University of Washington Press, 1979.

Collins, June McCormick. *Valley of the Spirits: The Upper Skagit Indians of Western Washington.* Seattle: University of Washington Press, 1974.

Combs, Richard. *A Guide to the Cathedral of St. John the Evangelist Spokane, Washington.* Spokane: St. John's Cathedral Bookstore and Gift Shop, 1983.

Cornish, Nellie C. *Miss Aunt Nellie, The Autobiography of Nellie C. Cornish.* Seattle: University of Washington Press, 1964.

Crittenden, Ann. *Sanctuary: A Study of American Conscience and the Law in Collision.* New York: Weidenfeld, Nicolson, 1988.

Dahl, Arthur. *Mark Tobey: Art and Belief.* Oxford: George Ronals, 1984.

Das, Rajana Kanta. *Hindustani Workers on the Pacific Coast.* Berlin: Walter De Gruyter & Co., 1923.

Deloria, Vine Jr. *Indians of the Pacific Northwest From the Coming of the White Man to the Present Day.* New York: Doubleday & Company, 1977.

Devine, Jean Porter. *From Settlement House to Neighborhood House: 1906-1976.* Seattle: Neighborhood House, Inc., 1976.

Duniway, Abigail Scott. *Path Breaking, An Autobiographical History of the Equal Suffrage Movement in Pacific Coast States.* 2nd ed. Portland: James, Kerns & Abbott Co., 1914.

Drury, Clifford Merrill. *Henry Harmon Spalding.* Caldwell, Idaho: The Caxton Printers, Ltd., 1936.

_____ . *Marcus and Narcissa Whitman, and the Opening of Old Oregon.* Glendale, California: A.H. Clark Co., 1973.

_____ . *Marcus Whitman, M.D.* Caldwell, Idaho: The Caxton Printers, 1937.

Du Bois, Cora. "The Feather Cult of the Middle Columbia." *General Series In Anthropology 7.* Menasha, Wisconsin: George Banta Publishing Company, Agent, 1936.

Dryden, Cecil P. *Give All to Oregon! Missionary Pioneers of the Far West.* New York: Hastings House Publishers, 1968.

Early, James. *On the Frontier of Leadership: The University of Puget Sound, 1888-1988.* Tacoma, Washington: University of Puget Sound, 1987.

Eells, Reverend Myron, D.D. *Biography of Reverend G.H. Atkinson, D.D.* Portland: F.W. Baltes and Company, Printers, 1893.

_____ . *Father Eells of the Results of Fifty-five Years of Missionary Labors in Washington and Oregon.* Boston: Congregational Sunday School and Publishing Society, 1894.

_____ . *History of the Congregational Association of Oregon, and Washington Territory.* Portland: Publishing House of Himes The Printer, 1881.

Eells, Myron, Edward William and Walter Earnest. *Eells Family History in America.* Privately Printed, 1966.

Esslemount, J.E. *Bah 'u'll h and the New Era: An Introduction to the Baha'i Faith.* Wilmette, Illinois: Baha'i Publishing Trust, 1970.

Fahey, John. *The Inland Empire: Unfolding Years 1879-1929.* Seattle: University of Washington Press, 1986.

Fitz-Gerald, Nathan Ward. *The New Revelation: Its Marvelous Message.* Tacoma, Washington: n.p., 1905.

Flanagan, Sister Mary Rita, O.P. *The Work of The Sisters of St. Dominic of the Congregation of St. Thomas Aquinas in the Diocese of Seattle 1881-1951.* Seattle: n.p., 1951.

Frazier, E. Franklin and C. Eric Lincoln. *The Negro Church in America and the Black Church since Frazier.* New York: Schocken Books, 1974.

Friedheim, Robert L. *The Seattle General Strike.* Seattle: University of Washington Press, 1964.

Gibson, James R. *Farming the Frontier: The Agricultural Opening of the Oregon Country 1786-1846.* Seattle: University of Washington Press, 1985.

Goodykoontz, Colin Brummitt. *Home Missions on the American Frontier.* Caldwell, Id: The Caxton Printers Ltd., 1939.

Gray, Alfred O. *Not By Might: The Story of Whitworth College, 1890-1965*. Spokane, WA: Whitworth College, 1965.

Guarneri, Carl and David Alvarez, eds. *Religion and Society in the American West: Historical Essays*. New York: University Press of America, 1987.

Haeberlin, Hermann and Erna Gunther. *The Indians of Puget Sound*. Seattle: University of Washington Press, 1973.

Hartwich, Ethelyn Miller. *The First Fifty Years: A History of University Unitarian Church*. Seattle: n.p., 1962.

Hards, Bea, ed. *A History of Gethsemane Lutheran Church Seattle, Washington*. Seattle: Gethsemane Lutheran Church, 1985.

Hatcher, William S. *Baha'i Faith: The Emerging Global Religion*. San Francisco: Harper and Row, 1984.

Hellan, Maurice, *There Were Giants*. Yakima, WA: Privately Printed, 1980.

Hines, H.K., D.D. *Missionary History of the Pacific Northwest*. Portland: Marsh Printing Company, 1899.

Hopper, Mary and E. Harriet Gipson. *A Frontier of the Spirit*. Seattle: North Seattle Printing Company, n.d.

Horne, J. Arthur. *Latter-day Saints in the Great Northwest*. Seattle: Graphic Arts Press, 1969.

Howard, Alma L. *Reflective Light: The 75-year Story of the University Unitarian Church of Seattle, 1913 to 1980*. Seattle: n.p., 1988.

Howell, Earl. *Methodism in the Northwest*. Nashville: The Parthenon Press, Printers, 1966.

Irving, Washington. *The Adventures of Captain Bonneville, U.S.A. in the Far West*. Norman: University of Oklahoma Press, 1986.

Ito, Kazuo. *Issei: A History of Japanese Immigrants in North America*. Seattle: Executive Committee for Publication of Issei: A History of Japanese Immigrants in North America, 1973.

Jessett, Thomas E. *Chief Spokan Garry, 1811-1892, Christian, Statesman and Friend of the White Man*. Minneapolis: T.S. Denison and Co., Inc., 1960.

_____ . *The Indian Side of the Whitman Massacre*. Fairfield, WA: Ye Galleon Press, 1973.

_____ . *Pioneering God's Country*. Tacoma, WA: The Church Lantern Press, 1953.

Johnson, Gertrude Wiencke, ed. *Travels of J.H. Wilbur*. Salem, OR: Willamette University, 1975.

Jones, Nard, *The Great Command*. Boston: Little, Brown and Company, 1959.

Lavender, David. *Westward Vision: The Story of the Oregon Trail*. New York: McGraw-Hill Book Company, 1971.

Leffler, The Very Reverend John C. *The Holy Box: The Story of St. Mark's Cathedral*. Seattle: n.p., 1979.

LeWarne, Charles Pierce. *And Be Ye Separate: The Lopez Island Colony of Thomas Gourley: Pacific Northwest Themes, Historical Essay in Honor of Keith A. Murray, James W. Scott, Editor*. Bellingham, WA: Center for Pacific Northwest Studies, 1978.

_____ . *Utopias on Puget Sound 1885-1915*. Seattle: University of Washington Press, 1975.

Loewenberg, Robert J. *Equality on the Oregon Frontier: Jason Lee and the Methodist Mission 1834-43*. Seattle: University of Washington Press, 1976.

Marty, Martin E. *The Public Church.* New York: The Crossroad Publishing Company, 1981.

Miller, Clifford R. *Baptists and the Oregon Frontier.* Portland: Oregon Baptist Convention, 1967.

Mooney, James. *The Ghost Dance Religion: The Shakers of Puget Sound.* Seattle: The Shorey Book Facsimile Reproduction, 1966.

Morgan, Murray. *Puget's Sound.* Seattle: University of Washington Press, 1979.

_____ . *Skid Road.* Seattle: University of Washington Press, 1982.

Morison, Samuel Eliot, Henry Steele Commager and William E. Leuchtenburg. Vol. 1 and 2 of *The Growth of the American Republic.* New York: Oxford University Press, 1980.

Mowry, William A. and Arthur May. *American Heros and Heroism.* New York: Silver, Burdett and Co., 1903.

Mumford, Esther Hall. *Seattle Black Victorians, 1852-1901.* Seattle: Ananse Press, 1980.

McCann, James. *A Study of the Jewish Community in the Greater Seattle Area.* Seattle: Jewish Federation of Greater Seattle, 1979.

McCrosson, Sister Mary Of The Blessed Sacrament. *The Bell and the River.* Palo Alto, CA: Pacific Books, Publishers, 1957.

McDowell, Esther. *Unitarians in the State of Washington 1870-1960.* n.p. Frand McCaffrey Publishers, 1966.

McMemee, A.J. *Brother Mack the Frontier Preacher.* Fairfield, WA: Ye Galleon Press, 1980.

Nichol, Francis D. *Reasons for Our Faith.* Washington D.C.: Review and Herald Publishing Association, 1947.

Newman, Peter C. Vol. 2 of *Caesars of the Wilderness: Company of Adventurers.* New York: Viking, 1987.

Nordquist, Philip A. "Lutherans in the West and Northwest." *New Partners, Old Roots.* Eds. Heidi Emerson et. al. Tacoma, WA: J & D Printing, Inc., 1986.

Nudel, Rabbi Julius J. *The Ties Between.* Portland: Temple Beth Israel, 1959.

Pash, Joseph J. *History of the Immaculate Conception Parish in the Colville Valley.* Colville, WA: The Statesman-Examiner, 1962.

Peterson, Orval D. *Washington-Northern Idaho Disciples.* St. Louis: Christian Board of Education, 1945.

Pierce, Richard A., ed. *The Russian Orthodox Religious Mission in America, 1794-1837.* Kingston, Ontario, Canada: The Limestone Press, 1978.

Raufer, Sister Maria Ilma, O.P. *Black Robes and Indians on the Last Frontier.* Milwaukee: The Bruce Publishing Company, 1966.

Ray, Mr. and Mrs. L.P. *Twice Sold, Twice Ransomed.* Freeport, N.Y.: Books For Libraries Press, 1971.

Rayner, Alice D. *The Path We Came By: A History of Plymouth Congregational Church, Seattle, Washington 1869-1937.* n.p.: 1937.

Relander, Click. *Drummers and Dreamers.* Seattle: Pacific Northwest National Parks & Forests Association, 1986.

Ruby, Robert H. and John A. Brown. *Half-Sun on the Columbia: A Biography of Chief Moses.* Norman, OK: University of Oklahoma Press, 1965.

_____ . *Myron Eells and the Puget Sound Indians.* Seattle: Superior Publishing Company, 1976.

Saint Demetrios Greek Orthodox Church Dedication Book, March 31, 1963. n.p.: 1963.

Sampson, Martin J. *Indians of Skagit County.* Mount Vernon, WA: Skagit County Historical Society, 1972.

Scheuerman, Richard D. *Pilgrims on the Earth.* Fairfield, WA: Ye Galleon Press, 1974.

Scheuerman, Richard D. and Clifford E. Trafzer, *The Volga Germans: Pioneers in the Northwest.* Moscow: The University Press of Idaho, 1980.

Schoenberg, Wilfred P. *A History of the Catholic Church in the Pacific Northwest.* Washington, D.C.: The Pastoral Press, 1987.

_____ . *Paths to the Northwest: A Jesuit Hisotry of the Oregon Province.* Chicago: Loyola University Press, 1982.

_____ . *The Three Bishops of Nesqually.* Vancouver: St. James Historical Society, 1983.

Scheller, Roscoe. *Courage and Water, a Story of Yakima Valley's Sunnyside.* Portland: Binfords & Mort, 1952.

Shook, Glenn A. *Mysticism, Science and Revelation.* Oxford: George Ronald Whemley, 1953.

Speir, Leslie. "The Prophet Dance of the Northwest and its Derivatives: The Source of the Ghost Dance." *General Series in Anthropology 1.* Menashe, WI: George Banta Publishing Company Agent, 1935.

St. Spiridon Orthodox Cathedral: 1895-1985. Seattle: Academy Press, 1985.

Suzuki, Lester E. *Ministry in the Assembly and Relocation Centers of World War II.* Berkeley: Yardbird Publishing Co., 1979.

Teit, James A. and Franz Boas. *The Salishan Tribes of the Western Plateaus.* Seattle: The Shorey Book Store Facsimile Reproduction, 1973.

Thomas, Lately. *Storming Heaven: The Lives and Turmoils of Minnie Kennedy and Aimee Semple McPherson.* New York: William Morrow and Co., Inc., 1970.

Thompson, Erwin N. *Whitman Mission: National Historic Site.* National Park Handbook Series 37. Washington D.C.: n.p., 1964.

Trafzer, Clifford E., ed. *American Indian Prophets: Religious Leaders and Revitalization Movements.* Sacramento: Sierra Oaks Publishing Company, 1986.

Turner, Dr. Dale E., *More Words of Wisdom.* Seattle: The Seattle Times, 1986.

Twain, Mark. *Christian Science.* 1907. Buffalo, N.Y.: Prometheus Books, 1986.

Vaughan, Miceal F. and Sheila C. Dietrich, eds. *Blessed Sacrament Parish: The Church and the People (1908-1983).* Seattle: North Seattle Printing Co., 1983.

Walla Walla College. *60 years of Progress.* College Place, WA: The Walla Walla College Press, 1952.

Wardin, Albert W., Jr. *Baptists in Oregon.* Portland: Judson Baptist College, 1969.

Whitner, Robert C. Two Essays on the History of Whitman College. Walla Walla, WA: The 1983 Trustees of Whitman College.

Wolfe, Rev. Edward A. *Diamond Historical and Jubilee Celebration, Pioneer Methodist Church.* Walla Walla, WA.: Private Printing, 1934.

Youngson, Dr. William Wallace. *Swinging Portals.* Portland: Oregon Conference of the Methodist Church, 1948.

Periodicals

Edwards, G. Thomas. "Whitman College and the Whitman Legacy." *Idaho Yesterdays* 31 (1987): 13-23.

Elmendorf. W.W. "The Structure of Twana Culture." *Washingotn State University Research Studies, Monograph Supplement* 28. n.p.: 1960.

Frachtenberg, Leo. J. "Eschatology of the Quileute Indians." *American Anthropologist* n.s. 22 (1920): 330-340.

Friedheim, Robert L. and Robin Friedheim. "The Seattle Labor Movement, 1919-20." *Pacific Northwest Quarterly* 55 (1964): 146-156.

Gill, John. "Superstitions and Ceremonies of Indians of Old Oregon." *Oregon Historical Quarterly* rpt. 29 (1928):

Gunther, Erna. "Klallam Ethnography." *University of Washington Publications in Anthropology* 1 (1927): 171-314.

Haeberlin, Herman K. "Sbetetda'q, A Shamanistic Performance of the Coast Salish." *American Anthropologist* n.s. 20 (1918): 249-257.

Hanson, Howard A. "Secondary Education in Washington Territory." *Pacific Northwest Quarterly* 41 (1950): 342-351.

Jeffrey, Julie Roy. "The Making of a Missionary: Narcissa Whitman and Her Vocation." *Idaho Yesterdays* 31 (1987): 75-85.

Jessett, Thomas E. "Anglican Indians in the Pacific Northwest Before the Coming of White Missionaries." rept. *Historical Magazine of the Protestant Episcopal Church* 45 (1986):

_____ . "A Concise History of the (Anglican) Church in the Pacific Northwest." *Historical Magazine of the Protestant Episcopal Church* 36 (1967):

Magnuson, Jon. "Affirming Native American Spirituality." *The Christian Century* 9 Dec. 1987: 1114-1117.

Ray, Verne F. "The Bluejay Character in the Plateau Spirit Dance." *American Anthropologist* 39 (1937): 593-601.

_____ . "Cultural Relations in the Plateau of Northwestern America." *Publications of the Frederick Webb Hodge Anniversiry Publication Fund* 3 Los Angeles: Southwest Museum, 1939.

_____ . " The Kolaskin Cult: A Prophet Movement of 1870 in Northeastern Washington." *American Anthropologist* 38 (1936): 67-75.

_____ . "The Sanpoil and Nespelem: Salishan Peoples of Northeastern Washington." *University of Washington Publications in Anthropology* 5. Seattle: n.p., 1932.

Schmeltzer, Michael. "Hutterites: A People Apart." *Washington Magazine* March-April 1987: 34-42, 65-67.

Schoenberg, Wilfred P. "The Bishops Blanchet and Their Role in the Whitman Massacre." *Idaho Yesterdays* 31 (1987): 3-12.

Slickpoo, Allen P., Sr. "The Nez Perce Attitude Toward the Missionary Experience." *Idaho Yesterdays* 31 (1987): 35-57.

Soden, Dale. "Mark Allison Matthews: Seattle's Minister Rediscovered." *Pacific Northwest Quarterly* 61 (1970): 77-86.

Watterman, Thomas Talbot. "The Paraphernalia of the Duwamish 'Spirit-Canoe' Ceremony." *Indian Notes* 7 (1930): 129-148, 295-312, 535-561.

Wolcott, John. "Muslims in the Northwest." *The Progress* 16 Jan. 1986: 12-13.

Manuscripts, Theses and Dissertations

Adatto, Albert. "Sephardim and the Seattle Sephardic Community." MA Thesis, University of Washington, 1939.

Eulenberg, Julia Niebuhr. "Samuel Koch: Seattle's Social Justice Rabbi." MA Thesis, University of Washington, 1984.

Fogelquist, Albin Hilding, Jr. *The Lutheran Presence in the Pacific Northwest Prior to the First World War.* Microfilm. Ann Arbor, MI: University Microfilms International, 1979.

Hinckley, Carol O. *A Glimpse into the History of the Church of Jesus Christ of Latter-day Saints in Puget Sound, Washington.* ts., ms., Seattle, 1988.

Jessett, Thomas Edwin. "The Influence of the Church in Washington State – Is This God's Country?" Speech. Spokane, WA, 1975.

Kenton, Jessie Kinnear. "Changing Values in Ecumenical Strategy in the Greater Seattle Area 1919-1984." MA Thesis San Francisco Theological Seminary, 1985.

Kuykendall, Elgin V. *"Father" James Harvey Wilbur: His Place in the History of the Northwest.* ms., Yakima, WA, 1942.

Soden, Dale Edward, "Mark Allison Matthews: Seattle's Southern Preacher." MA Thesis, University of Washington, 1980.

Quintard, Taylor, Jr. "A History of Blacks in the Pacific Northwest, 1788-1970." Diss, University of Minnesota, 1977.

A

Abernathy, George 51,61
Adams, Jimmy 110
Abdu'l-Baha 205, 230
Adventist 167, 205
Affiliated Tribes of Northwest Indians
 225
African Methodist-Episcopal Church
 144-145, 174, 176
Ahtanum Mission 89
Alaska 35, 146, 175, 190, 192
Aleut (Indians) 146
Aleutian Islands 35, 146
Alexander Vyacheslavov 149-150
Alexandrov, Father Vladimir 203
Alki 93
Alki Point 83
Allentown, Washington 5
American Association of General
 Practitioners 132
American Board of Commisioners for
 Foreign Missions, 24, 40, 42, 51-52,
 54, 58, 62, 68-69, 88, 90, 131, 201
American Federation of Labor 161
American Fur Company 38, 42, 51, 57
American Home Mission Society 106
American Home Missionary Society
 90, 152
American Lake 53
American Unitarian Association 127
Ames, Bishop E.R. 92
Amherst College 240
Amish 219
Amotqen 8, 17
Anarchism 138
Ancients 5
Anders, Emil Friedrickson 147
Anderson, Agnes Healy 172, 174
Anderson, Alfred H. 172, 174
Anderson, Guy 231
Andover Theological Seminary 90
Angelus Temple 134-135
Anglican 24, 37, 46, 241-242
Anglican Catechism 23
Anhyi 7
Annie Wright Seminary 101

Anti-Saloon League of Washington
 166
Apel, Rev. Gertrude 202, 235-237
Apocalypse 212
Apostolic Church of Jesus Christ 126
Aquarian Foundation 218
Ararat, Mt. 5
Armageddon 212
Armstrong, A.N. 90
Assembly of God 203
Astor, John Jacob 36
Astorian 54
Atis, John 68
Atkinson, George 90-91, 95, 152
Atkinson, Mary 90
Atwood, Rev. A. 100
Auburn 156, 213
Australia 206

B

Bachelors Hall 83
Bagley, Clarence 105
Bagley, Rev. Daniel H. 83, 105
Baha'i 205-206, 221, 229-231
Baha'u'llah 205
Balch, Lafayette 92-93
Ballard, Washington 125
Ballard, Arthur 5
Bannock (Indians) 107
Baptist 96-98, 101, 115-117, 145,
 152-153, 202-203, 217
Baptist Annals of Oregon 115-116
Baptist Historian of the Upper Coast
 115
Baptist Northern Convention 228
Baptist Women's Home 155
Barleycorn, John 177
Barnett, Eugene 238
Bates, Rev. 154
Battleground, Washington 213
Bayne Jr, Reverend Stephen Fielding,
 240-242
Bean, M.L. 179
Beaver, Jane 46
Beaver, Rev. Herbert 46, 50
Beck, Dave 241-242

C